Clean Data

Save time by discovering effortless strategies for cleaning, organizing, and manipulating your data

Megan Squire

[PACKT] PUBLISHING

BIRMINGHAM - MUMBAI

Clean Data

First published: May 2015

Production reference: 1190515

Published by Packt Publishing Ltd.
Livery Place
35 Livery Street
Birmingham B3 2PB, UK.

ISBN 978-1-78528-401-4

www.packtpub.com

Credits

Author
Megan Squire

Reviewers
J. Benjamin Cook
Richard A. Denman, Jr.
Oskar Jarczyk

Commissioning Editor
Akram Hussain

Acquisition Editor
Harsha Bharwani

Content Development Editor
Mamata Walkar

Technical Editor
Nilesh Mangnakar

Copy Editors
Puja Lalwani
Aditya Nair
Stuti Srivastava

Project Coordinator
Shipra Chawhan

Proofreaders
Stephen Copestake
Safis Editing

Indexer
Priya Sane

Production Coordinator
Shantanu N. Zagade

Cover Work
Shantanu N. Zagade

About the Author

Megan Squire is a professor of computing sciences at Elon University. She has been collecting and cleaning dirty data for two decades. She is also the leader of `FLOSSmole.org`, a research project to collect data and analyze it in order to learn how free, libre, and open source software is made.

About the Reviewers

J. Benjamin Cook, after studying sociology at the University of Nebraska-Lincoln, earned his master's in computational science and engineering from the Institute of Applied Computational Science at Harvard University. Currently, he is helping build the data science team at Hudl, a sports software company whose mission is to capture and bring value to every moment in sports. When he's not learning about all things data, Ben spends time with his daughters and his beautiful wife, Renee.

Richard A. Denman, Jr. is a senior consultant with Numb3rs and has over 30 years of experience providing services to major companies in the areas of data analytics, data science, optimization, process improvement, and information technology. He has been a member of the Association for Computing Machinery (ACM) and the Institute of Electrical and Electronics Engineers (IEEE) for over 25 years. He is also a member of the Institute for Operations Research and the Management Sciences (INFORMS) and the American Society for Quality (ASQ).

I would like to thank my wife, Barbara, my son, Ashford, and my daughter, Addie, for their support in producing this book.

Oskar Jarczyk graduated from Polish-Japanese Academy of Information Technology with an MSc Eng. degree in computer science (major databases). After three years of commercial work, he returned to academia to become a PhD student in the field of social informatics.

His academic work is connected with problems in the category of web intelligence, especially free/libre open-source software (FLOSS) and collaborative innovation networks (COINs). He specializes in analyzing the quality of work in open source software teams of developers that are on the GitHub portal. Together with colleagues from the WikiTeams research team, he coped with the problem of "clean data" on a daily basis while creating datasets in MongoDB and MySQL. They were later used with success for FLOSS scientific analyses in the R and Python language.

In his spare time, Oskar reads books about big data and practices kendo.

Table of Contents

Preface

"Pray, Mr. Babbage, if you put into the machine the wrong figures, will the right answer come out?"

– Charles Babbage (1864)

"Garbage in, garbage out"

– The United States Internal Revenue Service (1963)

"There are no clean datasets."

– Josh Sullivan, Booz Allen VP in Fortune (2015)

In his 1864 collection of essays, Charles Babbage, the inventor of the first calculating machine, recollects being dumbfounded at the "confusion of ideas" that would prompt someone to assume that a computer could calculate the correct answer despite being given the wrong input. Fast-forward another 100 years, and the tax bureaucracy started patiently explaining "garbage in, garbage out" to express the idea that even for the all-powerful tax collector, computer processing is still dependent on the quality of its input. Fast-forward another 50 years to 2015: a seemingly magical age of machine learning, autocorrect, anticipatory interfaces, and recommendation systems that know me better than I know myself. Yet, all of these helpful algorithms still require high-quality data in order to learn properly in the first place, and we lament "there are no clean datasets".

This book is for anyone who works with data on a regular basis, whether as a data scientist, data journalist, software developer, or something else. The goal is to teach practical strategies to quickly and easily bridge the gap between the data we want and the data we have. We want high-quality, perfect data, but the reality is that most often, our data falls far short. Whether we are plagued with missing data, data in the wrong format, data in the wrong location, or anomalies in the data, the result is often, to paraphrase rapper Notorious B.I.G., "more data, more problems".

Throughout the book, we will envision data cleaning as an important, worthwhile step in the data science process: easily improved, never ignored. Our goal is to reframe data cleaning away from being a dreaded, tedious task that we must slog through in order to get to the *real* work. Instead, armed with a few tried-and-true procedures and tools, we will learn that just like in a kitchen, if you wash your vegetables first, your food will look better, taste better, and be better for you. If you learn a few proper knife skills, your meat will be more succulent and your vegetables will be cooked more evenly. The same way that a great chef will have their favorite knives and culinary traditions, a great data scientist will want to work with the very best data possible and under the very best conditions.

What this book covers

Chapter 1, Why Do You Need Clean Data? motivates our quest for clean data by showing the central role of data cleaning in the overall data science process. We follow with a simple example showing some dirty data from a real-world dataset. We weigh the pros and cons of each potential cleaning process, and then we describe how to communicate our cleaning changes to others.

Chapter 2, Fundamentals – Formats, Types, and Encodings, sets up some foundational knowledge about file formats, compression, and data types, including missing and empty data and character encodings. Each section has its own examples taken from real-world datasets. This chapter is important because we will rely on knowledge of these basic concepts for the rest of the book.

Chapter 3, Workhorses of Clean Data – Spreadsheets and Text Editors, describes how to get the most data cleaning utility out of two common tools: the text editor and the spreadsheet. We will cover simple solutions to common problems, including how to use functions, search and replace, and regular expressions to correct and transform data. At the end of the chapter, we will put our skills to test using both of these tools to clean some real-world data regarding universities.

Chapter 4, Speaking the Lingua Franca – Data Conversions, focuses on converting data from one format to another. This is one of the most important data cleaning tasks, and it is useful to have a variety of tools at hand to easily complete this task. We first proceed through each of the different conversions step by step, including back and forth between common formats such as comma-separated values (CSV), JSON, and SQL. To put our new data conversion skills into practice, we complete a project where we download a Facebook friend network and convert it into a few different formats so that we can visualize its shape.

Chapter 5, Collecting and Cleaning Data from the Web, describes three different ways to clean data found inside HTML pages. This chapter presents three popular tools to pull data elements from within marked-up text, and it also provides the conceptual foundation to understand other methods besides the specific tools shown here. As our project for this chapter, we build a set of cleaning procedures to pull data from web-based discussion forums.

Chapter 6, Cleaning Data in PDF Files, introduces several ways to meet this most stubborn and all-too-common challenge for data cleaners: extracting data that has been stored in Adobe's Portable Document Format (PDF) files. We first examine low-cost tools to accomplish this task, then we try a few low-barrier-to-entry tools, and finally, we experiment with the Adobe non-free software itself. As always, we use real-world data for our experiments, and this provides a wealth of experience as we learn to work through problems as they arise.

Chapter 7, RDBMS Cleaning Techniques, uses a publicly available dataset of tweets to demonstrate numerous strategies to clean data stored in a relational database. The database shown is MySQL, but many of the concepts, including regular-expression based text extraction and anomaly detection, are readily applicable to other storage systems as well.

Chapter 8, Best Practices for Sharing Your Clean Data, describes some strategies to make your hard work as easy for others to use as possible. Even if you never plan to share your data with anyone else, the strategies in this chapter will help you stay organized in your own work, saving you time in the future. This chapter describes how to create the ideal data package in a variety of formats, how to document your data, how to choose and attach a license to your data, and also how to publicize your data so that it can live on if you choose.

Chapter 9, Stack Overflow Project, guides you through a full-length project using a real-world dataset. We start by posing a set of authentic questions that we can answer about that dataset. In answering this set of questions, we will complete the entire data science process introduced in *Chapter 1, Why Do You Need Clean Data?* and we will put into practice many of the cleaning processes we learned in the previous chapters. In addition, because this dataset is so large, we will introduce a few new techniques to deal with the creation of test datasets.

Chapter 10, Twitter Project, is a full-length project that shows how to perform one of the hottest and fastest-changing data collection and cleaning tasks out there right now: mining Twitter. We will show how to find and collect an existing archive of publicly available tweets on a real-world current event while adhering to legal restrictions on the usage of the Twitter service. We will answer a simple question about the dataset while learning how to clean and extract data from JSON, the most popular format in use right now with API-accessible web data. Finally, we will design a simple data model for long-term storage of the extracted and cleaned data and show how to generate some simple visualizations.

What you need for this book

To complete the projects in this book, you will need the following tools:

- A web browser, Internet access, and a modern operating system. The browser and operating system should not matter, but access to a command-line terminal window is ideal (for example, the Terminal application in OS X). In *Chapter 5, Collecting and Cleaning Data from the Web*, one of the three activities relies on a browser-based utility that runs in the Chrome browser, so keep this in mind if you would like to complete this activity.
- A text editor, such as Text Wrangler for Mac OSX or Notepad++ for Windows. Some integrated development environments (IDEs, such as Eclipse) can also be used as a text editor, but they typically have many features you will not need.
- A spreadsheet application, such as Microsoft Excel or Google Spreadsheets. When possible, generic examples are provided that can work on either of these tools, but in some cases, one or the other is required.
- A Python development environment and the ability to install Python libraries. I recommend the Enthought Canopy Python environment, which is available here: `https://www.enthought.com/products/canopy/`.
- A MySQL 5.5+ server installed and running.
- A web server (running any server software) and PHP 5+ installed.
- A MySQL client interface, either the command-line interface, MySQL Workbench, or phpMyAdmin (if you have PHP running).

Who this book is for

If you are reading this book, I guess you are probably in one of two groups. One group is the group of data scientists who already spend a lot of time cleaning data, but you want to get better at it. You are probably frustrated with the tedium of data cleaning, and you are looking for ways to speed it up, become more efficient, or just use different tools to get the job done. In our kitchen metaphor, you are the chef who just needs to brush up on a few knife skills.

The other group is made up of people doing the data science work but who never really cared about data cleaning before. But now, you are starting to think that maybe your results might actually get better if you had a cleaning process. Maybe the old adage "garbage in, garbage out" is starting to feel a little too real. Maybe you are interested in sharing your data with others, but you do not feel confident about the quality of the datasets you are producing. With this book, you will gain enough confidence to "cook in public" by learning a few tricks and creating new habits that will ensure a tidy, clean data science environment.

Either way, this book will help you reframe data cleaning away from being a symbol of drudgery and toward being your hallmark of quality, good taste, style, and efficiency. You should probably have a bit of programming background, but you do not have to be great at it. As with most data science projects, a willingness to learn and experiment as well as a healthy sense of curiosity and a keen attention to detail are all very important and valued.

Conventions

In this book, you will find a number of text styles that distinguish between different kinds of information. Here are some examples of these styles and an explanation of their meaning.

Code words in text, database table names, folder names, filenames, file extensions, pathnames, dummy URLs, user input, and Twitter handles are shown as follows: " The issue is that `open()` is not prepared to handle UTF-8 characters."

A block of code is set as follows:

```
for tweet in stream:
    encoded_tweet = tweet['text'].encode('ascii','ignore')
    print counter, "-", encoded_tweet[0:10]
    f.write(encoded_tweet)
```

When we wish to draw your attention to a particular part of a code block, the relevant lines or items are set in bold:

```
First name,birth date,favorite color,salary
"Sally","1971-09-16","light blue",129000
"Manu","1984-11-03","",159960
"Martin","1978-12-10","",76888
```

Any command-line input or output is written as follows:

```
tar cvf fileArchive.tar reallyBigFile.csv anotherBigFile.csv
gzip fileArchive.tar
```

New terms and **important words** are shown in bold. Words that you see on the screen, for example, in menus or dialog boxes, appear in the text like this: "Hold down the **Option** key and select the text in columns."

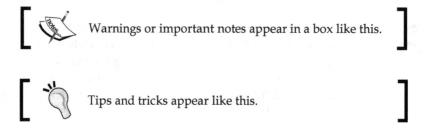

[Warnings or important notes appear in a box like this.]

[Tips and tricks appear like this.]

Reader feedback

Feedback from our readers is always welcome. Let us know what you think about this book—what you liked or disliked. Reader feedback is important for us as it helps us develop titles that you will really get the most out of.

To send us general feedback, simply e-mail `feedback@packtpub.com`, and mention the book's title in the subject of your message.

If there is a topic that you have expertise in and you are interested in either writing or contributing to a book, see our author guide at `www.packtpub.com/authors`.

Customer support

Now that you are the proud owner of a Packt book, we have a number of things to help you to get the most from your purchase.

Downloading the color images of this book

We also provide you with a PDF file that has color images of the screenshots/diagrams used in this book. The color images will help you better understand the changes in the output. You can download this file from `https://www.packtpub.com/sites/default/files/downloads/Clean_Data_Graphics.zip`.

Errata

Although we have taken every care to ensure the accuracy of our content, mistakes do happen. If you find a mistake in one of our books—maybe a mistake in the text or the code—we would be grateful if you could report this to us. By doing so, you can save other readers from frustration and help us improve subsequent versions of this book. If you find any errata, please report them by visiting `http://www.packtpub.com/submit-errata`, selecting your book, clicking on the **Errata Submission Form** link, and entering the details of your errata. Once your errata are verified, your submission will be accepted and the errata will be uploaded to our website or added to any list of existing errata under the Errata section of that title.

To view the previously submitted errata, go to `https://www.packtpub.com/books/content/support` and enter the name of the book in the search field. The required information will appear under the **Errata** section.

Piracy

Piracy of copyrighted material on the Internet is an ongoing problem across all media. At Packt, we take the protection of our copyright and licenses very seriously. If you come across any illegal copies of our works in any form on the Internet, please provide us with the location address or website name immediately so that we can pursue a remedy.

Please contact us at `copyright@packtpub.com` with a link to the suspected pirated material.

We appreciate your help in protecting our authors and our ability to bring you valuable content.

Questions

If you have a problem with any aspect of this book, you can contact us at `questions@packtpub.com`, and we will do our best to address the problem.

1
Why Do You Need Clean Data?

Big data, data mining, machine learning, and visualization—it seems like data is at the center of everything great happening in computing lately. From statisticians to software developers to graphic designers, everyone is suddenly interested in data science. The confluence of cheap hardware, better processing and visualization tools, and massive amounts of freely available data means that we can now discover trends and make predictions more accurately and more easily than ever before.

What you might *not* have heard, though, is that all of these data science hopes and dreams are predicated on the fact that data is messy. Usually, data has to be moved, compressed, cleaned, chopped, sliced, diced, and subjected to any number of other transformations before it is ready to be used in the algorithms or visualizations that we think of as the heart of **data science**.

In this chapter, we will cover:

- A simple six-step process you can follow for data science, including cleaning
- Helpful guidelines to communicate how you cleaned your data
- Some tools that you might find helpful for data cleaning
- An introductory example that shows how data cleaning fits into the overall data science process

A fresh perspective

We recently read that The New York Times called data cleaning **janitor work** and said that 80 percent of a data scientist's time will be spent doing this kind of cleaning. As we can see in the following figure, despite its importance, data cleaning has not really captured the public imagination in the same way as big data, data mining, or machine learning:

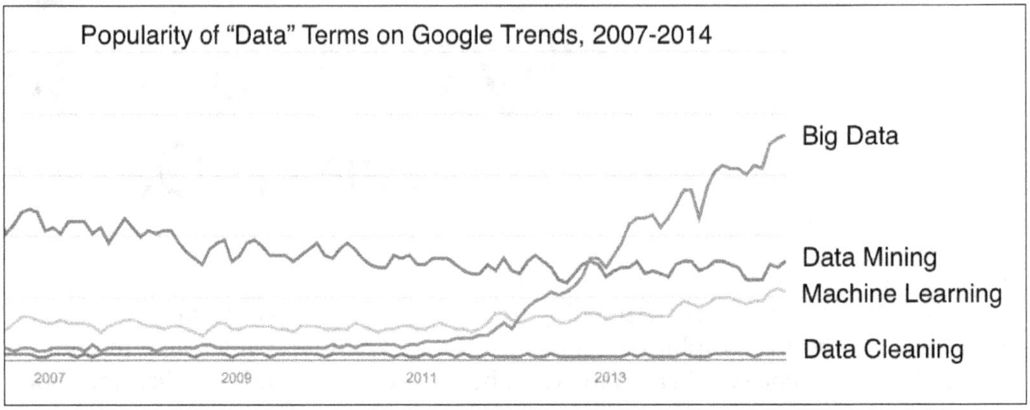

Who can blame us for not wanting to gather in droves to talk about how fun and super-cool janitor work is? Well, unfortunately—and this is true for actual housekeeping chores as well—we would all be a lot better off if we just got the job done rather than ignoring it, complaining about it, and giving it various demeaning names.

Not convinced yet? Consider a different metaphor instead, you are not a data janitor; you are a data chef. Imagine you have been handed a market basket overflowing with the most gorgeous heirloom vegetables you have ever seen, each one handpicked at the peak of freshness and sustainably produced on an organic farm. The tomatoes are perfectly succulent, the lettuce is crisp, and the peppers are bright and firm. You are excited to begin cooking, but you look around and the kitchen is filthy, the pots and pans have baked-on, caked-on who-knows-what, and, as for tools, you have nothing but a rusty knife and a soggy towel. The sink is broken and you just saw a beetle crawl out from under that formerly beautiful lettuce.

Even a beginner chef knows you should not cook in a place like this. At the very least, you will destroy that perfectly good delicious basket of goodies you have been given. And at worst, you will make people sick. Plus, cooking like this is not even fun, and it would take all day to chop the veggies with an old rusty knife.

Just as you would in a kitchen, it's definitely worth spending time cleaning and preparing your data science workspace, your tools, and your raw materials upfront. The old computer programming adage from the 1960s—garbage in, garbage out—is also true with data science.

The data science process

How does cleaning fit into the rest of the job of data science? Well, the short answer is that it's a critical piece, and it directly affects the processes that come before and after it.

The longer answer relies on describing the data science process in six steps, as shown in the following lists. Data cleaning is right in the middle, at step 3. But rather than thinking of these steps as a linear, start-to-finish framework, we will revisit the steps as needed several times over the course of a project in more of an iterative manner. It is also worth pointing out that not every project will have all the steps; for example, sometimes, we do not have a collection step or a visualization step. It really depends on the particular needs of the project:

1. The first step is to come up with the problem statement. Identify what the problem you are trying to solve is.
2. The next step is data collection and storage. Where did the data come from that is helping you answer this question? Where did you store it and in what format?
3. Then comes data cleaning. Did you change the data at all? Did you delete anything? How did you prepare it for the analysis and mining step next?
4. The next step is data analysis and machine learning. What kind of processing did you do to the data? What transformations? What algorithms did you use? What formulas did you apply? What machine learning algorithms did you use? In what order?
5. Representation and visualization is the next step. How do you show the results of your work? This can be one or more tables, drawings, graphs, charts, network diagrams, word clouds, maps, and so on. Is this the best visualization to represent the data? What alternatives did you consider?
6. The last step is problem resolution. What is the answer to the question or problem you posed in step 1? What limitations do you have on your results? Were there parts of the question that you could not answer with this method? What could you have done differently? What are the next steps?

It makes sense that data cleaning needs to happen before you attempt the analysis / mining / machine learning or visualization steps. Although, remember that, as this is an iterative process, we may revisit cleaning several times during the course of a project. Also, the type of mining or analysis we are going to do will often drive the way we clean the data. We consider cleaning to include a variety of tasks that may be dictated by the analysis method chosen, for example, swapping file formats, changing character encodings, or parsing out pieces of data to operate on.

Data cleaning is also going to be very closely tied to the collection and storage step (step 2). This means that you may have to collect raw data, store it, clean it, store the cleaned data again, collect some more, clean that, combine it with the previous data, clean it again, store it, and so on. As such, it is going to be very important to remember what you did and be able to repeat that process again if needed or tell someone else what you did.

Communicating about data cleaning

As the six-step process is organized around a story arc that starts with a question and ends with the resolution of the question, it works nicely as a reporting framework. If you decide to use the six-step framework as a way to report on your data science process, you will find that you get to write about your cleaning in the third step.

But even if you do not document your data science process in a formal report, you will find that it is extremely helpful to keep careful notes of what you did to the data and in what order.

Remember that even for the smallest, lowest-stakes project, you are always working for an audience of at least two people: you now and you 6 months from now. Believe me when I tell you that the you-in-six-months isn't going to remember what the you-of-today did to clean your data, much less why you did it or how to do it again!

The simplest solution for this is to just keep a **log** of what you did. The log should include links, screenshots, or copy and pastes of the specific commands you ran as well as a short explanation for why you did this. The following example shows a log for a very small text mining project with embedded links to the output files at each stage as well as links to the cleaning scripts. Don't worry if you are unfamiliar with some of the technologies mentioned in this log. This example shows you what a log might look like:

1. We wrote a SQL query to retrieve a list of every item and its description.
2. In order to conduct a term frequency analysis in Python, we needed data in a specific JSON format. We constructed a PHP script that looped through the results of our query, placing its results in a JSON file (version 1).

3. This file had some formatting errors, such as unescaped quotation marks and embedded HTML tags. These errors were corrected with a second PHP script, which when run, printed this cleaned JSON file (version 2).

Note that our log tries to explain what we did and why we did it. It is short and can include links when possible.

There are many more sophisticated solutions to communicate about data cleaning should you choose to use them, for example, if you are familiar with **version control systems** such as **Git** or Subversion, which are usually used to manage a software project, you can probably conceive how to extend them to keep track of your data cleaning. Whatever system you choose, even if it is a simple log, the most important thing is to actually use it. So, pick something that will encourage its use and not impede your progress.

Our data cleaning environment

The approach to data cleaning we are using in this book is a general-purpose, widely applicable one. It does not require or assume that you have any high-end specialty single-vendor database or data analysis products (in fact, these vendors and products may have their own cleaning routines or methods). I have designed the cleaning tutorials in this book around common, everyday issues that you might encounter when using real-world datasets. I have designed the book around real-world data that anyone can access. I'll show you how to clean data using open source, general-purpose software and technologies that are easy to get and are commonly used in the workplace.

Here are some of the tools and technologies that you should be ready to use:

- For nearly every chapter, we will use a terminal window and its command-line interface, such as the Terminal program on Mac OSX or bash on a Linux system. In Windows, some commands will be able to be run using Windows Command Prompt, but other commands may require the use of a more full-featured Windows command-line program, such as CygWin.
- For nearly every chapter, we will use a text editor or programmer's editor, such as Text Wrangler on a Mac, vi or emacs in Linux, or Notepad++ or Sublime Editor on Windows.
- For most chapters, we will need a Python 2.7 client, such as Enthought Canopy, and we will need enough permissions to install packages. Many of the examples will work with Python 3, but some will not, so if you already have that, you may wish to create an alternate 2.7 installation.

- For *Chapter 3, Workhorses of Clean Data – Spreadsheets and Text Editors,* we will need a spreadsheet program (we will focus on Microsoft Excel and Google Spreadsheets).
- For *Chapter 7, RDBMS Cleaning Techniques,* we will need a working MySQL installation and the client software to access it.

An introductory example

To get started, let's sharpen our chef's knife with a small example that integrates the six-step framework and illustrates how to tackle a few simple cleaning issues. This example uses the publicly available Enron e-mail dataset. This is a very famous dataset consisting of e-mail messages sent to, from, and between employees working at the now-defunct Enron Corporation. As part of the U.S. Government investigation into accounting fraud at Enron, the e-mails became part of the public record and are now downloadable by anyone. Researchers in a variety of domains have found the e-mails helpful for studying workplace communication, social networks, and more.

> You can read more about Enron and the financial scandal that led to its demise on its Wikipedia page at `http://en.wikipedia.org/wiki/Enron`, and you can read about the Enron e-mail corpus itself on its separate page at `http://en.wikipedia.org/wiki/Enron_Corpus`.

In this example, we will implement the six-step framework on a simple data science question. Suppose we want to reveal trends and patterns in e-mail usage over time within Enron Corporation. Let's start by counting messages that were sent to/from Enron employees by date. We will then show the counts visually on a graph over time.

First, we need to download the MySQL Enron corpus using the instructions at `http://www.ahschulz.de/enron-email-data/`. Another (backup) source for this file is `https://www.cs.purdue.edu/homes/jpfeiff/enron.html`. Following these instructions, we will need to import the data into a new database scheme called **Enron** on a MySQL server. The data is now ready to be queried using either the MySQL command-line interface or using a web-based tool such as PHPMyAdmin.

Our first count query is shown as follows:

```
SELECT date(date) AS dateSent, count(mid) AS numMsg
FROM message
GROUP BY dateSent
ORDER BY dateSent;
```

Right away, we notice that numerous e-mails have incorrect dates, for example, there are a number of dates that seem to predate or postdate the existence of the corporation (for example, 1979) or that were from years that were illogical (for example, 0001 or 2044). E-mail is old but not *that* old!

The following table shows an excerpt of a few of the weird lines (the complete result set is about 1300 rows long) All of these dates are formatted correctly; however, some of the dates are definitely wrong:

dateSent	numMsg
0002-03-05	1
0002-03-07	3
0002-03-08	2
0002-03-12	1
1979-12-31	6
1997-01-01	1
1998-01-04	1
1998-01-05	1
1998-10-30	3

These bad dates are most likely due to misconfigured e-mail clients. At this point, we have three choices for what to do:

- **Do nothing**: Maybe we can just ignore the bad data and get away with building the line graph anyway. But, as the lowest bad date was from the year 0001 and the highest was from the year 2044, we can imagine our line graph with the 1300 tick marks on the time axis, each showing a count of 1 or 2. This graph does not sound very appealing or informative, so doing nothing will not work.
- **Fix the data**: We could try to figure out what the correct date for each bad message was and produce a corrected dataset that we can then use to build our graph.
- **Throw out the affected e-mails**: We can just make an informed decision to discard any e-mail that has a date that falls outside a predetermined window.

In order to decide between options 2 and 3, we will need to count how many messages will be affected using only a 1999-2002 window. We can use the following SQL:

```
SELECT count(*) FROM message
WHERE year(date) < 1998 or year(date) > 2002;
Result: 325
```

325 messages with bad dates may initially seem like a lot, but then again, they are only about 1 percent of the entire dataset. Depending on our goals, we might decide to fix these dates manually, but let's assume here that we do not mind losing 1 percent of the messages. We can proceed cautiously toward option 3, throwing out the affected e-mails. Here is the amended query:

```
SELECT date(date) AS dateSent, count(mid) AS numMsg
FROM message
WHERE year(date) BETWEEN 1998 AND 2002
GROUP BY dateSent
ORDER BY dateSent;
```

The cleaned data now consists of 1,211 rows, each with a count. Here is an excerpt of the new dataset:

dateSent	numMsg
1998-01-04	1
1998-01-05	1
1998-10-30	3
1998-11-02	1
1998-11-03	1
1998-11-04	4
1998-11-05	1
1998-11-13	2

In this example, it looks like there are two questionable dates in January 1998 and no other messages until October, at which point, the messages start coming in more regularly. This seems weird, and it also points to another issue, is it important that we have every date on the *x* axis, even if there were no e-mails sent that day?

If we answer yes, it is important to show every date, even those with 0 counts; this may mean going through another round of cleaning in order to produce rows that show the date with a zero.

But then again, maybe we can be more strategic about this. Whether we need to have zero values in our raw data actually depends on what tool we are using to create the graph and what type of graph it is, for example, Google Spreadsheets will build a line or bar graph that can automatically detect that there are missing dates on the *x* axis and will fill in zero values even if they are not given in the initial dataset. In our data, these zero values would be the mysterious missing dates from most of 1998.

The next three figures show each of these tools and how they handle zero values on a date axis. Note the long zero tails at the beginning and end of the Google Spreadsheets representation of the data shown here:

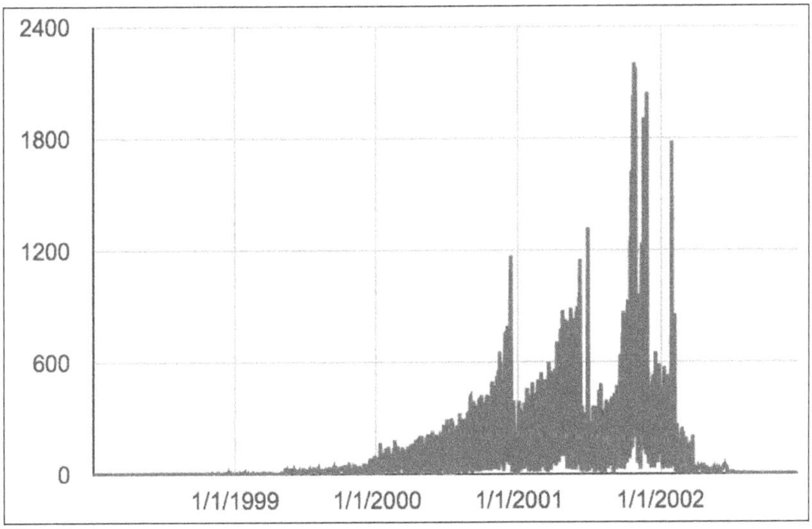

Google Spreadsheets automatically fills in any missing days with a zero.

The D3 JavaScript visualization library will do the same, filling in zero values for missing dates in a range by default, as shown in the next graph.

[For a simple D3 line graph example, take a look at this tutorial: `http://bl.ocks.org/mbostock/3883245`.]

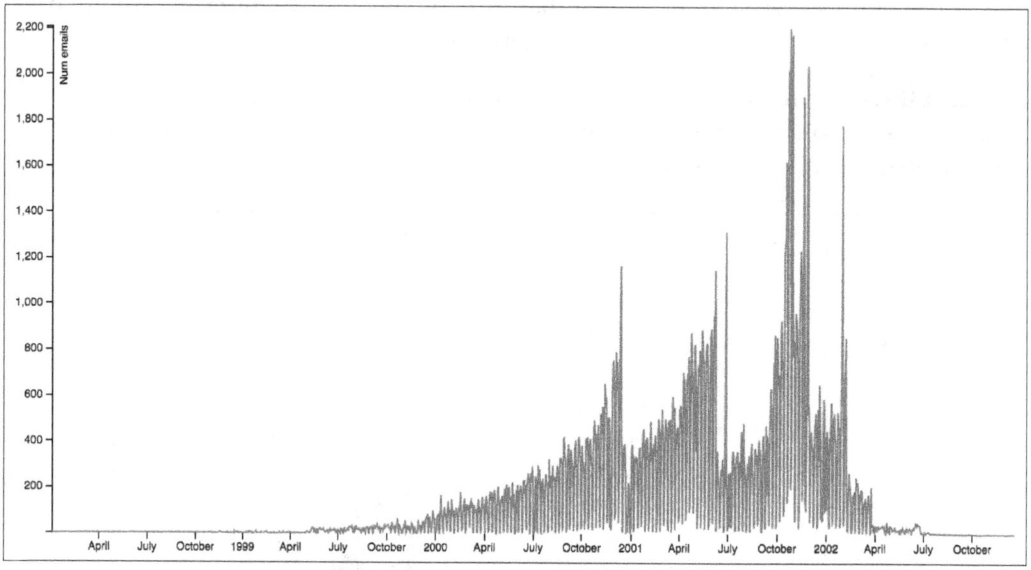

D3 automatically fills in any missing days with a zero.

Excel also has identical date-filling behavior in its default line graph, as shown here:

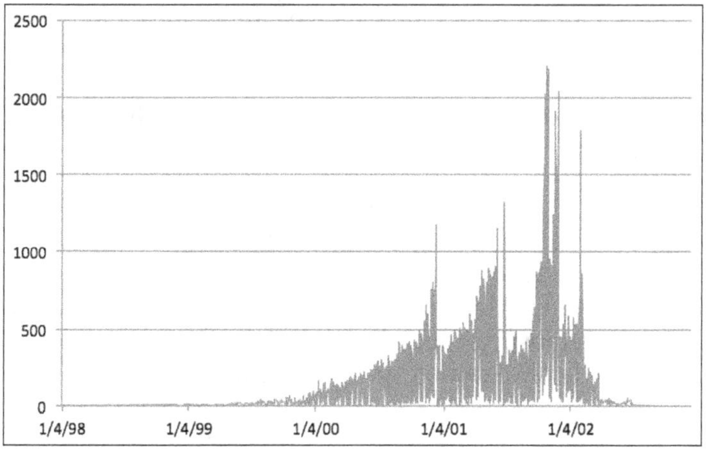

Excel automatically fills in any missing days with a zero.

Next, we need to consider whether, by allowing zero values for dates, we are also making our *x* axis substantially longer (my count query yielded 1211 rows, but there are a total of 1822 days in the range specified, which is 1998-2002). Maybe showing zero count days might not work; if the graph is so crowded, we cannot see the gaps anyway.

To compare, we can quickly run the same data into Google Spreadsheets (you can do this in Excel or D3 too), but this time, we will only select our count column to build the graph, thereby forcing Google Spreadsheets to *not* show dates on the *x* axis. The result is the true shape of only the data that came from the database count query with no zero count days filled in. The long tails are gone, but the overall shape of the important part of the graph (the middle) remains the same:

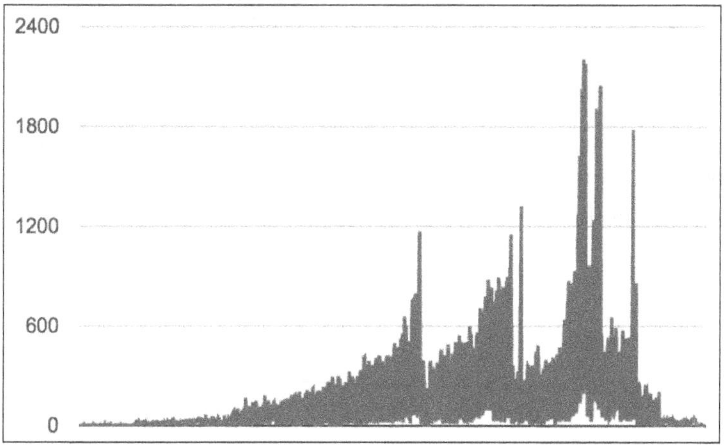

The graph now shows only dates with one or more message.

Lucky for us, the shape of the data is similar, save for a shorter head and tail on the graph. Based on this comparison, and based on what we plan to do with the data (remember that all we wanted to do was create a simple line graph), we can feel good about our decision to move forward without specifically creating a dataset showing zero count days.

When all is said and done, the line graphs reveal that Enron had several significant peaks in e-mail traffic. The largest peaks and heaviest traffic occurred in the October and November of 2001, when the scandal broke. The two smaller peaks occurred around June 26-27 of 2001 and December 12-13 of 2000, when similar newsworthy events involving Enron transpired (one involving the California energy crisis and another involving a leadership change at the company).

If you get excited by data analysis, you probably have all sorts of cool ideas for what to do next with this data. And now that you have cleaned data, it will make your analysis tasks easier, hopefully!

Summary

After all that work, it looks like The New York Times was right. As you can see from this simple exercise, data cleaning indeed comprises about 80 percent of the effort of answering even a tiny data-oriented question (in this case, talking through the rationale and choices for data cleaning took 700 words out of the 900-word case study). Data cleaning really is a pivotal part of the data science process, and it involves understanding technical issues and also requires us to make some value judgments. As part of data cleaning, we even had to take into account the desired outcomes of both the analysis and visualization steps even though we had not really completed them yet.

After considering the role of data cleaning as presented in this chapter, it becomes even more obvious how improvements in our cleaning effectiveness could quickly add up to substantial time savings.

The next chapter will describe a few of the fundamentals that will be required for any "data chef" who wants to move into a bigger, better "kitchen", including file formats, data types, and character encodings.

2

Fundamentals – Formats, Types, and Encodings

A few years ago, I received a very interesting present at my family's annual holiday gift exchange. It was a *garde manger* kitchen toolset that included a bunch of different knives as well as peelers, scoops, and zesters used to prepare vegetables and fruits. I learned to use each of the tools, and over time, I developed a special fondness for the channel knife and the tomato shark. This chapter is like your introductory data cleaning toolset. We will review:

- File formats, including compression standards
- The fundamentals of data types (including different types of missing data)
- Character encodings

We will need all these fundamentals as we progress to later chapters. Some of the concepts that we'll cover are so basic that you'll encounter them nearly every day, such as compression and file formats. These are so common; they are like a chef's knife. But some of these concepts, like character encodings, are more special-purpose and exotic, like a tomato shark!

File formats

This section describes the different file formats any data scientist is likely to encounter when dealing with data found in the wild—in other words, the kind of data you will *not* find in those carefully constructed datasets that so many books rely on. Here, we encounter some strategies and limitations to interacting with the most common file formats, and then we review the various compression and archiving formats you are likely to run into.

Text files versus binary files

When collecting data from online sources, you are likely to encounter data in one of these ways:

- The data will be downloadable in a file
- The data will be available via an interactive frontend to a storage system, for example, via a database system with a query interface
- The data will be available through a continuous stream
- The data will be available through an **Application Programming Interface** (**API**).

In any case, you may find yourself needing to create data files later on in order to share with others. Therefore, a solid foundation of the various data formats and their strengths and weaknesses is important.

First, we can think of computer files as belonging to two broad groups, commonly called **text files** and **binary files**. As all files consist of a sequence of bytes, one right after the other, strictly speaking, all files are binary. But if the bytes in the file are all text characters (for example, letters, numbers, and some control characters such as newlines, carriage returns, or tabs), then we say the file is a text file. In contrast, binary files are those files that contain bytes made up of mostly non-human-readable characters.

Opening and reading files

Text files can be read and written by a program called a text editor. If you try to open a file in a text editor and you can read it successfully (even if you do not understand it), then it is probably a text file. However, if you open the file in a text editor and it just looks like a jumble of garbled characters and weird illegible symbols, then it is probably a binary file.

Binary files are intended to be opened or edited with a particular application, not by a text editor. For example, a Microsoft Excel spreadsheet is intended to be opened and read by Microsoft Excel, and a photograph taken by a digital camera can be read by a graphics program, such as Photoshop or Preview. Sometimes, binary files can be read by multiple compatible software packages, for example, many different graphics programs can read and edit photos and even binary files designed for a proprietary format, such as Microsoft Excel or Microsoft Word files, can be read and edited by compatible software, such as Apache OpenOffice. There are also programs called binary editors, which will let you peek inside a binary file and edit it.

Sometimes, text files are also intended to be read by an application, yet you can still read them in a text editor. For example, web pages and computer source code consist of only text characters and can easily be edited in a text editor, yet they are difficult to understand without some training in the particular format, or layout, of the text itself.

It is usually possible to know what type of file you have even without opening it in an editor. For example, most people look for clues about the file, starting with the file's own name. Three-letter and four-letter file extensions are a common way to indicate the type of file it is. Common extensions that many people know include:

- `.xlsx` for Excel files, `.docx` for Word files, `.pptx` for Powerpoint files
- `.png`, `.jpg`, and `.gif` for image files
- `.mp3`, `.ogg`, `.wmv`, and `.mp4` for music and video files
- `.txt` for text files

There are also several websites that list file extensions and the programs that are affiliated with these particular extensions. One such popular site is `fileinfo.com`, and Wikipedia also has an alphabetical list of file extensions available at `https://en.wikipedia.org/wiki/List_of_filename_extensions_(alphabetical)`.

Peeking inside files

If you must open an unknown file to peek inside, there are several command-line options you can use to see the first few bytes of the file.

On OSX or Linux

On an OSX Mac or in Linux, go to your terminal window (on Mac, you can find the standard terminal application available by navigating to **Applications** | **Utilities** | **Terminal**), navigate to the location of your file using a combination of the print working directory (`pwd`) and change directory (`cd`) commands, and then use the `less` command to view the file page by page. Here is what my commands to perform this task looked like:

```
flossmole2:~ megan$ pwd
/Users/megan
flossmole2:~ megan$ cd Downloads
flossmole2:Downloads megan$ less OlympicAthletes_0.xlsx
"OlympicAthletes_0.xlsx" may be a binary file. See it anyway?
```

If you are prompted to "view anyway", then the file is binary and you should prepare yourself to see garbled characters. You can type `y` to see the file or just type `n` to run in the other direction. The next figure shows you the result of viewing a file called `OlympicAthletes_0.xlsx` using the `less` command, as shown in the dialogue. What a mess!

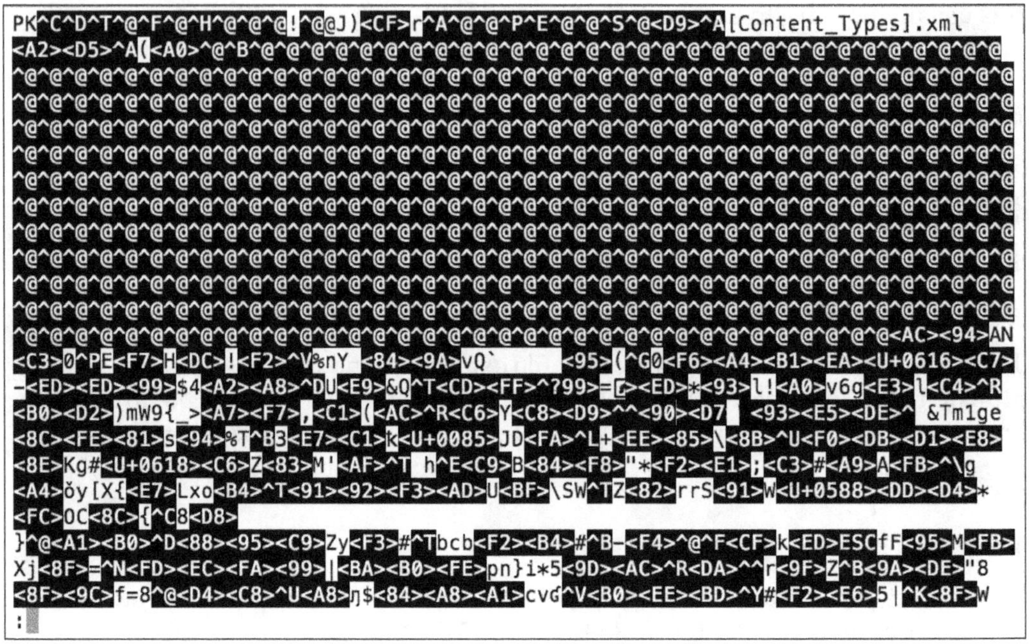

When you are done looking at it, you can type `q` to quit the `less` program.

On Windows

Windows has the `more` program available in its Command Prompt application as well. It works similarly to the `less` command described earlier (after all, *less is more*). You can access the Windows Command Prompt with **cmd** from the **Start** menu in Windows 7. In Windows 8, navigate to **Apps** | **Windows System** | **Command Prompt**. You can use `cd` and `pwd` to navigate to your file the same way as we did in the preceding example.

Common formats for text files

In this book, we are mostly concerned with text files rather than binary files. (Some special exceptions include compressed and archived files, which we will cover in the next section, and Excel and PDF files, each of which have their own chapters later in this book.)

The three main types of text files we will be concerned with in this book are:

- The delimited format (structured data)
- The JSON format (semi-structured data)
- The HTML format (unstructured data)

These files differ in layout (they just look different when we read them), and also in terms of how predictable their structures are. In other words, how much of the file is organized and has structured data? And how much of the data in the file is irregular or unstructured? Here, we discuss each of these text file formats individually.

The delimited format

Delimited files are extremely common as a way to share and transfer data. Delimited format files are just text files in which each data attribute (each *column*) and each instance of the data (each *row*) are separated by a consistent character symbol. We call the separator characters **delimiters**. The two most common delimiters are tabs and commas. These two common choices are reflected in the **Tab Separated Values** (**TSV**) and **Comma Separated Values** (**CSV**) file extensions, respectively. Sometimes, delimited files are also called **record-oriented** files, as the assumption is that each row represents a record.

Below are three instances of some data (three rows describing people), with data values separated by commas. The first row lists the names of the columns. This first row is also called the **header row**, and it has been highlighted in the data to show it more clearly:

```
First name,birth date,favorite color
Sally,1970-09-09,blue
Manu,1984-11-03,red
Martin,1978-12-10,yellow
```

Notice that with this example of delimited data, there is no *non-data* information. Everything is either a row or a data value. And the data is highly structured. Yet, there are still some options that can differentiate one delimited format from another. The first differentiator is how each instance of the data (each row) is separated. Usually at the end of a line, a new line, or a carriage return, or both are used depending on the operating environment in use during the creation of the file.

Seeing invisible characters

In the preceding example, the new line or carriage return is invisible. How do you see the invisible characters? We will read the same file in Text Wrangler on a Mac (similar full-featured editors such as Notepad++ are available for Windows), where we can use the **Show invisibles** option (located by navigating to **View | Text Display**).

```
First·name,birth·date,favorite·color¬
Sally,1970-09-09,blue¬
Manu,1984-11-03,red¬
Martin,1978-12-10,yellow¬
```

Another way to view the invisible characters is to use `vi` (a command-line text editor) on a Linux system or in the Terminal window on a Mac (this is not available on a Windows machine, by default). The process to view the invisible characters in a file using `vi` is as follows:

1. First, use the command:

   ```
   vi <filename>
   ```

2. Then, type `:` to enter the `vi` edit mode.
3. Then, type `set list` and press *Enter* to view the invisible characters.

The following screenshot shows the end-of-line characters that are revealed by `set list` in `vi`, showing line termination symbol $.

```
First name,birth date,favorite color$
Sally,1970-09-09,blue$
Manu,1984-11-03,red$
Martin,1978-12-10,yellow$
~
~
~
~
~
~
~
~
~
~
~
~
~
~
~
~
~
~
~
:set list
```

Enclosing values to trap errant characters

Another important option with delimited files is what character to use to enclose each value being separated. For example, comma-separated values are great unless you have numeric values with commas as the thousands separator. Consider the following example, where the salaries were given commas as their thousands separator, but commas are also the delimiter:

```
First name,birth date,favorite color,salary
Sally,1971-09-16,light blue,129,000
Manu,1984-11-03,red,159,960
Martin,1978-12-10,yellow,76,888
```

How can this be fixed at the point of file creation? Well, we have two options:

- **Option 1**: The person creating the delimited file would need to remove the commas in the final column before creating this table (in other words, no commas in salary amounts)
- **Option 2**: The person creating this file would need to use an additional symbol to enclose the data values themselves.

If option 2 is chosen, typically, a double quote separator is then added to enclose data values. So, `129,000` on the first line would become `"129,000"`.

Escaping characters

What if the data itself has quotation marks in it? What if Sally's favorite color were listed and shown as `light "Carolina" blue`? Take a look:

```
First name,birth date,favorite color,salary
"Sally","1971-09-16","light "Carolina" blue","129,000"
"Manu","1984-11-03","red","159,960"
"Martin","1978-12-10","yellow","76,888"
```

Internal quotation marks will have to be escaped through the use of another special character, the backslash \:

```
First name,birth date,favorite color,salary
"Sally","1971-09-16","light \"Carolina\" blue","129,000"
"Manu","1984-11-03","red","159,960"
"Martin","1978-12-10","yellow","76,888"
```

> Or, we could try encapsulating with a single quote instead of double quotes, but then we might have issues with possessives such as "it's" or names such as O'Malley. There's always something!

Delimited files are very convenient in that they are easy to understand and easy to access in a simple text editor. However, as we have seen, they also require a bit of planning in advance in order to ensure that the data values are truly separated properly and everything is formatted the way it was intended.

If you find yourself the unlucky recipient of a file with delimiting errors such as the preceding ones, we'll give you some tricks and tips in *Chapter 3, Workhorses of Clean Data – Spreadsheets and Text Editors*, for how to clean them up.

The JSON format

JavaScript Object Notation (JSON), pronounced *JAY-sahn*, is one of the more popular formats for what is sometimes called semi-structured data. Contrary to the implications in its name, JSON is not dependent upon JavaScript to be useful. The name refers to the fact that it was designed to serialize JavaScript objects.

A collection of data can be called semi-structured when its data values are labeled, but their order does not matter, and in fact, some of the data values may even be missing. A JSON file is just a collection of attribute-value pairs, such as this:

```
{
  "firstName": "Sally",
  "birthDate": "1971-09-16",
  "faveColor": "light\"Carolina\" blue",
  "salary":129000
}
```

The attributes are on the left-hand side of the colon, and the values are on the right-hand side. Each attribute is separated by a comma. The entire entity is enclosed in curly braces.

A few things about JSON are similar to delimited files, and a few things are different. First, string values must be double-quoted, and therefore, any double quotes internal to a string must be escaped with a backslash. (The escape character \ , when used as a regular character, must also be escaped!)

In JSON, commas cannot be included in numeric values unless the values are treated as strings and properly quoted. (Be careful when stringifying numbers, though—are you sure you want to do that? Then, refer to the *Data types* section in this chapter, which can help you with these issues.)

```
{
  "firstName": "Sally",
  "birthDate": "1971-09-16",
  "faveColor": "light\"Carolina\" blue",
  "salary": "129,000"
}
```

Multivalue attributes are acceptable, as are hierarchical values (neither of these are available very easily with delimited files). Here is an example of a JSON file with a multivalue attribute for `pet` and a hierarchy of data for `jobTitle`. Note that we've moved the `salary` data inside this new `job` hierarchy:

```
{
  "firstName": "Sally",
  "birthDate": "1971-09-16",
  "faveColor": "light\"Carolina\" blue",
  "pet":
  [
    {
      "type": "dog",
      "name": "Fido"
```

```
        },
        {
          "type": "dog",
          "name": "Lucky"
        }
      ],
      "job": {
        "jobTitle": "Data Scientist",
        "company": "Data Wizards, Inc.",
        "salary":129000
      }
    }
```

Experimenting with JSON

JSON is an extremely popular choice of data exchange format because of its extensibility, simplicity, and its support for multivalue attributes, missing attributes, and nested attributes / hierarchies of attributes. The increasing popularity of APIs for distributing datasets has also contributed to JSON's usefulness.

To see an example of how an API uses a search term to produce a **dataset** encoded in JSON, we can experiment with the iTunes API. iTunes is a music service run by Apple. Anyone can query the iTunes service for details about songs, artists, and albums. Search terms can be appended onto the iTunes API URL as follows:

```
https://itunes.apple.com/search?term=the+growlers
```

In this URL, everything after the `=` sign is a search term. In this case, I searched for a band I like, called The Growlers. Note that there is a + sign to represent the space character, as URLs do not allow spaces.

The iTunes API returns 50 results from its music database for my search keywords. The entire set is formatted as a JSON object. As with all JSON objects, it is formatted as a collection of **name-value** pairs. The JSON returned in this example appears very long, because there are 50 results returned, but each result is actually very simplistic—there are no multivalue attributes or even any hierarchical data in the iTunes data shown in this URL.

> For more details on how to use the iTunes API, visit the Apple iTunes developer documentation at `https://www.apple.com/itunes/affiliates/resources/documentation/itunes-store-web-service-search-api.html`.

The HTML format

HTML files, or web page files, are another type of text file that often have a lot of juicy data in them. How many times have you seen an interesting table, or list of information on a website, and wanted to save the data? Sometimes, copying and pasting works to try to create a delimited file from the web page, but most of the time, copying and pasting does not work effectively. HTML files can be terribly messy and thus, are a potentially painful way to extract data. For this reason, sometimes, we refer to web files as unstructured data. Even though web pages may have some HTML tags that could be used to attempt a delimiting type of pattern-based organization of data, they don't always. And there is also a lot of room for error in how these various HTML tags are applied, both across different websites and even within the same website.

The following figure shows just a small portion of the `http://weather.com` website. Even though there are pictures and colors and other non-text things in this screenshot, at its base level, this web page is written in HTML, and if we want to pull text data out of this page, we can do that.

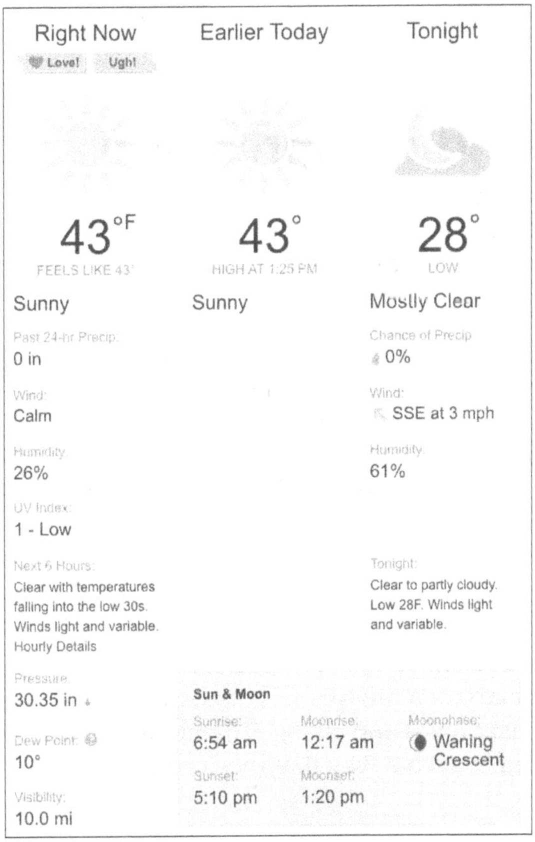

If we view the HTML source for the web page, we can locate a few lines of the nearly 1,000 lines of HTML code that comprise the data and layout instructions for the browser to show that particular weather table:

```
<div class="wx-temperature-label">FEELS LIKE
<span itemprop="feels-like-temperature-fahrenheit">43</span>&deg;</div>
</div>
<div class="wx-data-part">
<div class="wx-temperature">43<span class="wx-degrees">&deg;</span></div>
<div class="wx-temperature-label">HIGH AT 1:25 PM</div>
</div>
<div class="wx-data-part">
<div class="wx-temperature">28<span class="wx-degrees">&deg;</span></div>
<div class="wx-temperature-label">LOW</div>
</div>
```

Unstructured indeed! Of course, it is technically possible to pull the data value `43` (for the temperature in Fahrenheit) from this page, but it's not going to be a fun process, and we have no guarantee that our method to do that will be the same tomorrow or the day after that, as `http://weather.com` could change the source code for the site at any moment. Nonetheless, there is a ton of data on the Web, so in *Chapter 5, Collecting and Cleaning Data from the Web*, we cover a few strategies to extract data from web-based, unstructured files.

Archiving and compression

When is a text file also a binary file? When it's been compressed or archived, of course. What are archiving and compression? In this section, we'll learn what file archives and compressed files are, how archiving and compression work, and the various standards for each.

This is an important section as a lot of real-world data (especially, delimited data) will be compressed when you find it out in the real world. What are the most common compression formats that you as a data scientist are likely to run into? We will definitely find the answer to this question. You might also want to compress your data when you share it with others. How can you figure out which compression method is the best choice?

Archive files

An archive file is simply a single file that contains many files inside it. The files inside can be either text or binary or a mixture of both. Archive files are created by a special program that takes a list of files and changes them into a single file. Of course, the archive files are created in such a way that they can be expanded back into many files.

tar

The most common archived files that you are likely to encounter when doing data science work are so-called **Tape ARchive** (**TAR**) files, created using the tar program and usually given a `.tar` extension. Their original purpose was to create archives of magnetic tapes.

The tar program is available on Unix-like operating systems, and we can access it in the Mac OSX Terminal as well.

To create a tar file, you simply instruct the tar program which files you want included and what the output file name should be. (Program option `c` is used to indicate that we're creating a new archive file, and option `v` prints the filenames as they are extracted. The `f` option lets us specify the name of the output file.)

```
tar cvf fileArchive.tar reallyBigFile.csv anotherBigFile.csv
```

To "untar" a file (or expand it into the full listing of all the files), you just direct the tar program to the file you want expanded. The `x` letter in `xvf` stands for eXtract:

```
tar xvf fileArchive.tar
```

So, a `.tar` archive file includes multiple files, but how many and what are the files? You'll want to make sure that before you start extracting files, you have enough available disk space and that the files are really what you wanted to begin with. The `t` option in the tar command will show a list of the files inside a tar file:

```
tar -tf fileArchive.tar
```

There are many more archive programs apart from tar, but some of the interesting ones (for example, the built-in archiving ZIP compressor on OSX and the various ZIP and RAR utilities on Windows) also perform compression on the files, in addition to archiving, so we should probably discuss this concept next.

Compressed files

Compressed files are those files that have been made smaller so that they will take up less space. Smaller files mean less storage space on the disk and a faster transfer time if the file needs to be shared over the network. In the case of data files, like the ones we are interested in, the assumption is that the compressed file can be easily uncompressed back to the original.

How to compress files

There are numerous ways of creating compressed files, and which one you choose will depend on the operating system you are using and what compression software you have installed. On OSX, for example, any file or folder (or group) can easily be compressed by selecting it in **Finder**, right-clicking on it, and choosing **Compress** from the menu. This action will create a compressed (`.zip` extension) file in the same directory as the original file. This is shown in the following image:

How to uncompress files

The collection step of the data science process will often include downloading compressed files. These might be delimited text files, such as the ones we described earlier in this chapter, or they might be files containing multiple types of data files, such as spreadsheets or SQL commands used to build a database.

In any case, uncompressing a file returns the data to a state where we can use it to accomplish our goals. How do we know which program to use to uncompress the file? The first and biggest clue is the file's extension. This is a key tip-off as to what compression program created the file. Knowing how to uncompress the file is dependent on knowing how it was compressed.

In Windows, you can see the installed program that is associated with your file extension by right-clicking on the file and choosing **Properties**. Then, look for the **Open With** option to see which program Windows thinks will uncompress the file.

The remainder of this section will outline how to use command-line programs on OSX or a Linux system.

Compression with zip, gzip, and bzip2

zip, gzip and bzip2 are the most common compression programs. Their uncompression partners are called Unzip, Gunzip, and Bunzip2, respectively.

The following table shows a sample command-line for compressing and uncompressing in each of these programs.

	Compress	Uncompress
Zip	`zip filename.csv filename.zip`	`unzip filename.zip`
gzip	`gzip filename.csv filename.gz`	`gunzip filename.gz`
bzip2	`bzip2 filename.csv filename.bz2`	`bunzip2 filename.bz2`

Sometimes, you will see a file that includes both a `.tar` and a `.gz` extension or a `.bz2` extension like this: `somefile.tar.gz`. Other combinations that are common include: `.tgz` and `.tbz2`, as in `somefile.tgz`. These are files that have been tarred (archived) first and then compressed using gzip or bzip2. The reason for this is that gzip and bzip2 are not archiving programs; they are only compressors. Therefore, they can only compress a single file (or file archive) at a time. As tar's job is to make multiple files into single files, these programs are found together very often.

The tar program even has a built-in option that will gzip or bzip2 a file immediately after tarring it. To gzip the newly created `.tar` file, we can simply add `z` to the preceding tar command, and modify the filename:

```
tar cvzf fileArchive.tar.gz reallyBigFile.csv anotherBigFile.csv
```

Or, you can do this in two steps:

```
tar cvf fileArchive.tar reallyBigFile.csv anotherBigFile.csv
gzip fileArchive.tar
```

This sequence of commands will create the `fileArchive.tar.gz` file:

To uncompress a tar.gz file, use two steps:

```
gunzip fileArchive.tar.gz
tar xvf fileArchive.tar
```

These steps also work for bzip2 files:

```
tar cvjf fileArchive.tar.bz2 reallyBigFile.csv anotherBigFile.csv
```

To uncompress a tar.bz2 file, use two steps:

```
bunzip2 fileArchive.tar.bz
tar xvf fileArchive.tar
```

Compression options

When compressing and uncompressing, there are many other options you should take into consideration in order to make your data cleaning job easier:

- Do you want to compress a file and also keep the original? By default, most compression and archiving programs will remove the original file. If you want to keep the original file and also create a compressed version of it, you can usually specify this.
- Do you want to add new files to an existing compressed file? There are options for this in most archiving and compression programs. Sometimes, this is called **updating** or **replacing**.
- Do you want to encrypt the compressed file and require a password to open it? Many compression programs provide an option for this.
- When uncompressing, do you want to overwrite files in the directory with the same name? Look for a **force** option.

Depending on which compression software you are using and what its options are, you can use many of these options to make the job of dealing with files easier. This is especially true with large files—either large in size or large in number!

Which compression program should I use?

The concepts in this section on archiving and compression are widely applicable for any operating system and any type of compressed data files. Most of the time, we will be downloading compressed files from somewhere, and our main concern will be uncompressing these files efficiently.

However, what if you are creating compressed files yourself? What if you need to uncompress a data file, clean it, then recompress it and send it to a coworker? Or what if you are given a choice of files to download, each in a different compression format: zip, bz2, or gz? Which format should you choose?

Assuming that we are in an operating environment that allows you to work with multiple compression types, there are a few rules of thumb for what the various strengths and weaknesses of the different compression types are.

Some of the factors we use when making a compression decision are:

- The speed of compressing and uncompressing
- The compression ratio (how much smaller did the file get?)
- The interoperability of the compression solution (can my audience easily decompress this file?)

Rules of thumb

Gzip is faster to compress and decompress, and it is readily available on every OSX and Linux machine. However, some Windows users will not have a gunzip program readily available.

Bzip2 makes smaller files than gzip and zip, but it takes longer to do so. It is widespread on OSX and Linux. Windows users will probably struggle to handle bzip2 files if they have not already installed special software.

Zip is readily available on Linux, OSX, and Windows, and its speed to compress and decompress is not terrible. However, it does not create very favorable compression ratios (other compressors make smaller files). Still, its ubiquity and relative speed (compared to bzip2, for example) are strong points in its favor.

RAR is a widely available archiving and compression solution for Windows; however, its availability for OSX and Linux requires special software, and its compression speed is not as good as some of the other solutions.

Ultimately, you will have to decide on a compression standard based on the particular project you are working on and the needs of your audience or user, whether that is yourself, a customer, or a client.

Data types, nulls, and encodings

This section provides an overview of the most common data types that data scientists must deal with on a regular basis and some of the variations between these types. We also talk about converting between data types and how to safely convert without losing information (or at least understanding the risks beforehand).

This section also covers the mysterious world of empties, nulls, and blanks. We explore the various types of missing data and describe how missing data can negatively affect results of data analysis. We will compare choices and trade-offs for handling the missing data and some of the pros and cons of each method.

As much of our data will be stored as strings, we will learn to identify different character encodings and some of the common formats you will encounter with real-world data. We will learn how to identify character encoding problems and how to determine the proper type of character encoding for a particular dataset. We will write some Python code to convert from one encoding scheme to another. We will also cover the limitations of this strategy.

Data types

Whether we are cleaning data stored in a text file, a database system, or in some other format, we will start to recognize the same types of data make an appearance over and over: numbers of various kinds, dates, times, characters, strings of characters, and more. The upcoming sections describe a few of the most common data types, along with some examples of each.

Numeric data

In this section, we will discover that there are many ways to store a number, and some of them are easier to clean and manage than others. Still, numbers are fairly straightforward compared to strings and dates, so we will start with these before moving on to trickier data types.

Integers

Integers, or whole numbers, can be positive or negative, and just like the name implies, they do not have decimal points or fractions. Depending on what kind of storage system the integers are stored in, for example, in a **Database Management System** (**DBMS**), we may also have additional information about how large an integer can be stored as well as whether it is allowed to be signed (positive or negative values) or only unsigned (all positive values).

Numbers with decimals

In our data cleaning work, numbers with a fractional component—such as prices, averages, measurements, and the like—are typically expressed using a decimal point (rather than a numerator/denominator). Sometimes, the particular storage system in place also has rules specifying the number of digits that are allowed to come after the decimal point (**scale**) as well as the total number of digits allowed in the number (**precision**). For example, we say that the number 34.984 has a precision of 3 and a scale of 5.

Different data storage systems will also allow for different types of decimal numbers. For example, a DBMS may allow us to declare whether we will be storing floating-point numbers, decimal numbers, and currency/money numbers at the time we set up our database. Each of these will act slightly differently—in math problems, for instance. We will need to read the guidance provided by the DBMS for each data type and stay on top of changes. Many times, the DBMS provider will change the specifications for a particular data type because of memory concerns or the like.

Spreadsheet applications, on the other hand, unlike DBMS applications, are designed to display data in addition to just storing it. Therefore, we may actually be able to store a number in one format and display it in another. This can cause some confusion if formatting has been applied to data cells in a spreadsheet. The following figure shows an example of some decimal display properties being set for a cell. The formula bar shows the full number 34.984, but the cell shows that the number appears to have been rounded down.

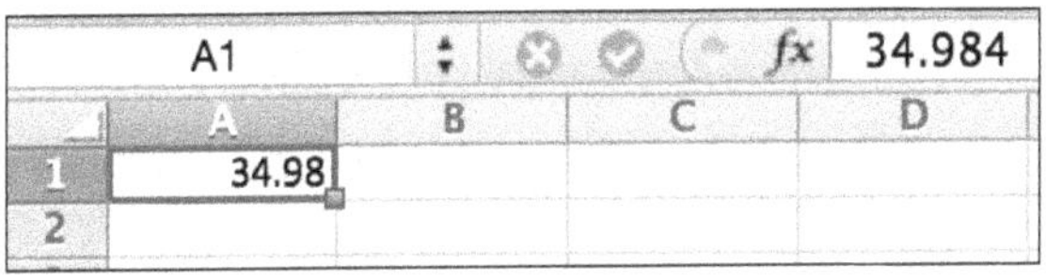

> In many locations around the world, the comma character separates the decimal from the nondecimal portion of a number rather than a dot or period character. This is a good reminder that it is always worth inspecting the localization settings of the system you are on and making sure that they match the expectations of the data you are working with. For example, in OSX, there is a **Language & Region** dialogue located in the **Systems Preferences** menu. From here, you can change your localization settings if you need to.

Unlike in a DBMS, a raw text file has no options to specify the size or expectations of a number field, and unlike a spreadsheet, the text file has no display options for a given data value either. If a text file shows a value of 34.98, then that may be all we know about that number.

When numbers are not numeric

Numeric data is first and foremost comprised of sequences of digits 0-9 and, sometimes, a decimal point. But a key point about true numeric data is that it is primarily designed to have calculations performed on it. We should choose numeric storage for our data when we expect to be able to *do math* on a data value, when we expect to compare one value to another numerically, or when we want items to be sorted in numeric order. In these cases, the data values need to be stored as numbers. Consider the following list of numbers sorted by their number value, low to high:

- 1
- 10
- 11
- 123
- 245
- 1016

Now, consider the same list sorted as if they are text values in an address field:

- 1 Elm Lane
- 10 Pine Cir.
- 1016 Pine Cir.
- 11 Front St.
- 123 Main St.
- 245 Oak Ave.

Telephone numbers and postal codes (and house numbers in street addresses as in the previous example) are often comprised of numeric digits, but when we think of them as data values, do they have more in common with text or with numeric data? Do we plan to add them, subtract them, or take their averages or standard deviations? If not, they may more appropriately be stored as text values.

Dates and time

You are probably familiar with many different ways of writing the same date, and you probably have some that you prefer over others. For instance, here are a few common ways of writing the same date:

- 11-23-14
- 11-23-2014
- 23-11-2014
- 2014-11-23
- 23-Nov-14
- November 23, 2014
- 23 November 2014
- Nov. 23, 2014

Regardless of our preference for writing dates, a complete date is made up of three parts: month, day, and year. Any date should be able to be parsed into these component parts. Areas of confusion with dates are usually in two areas: lack of clarity about the month signifier and a day signifier for numbers below 12, and confusion about specifying years. For example, if we only see "11-23", we can assume November 23, as there is no month abbreviated "23", but what year is it? If we see a date of "11-12", is that the 12th of November or the 11th of December? And in what year? Does a year of 38 signify 1938 or 2038?

Most DBMSes have a particular way you should import data if you have specified it as a date, and if you export data, you will get it back in that date format too. However, these systems also have many functions that you can apply to reformat dates or pull out just the pieces you want. For example, MySQL has many interesting date functions that allow us to pull out just the month or day, as well as more complicated functions that allow us to find out what week in the year a particular date falls in or what day of the week it was. For example, the following SQL counts the messages in the Enron dataset from *Chapter 1, Why Do You Need Clean Data?*, that were sent on May 12 each year, and it also prints the day of the week:

```
SELECT YEAR(date) AS yr, DAYOFWEEK(date) AS day, COUNT(mid)
FROM message WHERE MONTHNAME(date) = "May" AND DAY(date) = 12

GROUP BY yr, day

ORDER BY yr ASC;
```

Some spreadsheet programs, such as Excel, internally store dates as numbers but then allow the user to display the values in any format that they like using either built-in or custom formats. Excel stores a given date value as a fractional number of days since Dec 31, 1899. You can see the internal representation of a date in Excel by entering a date and asking for **General** formatting, as shown in the following figure. Excel stores May 21, 1986 as **31553**.

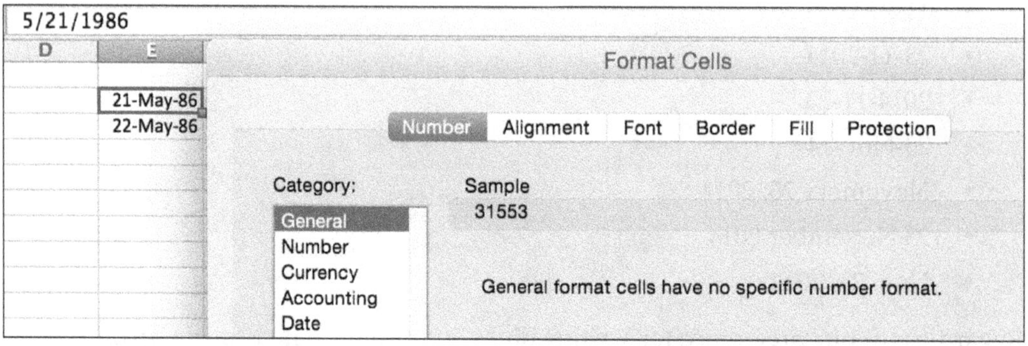

So, when you convert back and forth between different formats, switching the slashes to dashes, or swapping the order of months and days, Excel is just applying a different *look* to the date as you see it, but underneath, its internal representation of the date value has not changed.

Why does Excel need a fractional number to store the date since 1899? Isn't the number of days a whole number? It turns out that the fraction part is the way Excel stores time.

E	F
formatted as a date and time	formatted as 'general'
5/21/86 12:00 AM	31553
5/21/86 12:00 PM	31553.5
5/21/86 6:00 PM	31553.75

In the preceding figure, we can see how an internal date of 31553 is mapped to midnight, but 31553.5 (halfway through the day) is noon, and 31553.75 is 6 p.m. The greater precision we add to the decimal points, the greater time specificity we will get in the internal representation.

But not all data storage systems store dates and time as fractions, and they do not all start at the same spot. Some systems store dates and time as a number of seconds since the Unix epoch (00:00:00, January 1, 1970, universal time), and a negative number is used to store time before the epoch.

Both DBMS and spreadsheet applications allow for some date math, just like with numbers. In both types of systems, there are functions that allow dates to be subtracted to find a difference, or other calculations, such as adding a number of weeks to a day and getting a new day value.

Strings

Strings represent sequences of any character data, including alphabetic letters, numbers, spaces and punctuation, characters in hundreds of languages, and all kinds of special purpose symbols. Strings are very flexible, and this makes them the most common way to store data. Plus, as they can store nearly any other type of data (not necessarily efficiently), strings become the lowest common denominator to communicate data or move it from one system to another.

As with numeric data, the storage mechanism we are using at the moment may have some guidelines we are expected to use with strings. For example, a DBMS or spreadsheet may require that we state in advance what size we expect our strings to be or what types of characters we are expecting. Character encoding is an interesting and important area on its own, so we have a whole section on it coming up later in this chapter.

Or, there may be guidelines for the size of the data we are allowed to work with in a particular environment. In the world of databases, there are fixed and variable width character columns, which are designed to hold shorter strings, and some DBMS vendors have designed a text type that is intended to hold longer strings.

> Generically, many data scientists extend this terminology. As string data gets bigger and more unwieldy, it is referred to as text data, and its analysis becomes text analysis or text mining.

String (or text) data can be found in any of the file formats we talked about earlier in the chapter (delimited files, JSON, or web pages) and can be stored in or accessed by many of the storage solutions we talked about (APIs, DBMS, spreadsheets, and flat files). But no matter what the storage and delivery mechanism, it seems as though strings are most often discussed in same breath as big, messy, unstructured data. An Excel expert will be unfazed if asked to parse out the pieces of a few hundred street addresses or sort a few thousand book titles into categories. No statistician or programmer is going to blink if asked to count the character frequency in a word list. But when string manipulation turns into "extract the source code found embedded in 90 million e-mail messages written in Russian" or "calculate the lexical diversity of the entire contents of the Stack Overflow website", things get a lot more interesting.

Other data types

Numbers, dates/times, and strings are the *big three* data types, but there are many other types of exotic data that we will run into depending on what environment we are working in. Here is a quick rundown of some of the more interesting ones:

- **Sets/enums**: If your data seems to only have a few choices for possible data values, you may be looking at a set or enumerated (enum) type. An example of enumerated data might be the set of possible final grades in a college course: {A, A-, B+, B, B-, C+, C, C-, D+, D, D-, F, W}.
- **Booleans**: If your data is limited to one of just two selections, and they evaluate to 0/1 or true/false, you may be looking at Boolean data. A database column called `package_shipped` might have values of either yes or no, indicating whether a package has been shipped out.
- **Blobs (binary large objects)**: If your data is binary, for example, you are storing the actual bytes for a picture file (not just the link to it) or the actual bytes for an mp3 music file, then you are probably looking at blob data.

Converting between data types

Conversions between data types are an inevitable part of the cleaning job. You may be given string data, but you know that you need to perform math on it, so you wish to store it as a number. You may be given a date string in one format but you want it in a different date format. Before we go any further, though, we need to discuss a potential problem with conversions.

Data loss

There is a risk of losing data when converting from one data type to another. Usually, this happens when the target data type is not capable of storing as much detail as the original data type. Sometimes, we are not upset by data loss (in fact, there may even be times when a cleaning procedure will warrant some intentional loss), but if we are not expecting the data loss, it can be devastating. Risk factors include:

- **Converting between different sizes of the same data type**: Suppose you have a string column that is 200 characters long and you decide to move the data to a column that is only 100 characters long. Any data that exceeds 100 characters might be chopped off or truncated. This can also happen when switching between different sizes of numeric columns, for example, when going from big integers to regular integers or from regular integers to tiny integers.

- **Converting between different levels of precision**: Suppose you have a list of decimal numbers that are precise to four digits, and then you convert them to two digits of precision, or even worse, to integers. Each number will be rounded off or truncated, and you will lose the precision that you had.

Strategies for conversion

There are many strategies to handle data type conversions, and which one you use depends on where the data is being stored at the moment. We are going to cover two of the most common ways in which we encounter data type conversions in the data science cleaning process.

The first strategy, SQL-based manipulation, will apply if we have data in a database. We can use database functions, available in nearly every database system, to slice and dice the data into a different format, suitable for either exporting as a query result or for storing in another column.

The second strategy, file-based manipulation, comes into play when we have been given a flat file of data—for example, a spreadsheet or JSON file—and we need to manipulate the data types in some way after reading them out of the file.

Type conversion at the SQL level

Here, we will walk through a few common cases when SQL can be used to manipulate data types.

Example one – parsing MySQL date into a formatted string

For this example, we will return to the Enron e-mail dataset we used in *Chapter 1, Why Do You Need Clean Data?*. As with the previous example, we are going to look in the message table, where we have been using the date column, which is stored as a `datetime` MySQL data type. Suppose we want to print a full date with spelled-out months (as opposed to numbers) and even the day of the week and time of day. How can we best achieve this?

For the record with the message ID (mid) of 52, we have:

```
2000-01-21 04:51:00
```

We want is this:

```
4:51am, Friday, January 21, 2000
```

- Option 1: Use `concat()` and individual date and time functions, as shown in the following code sample. The weakness of this option is that the a.m./p.m. is not printed easily:

```
SELECT concat(hour(date),
':',
minute(date),
', ',
dayname(date),
', ',
monthname(date),
' ',
day(date),
', ',
year(date))
FROM message
  WHERE mid=52;
```

Result:

```
4:51, Friday, January 21, 2000
```

If we decided that we really wanted the a.m./p.m., we could use an if statement that tests the hour and prints "a.m". if the hour is less than 12 and "pm" otherwise:

```
SELECT concat(
  concat(hour(date),
    ':',
    minute(date)),
  if(hour(date)<12,'am','pm'),
  concat(
    ', ',
    dayname(date),
    ', ',
    monthname(date),
    ' ',
    day(date),
    ', ',
    year(date)
```

```
    )
)
FROM message
WHERE mid=52;
```

Result:

```
4:51am Friday, January 21, 2000
```

> MySQL date and time functions, such as `day()` and `year()`, are described in their documentation: `http://dev.mysql.com/doc/refman/5.7/en/date-and-time-functions.html`, and their string functions, such as `concat()`, can be found here: `http://dev.mysql.com/doc/refman/5.7/en/string-functions.html`. Other database management systems will have similar versions of these functions.

- Option 2: Use the more sophisticated `date_format()` MySQL function. This function takes a series of string specifiers for how you want the date to be formatted. There is a very long list of these specifiers in the MySQL documentation. A completed example to convert the date into our desired format is shown in the following code:

```
SELECT date_format(date, '%l:%i%p, %W, %M %e, %Y')
FROM message
WHERE mid=52;
```

Result:

```
4:51AM, Friday, January 21, 2000
```

This is pretty close to what we said we wanted, and it is much shorter than Option 1. The only difference is that the a.m./p.m. is capitalized. If we really want it lowercased, we can do this:

```
SELECT concat(
  date_format(date, '%l:%i'),
  lower(date_format(date,'%p ')),
  date_format(date,'%W, %M %e, %Y')
)
FROM message
WHERE mid=52;
```

Result:

```
4:51am, Friday, January 21, 2000
```

Example two – converting a string into MySQL's date type

For this example, let's look at a new table in the Enron schema: the table called `referenceinfo`. This table shows the messages to which the other messages refer. For example, the first entry in that table, with a `rfid 2`, contains the text of the e-mail to which message 79 refers. The column is a string, and its data looks like this (in part):

```
> From: Le Vine, Debi> Sent: Thursday, August 17, 2000 6:29 PM> To:
ISO Market Participants> Subject: Request for Bids - Contract for
Generation Under Gas> Curtailment Conditions>> Attached is a Request
for Bids to supply the California ISO with> Generation
```

This is a very messy string! Let's take on the job of extracting the date shown on the top line and converting it into a MySQL date type, suitable for inserting into another table or for performing some date math.

To do this, we will use the built-in `str_to_date()` MySQL function. This function is a bit like `date_format()` that we saw earlier, except that it's backwards. Here is a working example that will look for the word `Sent:` and extract the following characters up to the > symbol and then turn these characters into a real MySQL datetime data type:

```
SELECT
str_to_date(
  substring_index(
    substring_index(reference,'>',3),
    'Sent: ',
    -1
  ),
  '%W,%M %e, %Y %h:%i %p'
)
FROM referenceinfo
WHERE mid=79;
```

Result:

```
2000-08-17 18:29:00
```

Now we have a datetime value that is ready for inserting into a new MySQL column or for performing more date functions or calculations on it.

Example three – casting or converting MySQL string data to a decimal number

In this example, let's consider how to convert numbers hiding inside a text column into a format suitable for calculations.

Suppose we were interested in extracting the price for a barrel of oil (abbreviated *bbl*) from some e-mail messages sent to Enron from a mailing list. We could write a query such that every time we see the `/bbl` string in an e-mail message from a certain sender, we look for the preceding dollar sign and extract the attached numeric value as a decimal number.

Here is a sample snippet from an e-mail message in the Enron message table with a message ID (`mid`) of 270516, showing how the number looks inside the string:

```
March had slipped by 51 cts at the same time to trade at $18.47/bbl.
```

The MySQL command to perform this string extraction and conversion to a decimal is as follows:

```
SELECT convert(
          substring_index(
            substring(
              body,
              locate('$',body)+1
            ),
            '/bbl',
            1
          ),
          decimal(4,2)
      ) as price
FROM message
WHERE body LIKE "%$%" AND body LIKE "%/bbl%" AND sender =
  'energybulletin@platts.com';
```

The `WHERE` clause restrictions are added so that we make sure we are only getting messages that have bbl oil prices in them.

The `convert()` function is similar to `cast()` in MySQL. Most modern database systems will have a way of converting data types into numbers like this.

Type conversion at the file level

In this section, we will show some common cases when data types will need to be manipulated at the file level.

> This material really only applies to file types where there is an implicit typing structure, for example, spreadsheets and semi-structured data like JSON. We have no examples here that use delimited (text-only) flat files, as in a text file, all data is text data!

Example one – type detection and converting in Excel

You may be familiar with type converting in Excel and similar spreadsheet applications via the cell formatting menu options. The typical procedure involves selecting the cells you want to change and using the drop-down menu located on the ribbon.

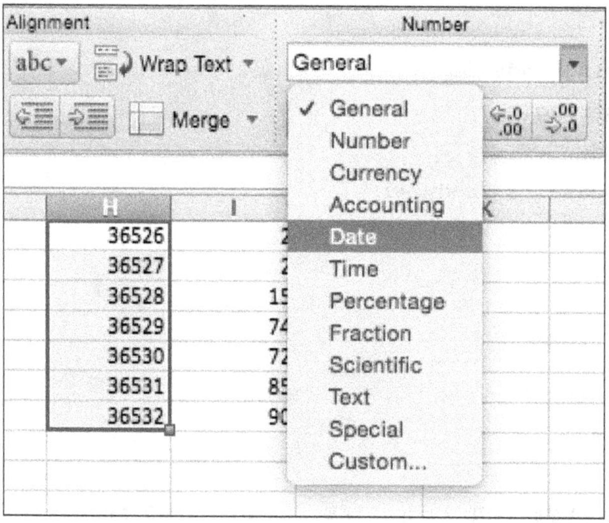

Or, if that does not offer enough options, there is also the **Format Cells** dialogue, located in the format menu, which offers more granular control over the output of the conversion process.

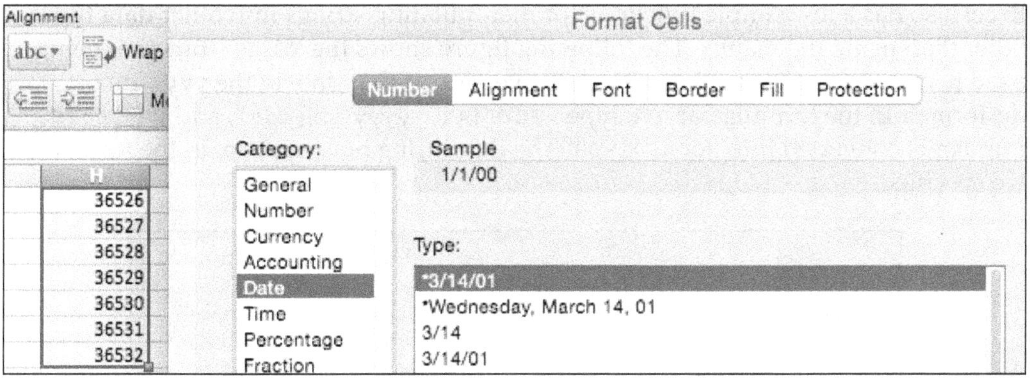

The lesser-known `istext()` and `isnumber()` functions may also be useful in formatting data in Excel.

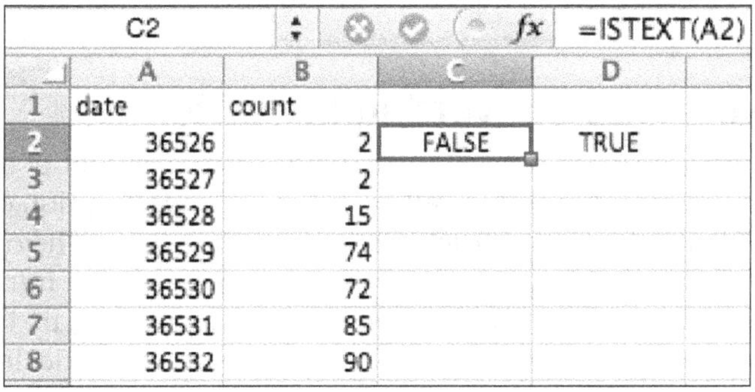

C2
fx
=ISTEXT(A2)
A
B
C
D
1 date count
2 36526 2 FALSE TRUE
3 36527 2
4 36528 15
5 36529 74
6 36530 72
7 36531 85
8 36532 90

These functions can be applied to any cell, and they return **TRUE** or **FALSE** depending on whether the data is text or not, or in the case of `isnumber()`, whether the number is really a number or not. Paired with a feature like conditional formatting, these two formulas can help you locate bad values or incorrectly typed values in small amounts of data.

Excel also has a few simple functions for manipulating strings into other data types, other than using the menus. The following figure shows the `TEXT()` function being used to convert a numeric date to a string version of that date in the yyyy-mm-dd format. In the formula bar, we type `=TEXT(A4,"yyyy-mm-dd")`, and the `36528` number is converted into `2000-01-03`. The date string now appears in the format we specified.

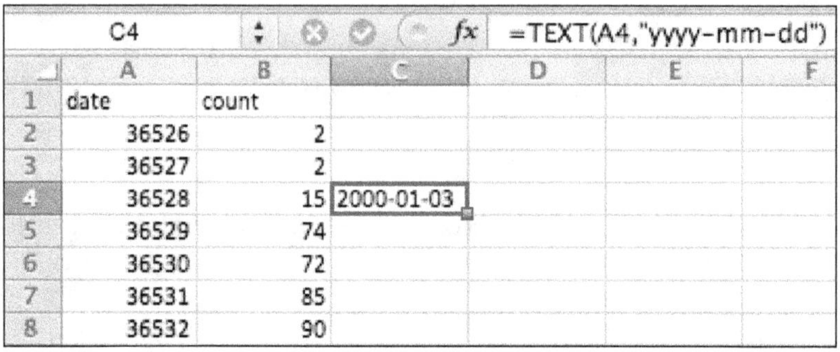

	A	B	C	D	E	F
1	date	count				
2	36526	2				
3	36527	2				
4	36528	15	2000-01-03			
5	36529	74				
6	36530	72				
7	36531	85				
8	36532	90				

Example two – type converting in JSON

JSON, as a semi-structured text-based format, does not offer a lot of options in the way of formatting and data types. Recall from the JSON description earlier in this chapter that JSON objects are constructed as name-value pairs. The only options for formatting the value part of a name-value pair are a text string, a number, or a list. While it is possible to build JSON objects by hand—for example, by typing them out in a text editor—usually, we build JSON objects programmatically, either by exporting JSON from a database or by writing a small program to convert a flat text file into JSON.

What happens if our program that is designed to generate JSON is flawed? Suppose the program gives us strings instead of numbers. This happens occasionally and it can have unintended consequences for any program designed to consume JSON. The following is an example showing some simple PHP code that is designed to generate JSON, which will later be read into D3 to build a graph.

The PHP code to generate a JSON representation of a dataset from a database is straightforward. The sample code, as shown in the following example, connects to the Enron database, builds a query, runs the query, puts each part of the query result into an array, and then encodes the array values as JSON name-value pairs. Here is the code to build a list of dates and counts, just like the dates and counts we used in *Chapter 1, Why Do You Need Clean Data?*:

```
<?php
// connect to db
$dbc = mysqli_connect('localhost','username','password','enron')
```

```
        or die('Error connecting to database!' . mysqli_error());

// the same sample count-by-date query from chapter 1
$select_query = "SELECT date(date) AS dateSent, count(mid) AS
numMsg FROM message GROUP BY 1 ORDER BY 1";
$select_result = mysqli_query($dbc, $select_query);
// die if the query failed
if (!$select_result)
        die ("SELECT failed! [$select_query]" .  mysqli_error());
// build a new array, suitable for json printing
$counts = array();
while($row = mysqli_fetch_array($select_result))
{
      array_push($counts, array('dateSent' => $row['dateSent'],
        'numMsg'    => $row['numMsg']));
}
echo json_encode($counts);
?>
```

> Note that the `json_encode()` function requires PHP version 5.3 or higher, and this example relies on the same working Enron database that we built in *Chapter 1, Why Do You Need Clean Data?*.

The problem here is that the result is stringified—PHP has placed the numeric values for `numMsg` in quotation marks, which in JSON means string values:

```
[
  {"dateSent":"0001-05-30","numMsg":"2"},
  {"dateSent":"0001-06-18","numMsg":"1"}
]
```

To nudge the PHP function to be really careful about numeric values and not just assume that everything is a string, we will need to specifically convert the values to numbers before printing them to the screen. Simply change the way we call `json_encode()` so that it looks like this:

```
echo json_encode($counts, JSON_NUMERIC_CHECK);
```

Now the JSON result includes actual numbers for `numMsg`:

```
[
  {"dateSent":"0001-05-30","numMsg":2},
  {"dateSent":"0001-06-18","numMsg":1}
]
```

PHP includes similar functions for converting big integers to strings as well. This can be useful when you have extremely large numbers but you need them to be stored as string data for some reason, for example, when storing session values or Facebook or Twitter user ID values.

If we do not control the PHP code that is generating the JSON output—for example, if we are accessing the JSON via an API and we don't have any control over its generation—then we'll have to perform a conversion after the JSON has already been built. In this case, we need to ask our D3 JavaScript code to coerce the strings into numbers using a + operator on that data value. In this example, we have read the JSON output and are preparing to build a graph. The `numMsg` value has been coerced from a string to a number:

```
d3.json("counts.json", function(d) {
  return {
    dateSent: d.dateSent,
    numMsg: +d.numMsg
  };
}, function(error, rows) {
  console.log(rows);
});
```

If a null falls in a forest...

In this section, we are going to dip our chef's ladle into the mysterious stew of zeroes, empties, and nulls.

What is the difference between these? Well, as I mentioned stew, consider this illustration first. Imagine you have a top-of-the-line stove in your fancy chef's kitchen, and on that stove, you are going to prepare a pot of thick, hearty stew. Your sous chef asks you, "How much stew is in the pot?". Take a look at these options:

1. At the beginning of the day, you observe that there is no pot on the stove. The question "how much stew is in the pot?" is unanswerable. There is no pot! The answer is not a positive value, it is not a zero value, and it is not even empty. The value is **NULL**.
2. A few hours later, after much cleaning and chopping, you look in the pot and see three liters of delicious stew. Great; you now have an answer to the question. In this case, our answer is a **data value of 3**.

3. After the lunch rush, you look in the pot again and discover that there is no more stew. Every last drop has been sold. You looked, you measured, and you found the answer to "how much stew is in the pot?" is a **zero** value. You send the pot to be washed at the sink.
4. Just before the evening meal, you grab the clean pot from the sink. As you walk across the kitchen, the sous chef asks, "What's in the pot?" Currently, the pot is **empty**. There is nothing in the pot. Note that the answer is not zero, because the question he asked was not a numeric one. The answer is also not NULL because we *DO* have a pot, and we *DID* look inside it, but there was just no answer.

Different data and programming environments (DBMS, storage systems, and programming languages) treat these zero, empty, and NULL concepts slightly differently. Not all of them clearly distinguish between all four cases. Therefore, this chapter is written somewhat generically, and when examples are given, we try to point out which environment we are applying them to. It is important to be aware of what *you* mean in each environment when you say that something is null, empty, or zero. And when you see these values in real-world datasets, it is important to be clear about what you can (and cannot) assume about each.

> A special caveat for those dealing with Oracle databases: empty, blank, and NULL are different in Oracle when compared to many other systems. Proceed with caution through this section and consult your database documentation for details specific to Oracle.

Zero

First things first. Of the zeroes, empties, and NULLs, the easiest to deal with is the zero value. Zero is a measurable quantity and has meaning in a numeric system. We can sort zeroes (they come before 1, 2, 3...), and we can compare other numbers to zero using the handy number line (-2, -1, 0, 1, 2, 3...). We can also perform math on zeroes (except for division by zero, which is always awkward).

As a legitimate value, zero works best as numeric data. A string value of zero does not make much sense as it would end up just needing to be interpreted as 0, or the character of 0, which is probably not really the spirit of what we intended.

Empties

Empties are a bit more tricky to work with than zeroes, but they make a lot of sense in some cases, for instance, when working with strings. For example, suppose we have an attribute called middle name. Well, I have no middle name so I would always like to leave this field empty. (Fun fact: my mother still tells the story of how my Kindergarten graduation certificate shows a middle name that I made up on the spot, too shy to admit to my teacher that I lacked a middle name.) Filling in a space or a hyphen (or making up something) for a value that is truly empty does not make a lot of sense. Space is not the same thing as empty. The correct value in the case of an empty string may, in fact, be "empty".

In a CSV or delimited file, an empty value can look like this—here, we have emptied out the favorite color values for the second two records:

```
First name,birth date,favorite color,salary
"Sally","1971-09-16","light blue",129000
"Manu","1984-11-03","",159960
"Martin","1978-12-10","",76888
```

In an `INSERT` database, for example, to put the `Manu` record into a MySQL system, we would use some code like this:

```
INSERT INTO people (firstName, birthdate, faveoriteColor, salary)
  VALUES ("Manu","1984-11-03","",159960);
```

Sometimes, semi-structured data formats, such as JSON, will allow a blank object and blank strings. Consider this example:

```
{
  "firstName": "Sally",
  "birthDate": "1971-09-16",
  "faveColor": "",
  "pet": [],
  "job": {
    "jobTitle": "Data Scientist",
    "company": "Data Wizards, Inc.",
    "salary":129000
  }
}
```

Here, we have taken away Sally's pets and made her favorite color an empty string.

Blanks

Be aware that " " (two double quotes with a space in between, sometimes called a blank but more appropriately called a **space**) is not necessarily the same thing as "" (two double quotes right next to each other, sometimes also called a blank but more appropriately called **empty**). Consider the difference between these two MySQL INSERT statements:

```
-- this SQL has an empty for Sally's favoriteColor and a space for
Frank's
INSERT INTO people (firstName, birthdate, faveoriteColor, salary)
VALUES ("Sally","1971-09-16","",129000),
       ("Frank","1975-10-23"," ",76000);
```

In addition to spaces, other invisible characters that sometimes get accidentally interpreted as empty or blank include tabs and carriage returns / line feeds. Be careful of these, and when in doubt, use some of the tricks introduced earlier in this chapter to uncover invisible characters.

Null

I know that if you look up **null** in the dictionary, it might say that it means zero. But do not be fooled. In computing, we have a whole host of special definitions for NULL. To us, NULL is not nothing; in fact, it is the absence of even nothing.

How is this different than empty? First, empty can be equal to empty, as the length of the empty string will be 0. So, we can imagine a value existing, against which we can perform comparisons. However, NULL cannot be equal to NULL, and NOT NULL will not be equal to NOT NULL either. I have heard it suggested that we should all repeat as a mantra that *NULL is not equal to anything, even itself.*

We use NULL when we legitimately want no entry of any kind for the data value. We do not even want to put the pot on the stove!

Why is the middle name example "empty" and not NULL?

Good question. Recall from the stew pot analogy that if we ask the question and the answer is empty, it is different from never getting an answer (NULL). If you asked me what my middle name was and I told you I did not have one, then the data value is empty. But if you just do not know whether I have a middle name or not, then the data value is NULL.

Is it ever useful to clean data using a zero instead of an empty or null?

Maybe. Remember in the e-mail example from *Chapter 1, Why Do You Need Clean Data?*, when we discussed adding missing dates to our line graph and how the various spreadsheet programs automatically filled in a count of zero when creating a line graph with missing dates? Even though we had not counted the e-mails on those dates, our graphs interpolated the missing values as if they were zeroes. Are we OK with this? Well, it depends. If we can confirm the fact that the e-mail system was live and working on these dates, and we are confident that we have the full collection of e-mails sent, then the count for these dates could truly be inferred to be zero. However, in the case of the Enron e-mails we were using in *Chapter 1, Why Do You Need Clean Data?*, we were pretty sure that was *not* the case.

Another case where it might be useful to store a zero-type data instead of empty is when we have a dummy date or only part of a date, for example, if you know the month and year, but not the day, and you have to insert data into a full date column. Filling in 2014-11-00 might be the way to go in that instance. But you should, of course, document this action (refer to the *Communicating about data cleaning* section in *Chapter 1, Why Do You Need Clean Data?*) because what you did and why is probably not going to be obvious to you looking at this data six months from now!

Character encodings

In the olden days of computing, every string value had to be constructed from only 128 different symbols. This early encoding system, called **American Standard Code for Information Exchange** (**ASCII**), was largely based on the English alphabet, and it was set in stone. The 128 characters included a-z, A-Z, 0-9, some punctuation and spaces, as well as some now-useless Teletype codes. In our data science kitchen, using this type of encoding system today would be like cooking a frozen dinner. Yes, it is cheap, but it also lacks variety and nutrition, and you really cannot expect to serve it to a guest.

In the early 1990s, a variable length encoding system, now called **UTF-8**, was proposed and standardized. This variable length scheme allows many more natural language symbols to be encoded properly as well as all the mathematical symbols and provides plenty of room to grow in the future. (The list of all these symbols is called **Unicode**. The encoding for the Unicode symbols is called UTF-8.) There is also now a UTF-16 encoding, where each character takes a minimum of two bytes to encode. At the time of writing this, UTF-8 is the predominant encoding for the Web.

For our purposes in this book, we are mostly concerned with what to do with data that exists in one encoding and must be cleaned by converting it to another encoding. Some example scenarios where this could be relevant include:

- You have a MySQL database that has been created using a simple encoding (such as one of the 256-bit Latin-1 character sets that are the default on MySQL), and which stores UTF-8 data as Latin-1, but you would now like to convert the entire table to UTF-8.
- You have a Python 2.7 program that uses functions designed for ASCII but must now handle UTF-8 files or strings.

In this section, we will work through a few basic examples based on these scenarios. There are many more equally likely situations where you will encounter character encoding issues, but this will be a starting point.

Example one – finding multibyte characters in MySQL data

Suppose we have a column of data and we are curious about how many values in that column actually have multibyte encoding. Characters that appear as a single character but take multiple bytes to encode can be discovered by comparing their length in bytes (using the `length()` function) to their length in characters (using the `char_length()` function).

> The following example uses the MyISAM version of the MySQL World database that is available as part of the MySQL documentation at `http://dev.mysql.com/doc/index-other.html`

By default, the MyISAM version of the MySQL World test database uses the `latin1_swedish_ci` character encoding. So, if we run a query on a country name that has a special character in it, we might see something like the following for Côte d'Ivoire:

```
SELECT Name, length(Name)
FROM Country
WHERE Code='CIV';
```

This shows the length of 15 for the country, and the name of the country Côte d'Ivoire is encoded as CÃ™te dÃIvoire. There are several other entries in various columns that are encoded strangely as well. To fix this, we can change the default collation of the name column to `utf8` with the following SQL command:

```
ALTER TABLE  Country
  CHANGE Name `Name` CHAR(52)
  CHARACTER SET utf8
  COLLATE utf8_general_ci
  NOT NULL DEFAULT  '';
```

Now we can empty the table and insert the 239 Country rows again:

```
TRUNCATE Country;
```

Now we have `Country` names that use UTF-8 encoding. We can test to see whether any of the countries are using a multibyte character representation for their name now by running the following SQL:

```
SELECT *
  FROM Country
  WHERE length(Name) != char_length(Name);
```

It shows that the Côte d'Ivoire and the French island Réunion both have multibyte character representations.

Here is another example if you do not have access to the world dataset, or in fact, any dataset at all. You can run a comparison of multibyte characters as a MySQL select command:

```
SELECT length('私は、データを愛し'), char_length('私は、データを愛し');
```

In this example, the Japanese characters have a length of 27 but a character length of 9.

This technique is used when we want to test the character set of our data—maybe you have too many rows to look one at a time, and you simply want a SQL statement that can show you all the multibyte entries at once so that you can make a plan for how to clean them. This command shows us the data that currently has a multibyte format.

Example two – finding the UTF-8 and Latin-1 equivalents of Unicode characters stored in MySQL

The following code will use the `convert()` function and the `RLIKE` operator to print the UTF-8 equivalent of Unicode strings that have been saved to MySQL using Latin-1. This is useful if you have multibyte data that has been stored in Latin-1 encoded text columns in MySQL, an unfortunately common occurrence as Latin-1 is still the default (as of MySQL 5).

This code uses the publicly available and widely used Movielens database of movies and their reviews. The entire movielens dataset is widely available on many websites, including from the original project site: `http://grouplens.org/datasets/movielens/`. Another SQL-friendly link is here: `https://github.com/ankane/movielens.sql`. To make it easier to work through these examples, the `CREATE` and `INSERT` statements for just a small subset of the relevant rows have been made available on the author's GitHub site for this book: `https://github.com/megansquire/datacleaning/blob/master/ch2movies.sql`. This way, if you prefer, you can simply create this one table using that code and work through the following example.

```
SELECT convert(
  convert(title USING BINARY) USING latin1
  ) AS 'latin1 version',
convert(
  convert(title USING BINARY) USING utf8
) AS 'utf8 version'
FROM movies
  WHERE convert(title USING BINARY)
    RLIKE concat(
    '[',
    unhex('80'),
    '-',
    unhex('FF'),
    ']'
  );
```

The following screenshot shows the results for the first three movies after running this command in phpMyAdmin on the Latin-1 encoded title column in the movies table within the Movielens database:

latin-1 version	utf-8 version
City of Lost Children, The (CitÃ© des enfants perd...	City of Lost Children, The (Cité des enfants perdu...
MisÃ©rables, Les (1995)	Misérables, Les (1995)
Happiness Is in the Field (Bonheur est dans le prÃ...	Happiness Is in the Field (Bonheur est dans le pré...

> Any advice for converting an existing database to UTF-8?
>
> Because of the ubiquity of UTF-8 on the Web and its importance in accurately conveying information written in natural languages from around the world, we strongly recommend that you create new databases in a UTF-8 encoding scheme. It will be far easier to start off in a UTF-8 encoding than not.
>
> However, if you have the tables already created in a non-UTF-8 encoding, but they are not yet populated with data, you will have to alter the table to a UTF-8 encoding and change the character set of each column to a UTF-8 encoding. Then, you will be ready to insert UTF-8 data.
>
> The hardest case is when you have a large amount of data already in a non-UTF-8 encoding, and you want to convert it in place in the database. In this case, you have some planning to do. You'll have to take a different approach depending on whether you can get away with running commands on a few tables and/or a few columns or whether you have a very long list of columns and tables to adjust. In planning this conversion, you should consult the documentation specific to your database system. For example, when performing MySQL conversions, there are solutions that use either the `mysqldump` utility or those that use a combination of `SELECT`, `convert()`, and `INSERT`. You will have to determine which of these is right for your database system.

Example three – handling UTF-8 encoding at the file level

Sometimes, you will need to adjust your code to deal with UTF-8 data at file level. Imagine a simple program designed to collect and print web content. If the majority of web content is now UTF-8 encoded, then our program internals need to be ready to handle that. Unfortunately, many programming languages still need a little bit of coaxing in order to handle UTF-8 encoded data cleanly. Consider the following example of a Python 2.7 program designed to connect to Twitter using its API and write 10 tweets to a file:

```
import twitter
import sys

####################
def oauth_login():
    CONSUMER_KEY = ''
    CONSUMER_SECRET = ''
    OAUTH_TOKEN = ''
    OAUTH_TOKEN_SECRET = ''
    auth = twitter.oauth.OAuth(OAUTH_TOKEN, OAUTH_TOKEN_SECRET,
                               CONSUMER_KEY, CONSUMER_SECRET)
    twitter_api = twitter.Twitter(auth=auth)
    return twitter_api
###################

twitter_api = oauth_login()
codeword = 'DataCleaning'
twitter_stream = twitter.TwitterStream(auth=twitter_api.auth)
stream = twitter_stream.statuses.filter(track=codeword)

f = open('outfile.txt','wb')
counter = 0
max_tweets = 10
for tweet in stream:
    print counter, "-", tweet['text'][0:10]
    f.write(tweet['text'])
    f.write('\n')
    counter += 1
    if counter >= max_tweets:
        f.close()
        sys.exit()
```

If you are worried about setting up Twitter authentication in order to get the keys and tokens used in this script, do not worry. You can either work your way through the simple setup procedure at `https://dev.twitter.com/apps/new`, or we have a much longer, in-depth example of Twitter mining in *Chapter 10, Twitter Project*. In that chapter, we walk through the entire setup of a Twitter developer account and go over the tweet collection procedure in much more detail.

This little program finds 10 recent tweets that use the keyword **DataCleaning**. (I chose this keyword because I recently posted several tweets full of emojis and UTF-8 characters using this hashtag, I was pretty sure it would quickly generate some nice results characters within the first 10 tweets.) However, asking Python to save these tweets to a file using this code results in the following error message:

```
UnicodeEncodeError: 'ascii' codec can't encode character u'\u00c9' in
position 72: ordinal not in range(128)
```

The issue is that `open()` is not prepared to handle UTF-8 characters. We have two choices for a fix: strip out UTF-8 characters or change the way we write files.

Option one – strip out the UTF-8 characters

If we take this route, we need to understand that by stripping out characters, we have lost data that could be meaningful. As we discussed earlier in this chapter, data loss is generally an undesirable thing. Still, if we did want to strip these characters, we could make the following changes to the original `for` loop:

```
for tweet in stream:
    encoded_tweet = tweet['text'].encode('ascii','ignore')
    print counter, "-", encoded_tweet[0:10]
    f.write(encoded_tweet)
```

This new code changes an original tweet written in Icelandic like this:

```
Ég elska gögn
```

To this:

```
g elska ggn
```

For text analysis purposes, this sentence no longer makes any sense as g and ggn are not words. This is probably not our best option for cleaning the character encoding of these tweets.

Option two – write the file in a way that can handle UTF-8 characters

Another option is to just use the `codecs` or `io` libraries, which allow UTF-8 encoding to be specified at the time the file is opened. Add an import codec line at the top of the file, and then change the line where you open the file like this:

```
f = codecs.open('outfile.txt', 'a+', 'utf-8')
```

The `a+` parameter states we want to append the data to the file if it has already been created.

Another option is to include the `io` library at the top of your program and then use its version of `open()`, which can be passed a particular encoding, as follows:

```
f= io.open('outfile.txt', 'a+', encoding='utf8')
```

> Can we just use Python 3? Why are you still using 2.7?
>
> It is true that Python 3 handles UTF-8 encodings more easily than Python 2.7. Feel free to use Python 3 if the rest of your development environment can handle it. In my world, I prefer to use Enthought Canopy to work in data analysis and data mining and to teach my students. Many distributions of Python—Enthought included—are written for 2.7 and will not be moved to Python 3 for quite some time. The reason for this is that Python 3 made some major changes to the internals of the language (for example, in supporting UTF-8 encodings naturally, as we just discussed), and this means that there were a lot of important and useful packages that still have to be rewritten to work with it. This rewriting process takes a long time. For more on this issue, visit `https://wiki.python.org/moin/Python2orPython3`

Summary

This chapter covered a whirlwind of fundamental topics that we will need in order to clean data in the rest of this book. Some of the techniques we learned here were simple, and some were exotic. We learned about file formats, compression, data types, and character encodings at both the file level and database level. In the next chapter, we will tackle two more workhorses of clean data: the spreadsheet and the text editor.

3

Workhorses of Clean Data – Spreadsheets and Text Editors

When designing a home kitchen, the typical layout invokes the classic work triangle, the points of which are the refrigerator, sink, and stove. In our Clean Data kitchen, we have a few indispensible devices as well. Two of these are the humble **spreadsheet** and the **text editor**. Although these unpretentious tools are often overlooked, full knowledge of their features can make many cleaning tasks quicker and easier. In *Chapter 2, Fundamentals – Formats, Types, and Encodings*, we briefly introduced these two tools in the context of learning about data types and file types, but in this chapter, we are ready to dig deeper into:

- Useful functions in Excel and Google Spreadsheets that can help us manipulate data, including text to columns, splitting and concatenating strings, searching and formatting to find unusual values, sorting, importing spreadsheet data into MySQL, and even generating SQL using a spreadsheet
- Typical features of a text editor that can automatically extract and manipulate data into a more useful format, including searching and replacing with regular expressions, altering line beginnings and endings, and column-based editing
- A small project where we use features of both of these tools to clean some real-world data

Spreadsheet data cleaning

The utility of the spreadsheet for data cleaning comes from two things: its ability to organize data into columns and rows and its suite of built-in functions. In this section, we will learn how to use the spreadsheet to its fullest in our quest for clean data.

Text to columns in Excel

As spreadsheets are designed to hold data in columns and rows, one of the first cleaning tasks we might need to do is arrange our data accordingly. For instance, if you paste a large amount of data into Excel or Google Spreadsheets, the software will first try to look for a delimiter (such as a comma or tab) and divide the data into columns that way. (Refer to *Chapter 2, Fundamentals – Formats, Types, and Encodings*, for a review of delimited data.) Sometimes, the spreadsheet software will not find a delimiter, so we will have to provide it more guidance about how to divide the data into columns. Consider the following snippet of text from a list of several thousand Internet Relay Chat channel topics on Freenode:

```
[2014-09-19 14:10:47] === #eurovision   4   Congratulations to
Austria, winner of the Eurovision Song Contest 2014!
[2014-09-19 14:10:47] === #tinkerforge   3
[2014-09-19 14:10:47] === ##new   3   Welcome to ##NEW
```

> To generate a list of channels and their topics in an IRC chat server, use the `alis` command, which can be sent as part of either `/query` or `/msg`, depending on your server's settings. On Freenode, the `/msg alis *` command will generate a list of channels. More information on IRC chat can be found here: `https://freenode.net/services.shtml`

We can see with our human eyes that the first chunk of data is a timestamp, followed by `===`, `#` and a channel name, a number (the count of users on the channel at the moment the list was constructed), and a description of the channel. However, if we paste these lines into Excel or Google Spreadsheets, it is unable to automatically make the same observations about what columns should be. The rows are detected correctly by the spreadsheet, but the delimiting is too inconsistent for columns to be detected automatically. How the data looks when pasted into Google Spreadsheets is given in the following image. By highlighting cell A1, we can see that the entire line is shown in the formula bar, indicating that the entire row has been pasted into cell A1:

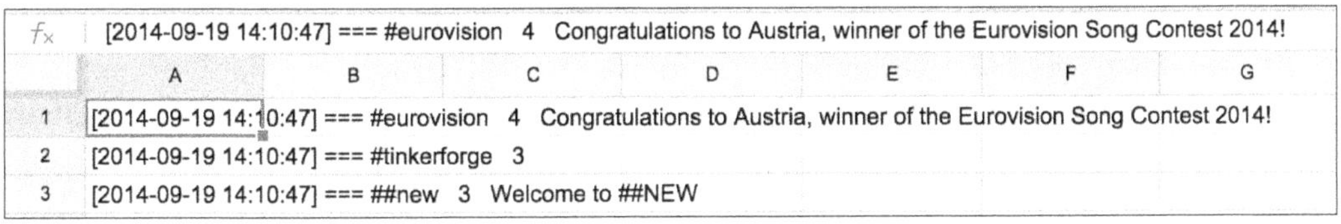

How can we easily create columns from this data in the spreadsheet? We would like each separate data item to be in its own column. By doing this, we will be able to, for example, take an average of the number of users on the channels or sort the data by the channel names. Right now, we cannot easily sort or use formulas on this data as it is all in one giant text string.

One strategy will be to use Excel's text-to-columns wizard to split the data into recognizable chunks; then, we can reassemble them and strip out extra characters if needed. This is shown in the steps mentioned as follows:

1. Highlight column `A`, and launch the text-to-columns wizard (located in the Data menu). In step 1, choose a fixed width, and in step 2, double-click on all the lines that have been drawn to delimit the description field. The following figure shows you how the data should look after delimiting the first few columns and removing all the extra lines:

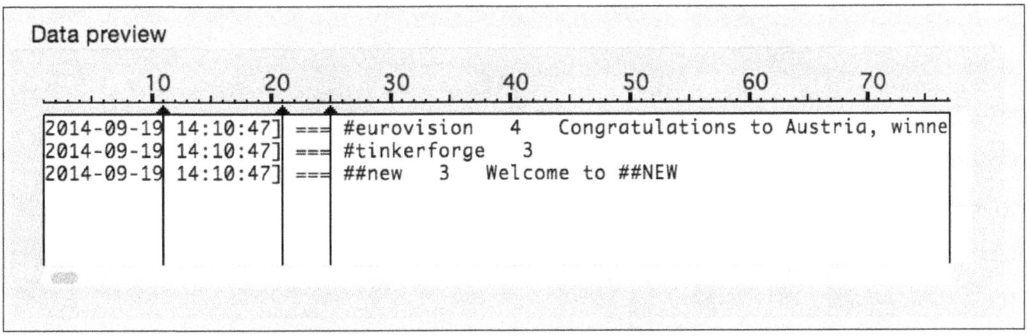

Fixed-width splitting in Excel.

The resulting data looks like the following figure. The first three columns are good, but the fixed-width delimiting did not work to separate the count of users and channel names in column D. This happened because the channel names are not as predictable in length as the previous columns.

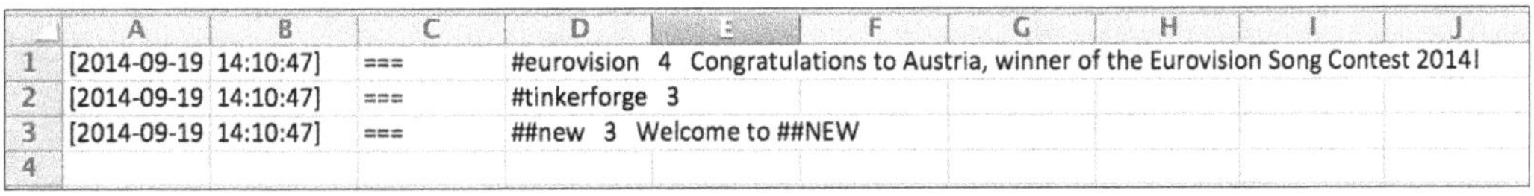

This is the result after the first round of text-to-columns splitting.

2. We will have to run text-to-columns again but just on column D this time, and we will use delimited instead of fixed-width procedure. First, note that there are two spaces between the channel name **#eurovision** and the number of users (**4**) and two spaces again between **4** and the channel description. Even though text-to-columns does not allow us to type two spaces as a delimiter (it allows single characters only), we can use the **Find-Replace** dialogue to replace all cases of two spaces with a symbol that is not used anywhere else in our text. (Perform a **Find** operation first to make sure.) I chose a ^ symbol.

   This particular step seems a little sloppy, so if you are interested in an alternate approach, I do not blame you one bit. Excel is more limited than other tools in its ability to find and replace bad text. We will learn how to use regular expressions in the *Text editor data cleaning* section later in this chapter.

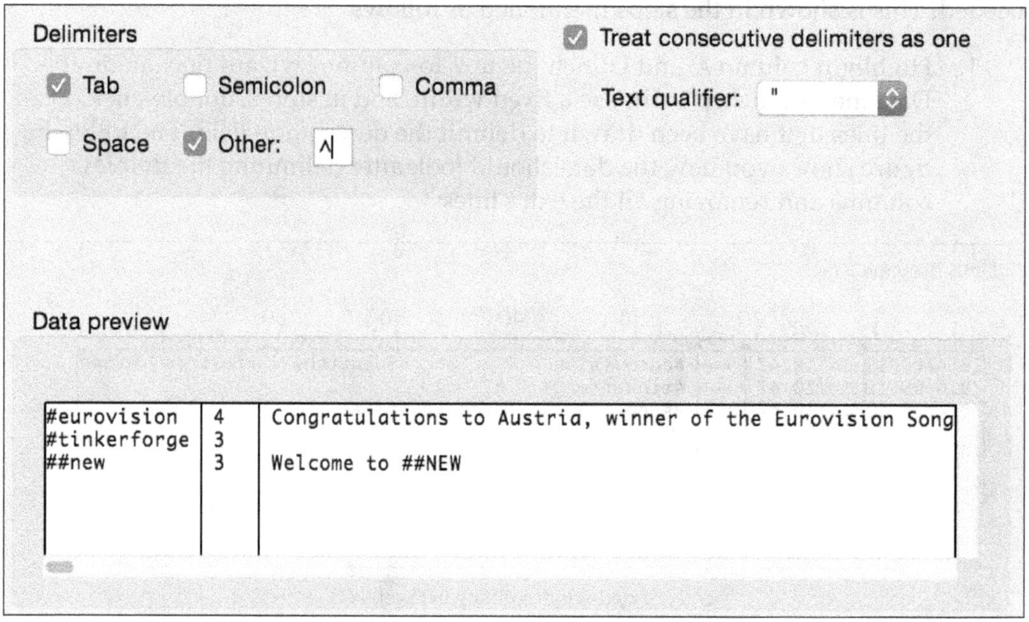

Adding an unusual delimiting character allows us to split apart the remaining columns.

3. Now, use **Find-Replace** to remove the `[` and `]` characters from columns A and B, replacing them with nothing. (Highlight these columns before starting find-replace so that you do not accidentally remove symbols throughout the whole sheet.)

   Unfortunately, Excel, in its eternal quest to try to help us, turns these into dates formatted in a way we might not like: 9/19/2014. If you want these to go back to the way they were (2014-09-19), select the entire column and use the custom format dialogue to specify the date format as yyyy-mm-dd.

4. The strings in column **F** still have extra space at the beginning. We can strip the extra spaces from the front of each string value using the `trim()` function. Insert a new column to the left of **F**, and apply the `trim()` function, shown as follows:

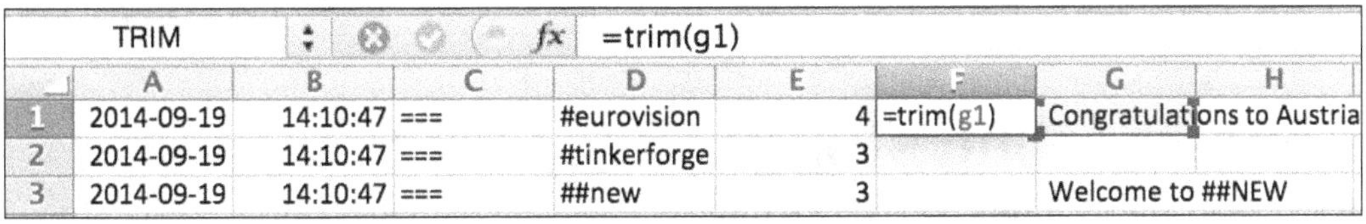

   This is the result of applying the `trim()` function to strip out leading or trailing spaces.

5. We can also apply the `clean()` function to the trimmed text. This will remove any of the first 32 ASCII characters: all non-printing control characters that may have somehow made their way into these channel descriptions. You can apply `clean()` outside `trim()` functions like this: `clean(trim(g1))`.

6. Drag the corner of the F1 box down to apply `clean(trim())` to the rest of the cells in column **F**.

7. Select column **F**, copy it, and use **Paste Special Values Only** in column **F** so that we can delete column **G**.

8. Delete column **G**. Voila, now you have perfectly cleaned data.

Splitting strings

A lightweight version of the text to columns feature, available in Google Spreadsheets but not in Excel, is the `split()` function. This function just takes a string value and splits it into its component pieces. Be aware that you need to provide enough new columns for the newly split data to fit into. In the following example, we have used the same data as the previous example but created three new columns to hold the split values from **D**.

fx =split(D1,"-")

	A	B	C	D
1	2014	9	19	2014-09-19
2	2014	9	19	2014-09-19
3	2014	9	19	2014-09-19

Concatenating strings

The `concatenate()` function takes a number of strings, either as cell references or as quoted strings, and attaches them together inside a new cell. In the following example, we use the `concatenate()` function to join the date and time strings into one. This function is available in both Excel and Google Spreadsheets, as shown in the following figure:

fx =CONCATENATE(B1," ",C1)

	A	B	C
1	2014-09-19 14:10:47	2014-09-19	14:10:47
2	2014-09-19 14:10:47	2014-09-19	14:10:47
3	2014-09-19 14:10:47	2014-09-19	14:10:47

Conditional formatting to find unusual values

Both Excel and Google spreadsheets have **conditional formatting** features. Conditional formatting uses a set of rules to change the appearance (format) of a cell or cells depending on whether some criteria are met (condition). We can use this to find data that is too high, too low, missing, or otherwise strange. Once we have identified it, we can clean it.

Here is an example of how to use conditional formatting in Google Spreadsheets to find a row in our sample data that does not include # in the channel name and has an empty value for the number of chat participants:

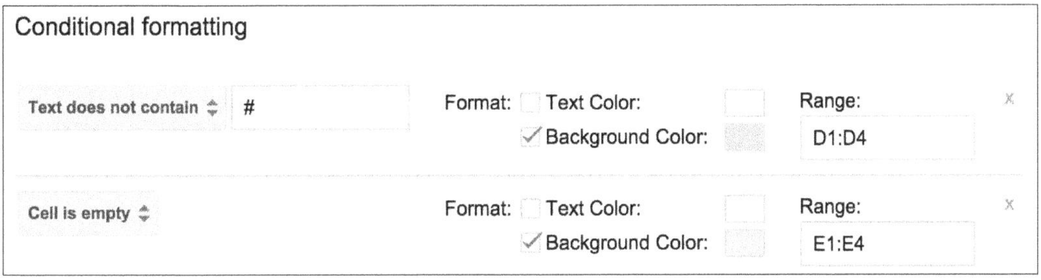

Here is the result after the background cell colors have been changed to locate cells in **D** that do not start with # and cells in **E** that are empty. Now these problem values can be found easily with a visual inspection.

	A	B	C	D	E	F
1	2014-09-19 14:10:47	2014-09-19	14:10:47	#eurovision	4	Congratulations to Au
2	2014-09-19 14:10:47	2014-09-19	14:10:47	#tinkerforge	3	
3	2014-09-19 14:10:47	2014-09-19	14:10:47	##new	3	Welcome to ##NEW
4	2014-09-20 14:10:48	2014-09-20	14:10:48	/END OF LIST		

Sorting to find unusual values

If there is too much data for a visual inspection, then we could try to employ sorting to find the troublesome data. In either Google Spreadsheets or Excel, select the columns you want to sort, which can be the entire sheet, and use the **Sort** option in the **Data** menu. This works fairly easily for most of the columns, especially if you are looking for data like cell D4.

But what happens if you try to sort by column **E** in order to find that missing value? Maybe we would like to put all the missing data together so that we can delete these rows of data. The value for E4 is empty. Remember from *Chapter 2, Fundamentals – Formats, Types, and Encodings*, that NULL (empty in Google Spreadsheets parlance) cannot be compared to any other value, so it remains at the bottom of the sorted list no matter whether you sort the values in column **E** from low to high or high to low.

Importing spreadsheet data into MySQL

Now that you have a lovely spreadsheet full of clean data, you might wish to store it in a database for the long term.

Creating CSV from a spreadsheet

Many database systems will accept data via an import routine built around CSV files. If you are using MySQL, there is a `LOAD DATA IN FILE` command that will slurp data right into the database from a delimited file, and you can even set your own delimiter. First, let's take a look at an example of the command, and then we can create the file in Excel according to the parameters we want.

From the MySQL command line, we can run:

```
load data local infile 'myFile.csv'
  into table freenode_topics
  fields terminated by ','
  (dateOfTopic, channel, numUsers, message);
```

This, of course, assumes that a table has already been created. In this case, it is called `freenode_topics`, and it has four columns in it, which appear on the last line of this SQL query.

The CSV file referenced in this query, `myFile.csv`, will therefore need to have the columns in this order and separated by commas.

In Excel, a CSV can be created from the current sheet in a workbook by navigating to **File** | **Save As** and then choosing **CSV (MS-DOS)** from the list of format options. In Google Spreadsheets, you can accomplish the same thing by navigating to **File** | **Downloads** | **CSV**. In both cases, save the file to your local system and then launch the MySQL client and proceed through the command line shown previously.

> If you do not like using the MySQL command-line client, CSV files can also be uploaded to a server using MySQL's own Workbench graphical client or using a tool like PhpMyAdmin. PhpMyAdmin does have a size limit on the upload file (currently, 2 MB).

Generating SQL using a spreadsheet

Another way to get data into a database seems strange at first, but it can be a real timesaver if you are unable—for whatever reason, maybe because of the wrong permissions or because of file size limits—to load it via the CSV discussed previously. In this method, we will build `INSERT` statements inside the spreadsheet itself and then run these commands in the database.

If each column in the spreadsheet represents a column in the database, then we can simply add the structural components of a SQL `INSERT` command (quoted strings, parenthesis, commands, and line-terminating semicolons) around the columns in the spreadsheet and concatenate the result together into a giant string of `INSERT` commands.

fx INSERT INTO freenode_topics (dateOfTopic, channel,num_users,message) VALUES('

	A	B	C	D	E	F	G	H	I
1	INSERT INTO freenode_topic	2014-09-19 14:10:47	','	#eurovision	',	4	,'	Congratulations to Aus	');
2	INSERT INTO freenode_topic	2014-09-19 14:10:47	','	#tinkerforge	',	3	,'		');
3	INSERT INTO freenode_topic	2014-09-19 14:10:47	','	##new	',	3	,'	Welcome to ##NEW	');

After using the `concatenate(A1:I1)` function to attach all the strings in columns A:I, we end up with `INSERT` statements that look like this:

```
INSERT INTO freenode_topics (dateOfTopic, channel, num_users,
  message) VALUES('2014-09-19 14:10:47', '#eurovision',4,
  'Congratulations to Austria, winner of the Eurovision Song Contest
  2014!');
```

These can be pasted into a user-friendly frontend, such as PhpMyAdmin or MySQL Workbench. Or, you can save this as a text file (using your text editor), one `INSERT` statement after the other. I called my file `inserts.sql`. This file can now be imported into the database using the command line and MySQL client, as follows:

```
$mysql -uusername -p -hhostname databasename < inserts.sql
```

Or, it can be imported using the `source` command in the MySQL command-line client like this:

```
$mysql -uusername -p -hhostname
[enter your password]
> use databasename;
> source inserts.sql
```

Either one of these will work to get the data into MySQL. If the script is small enough, you can also use one of the graphical clients, such as MySQL Workbench. Be careful of loading very large scripts into the graphical client, however, as the amount of memory on your client machine may not be sufficient to load hundreds of gigabytes of SQL. I prefer the second method (`source`) because it prints out a success message following each successful insert, so I know my commands are good.

If you are a little unclear about how you would go about creating a text file called `inserts.sql`, then the next section is for you. We are going to cover more than you ever thought you would want to know about text editors!

Text editor data cleaning

We learned in *Chapter 2, Fundamentals – Formats, Types, and Encodings*, that text editors are the preferred way of reading and creating text files. This sounds reasonable and makes perfect sense. What we did not really explain back then was that a text editor is sometimes also called a programmer's editor because it has many cool features that help folks such as programmers, as well as data cleaners, who must deal with text files all day long. We are going to take a tour of some of the most useful features now.

> There are dozens of text editors available for every operating system. Some of them cost money, but many are available at no cost. For this chapter, I am going to use Text Wrangler, a no cost editor available for OSX (available here: `http://www.barebones.com/products/textwrangler`). The features shown in this chapter are widely available in most other editors, such as Sublime Editor, but you should check the documentation for whatever editor you have chosen if the location of a particular feature or tool is not obvious.

Text tweaking

Our text editor of choice has a number of useful functions built into it for text manipulation. The ones outlined here represent some of the most commonly used ones for data cleaning tasks. Keep in mind that you might run dozens of cleaning routines on a single text file in the course of cleaning it, so the tips we gave in *Chapter 1, Why Do You Need Clean Data?*, for how to clearly communicate the changes you made will really come in handy here.

Changing case is a very common request in data cleaning. Many times, we will inherit data that is all lowercase or all uppercase. The following image shows a dialogue within Text Wrangler to perform case changes on a selection of text. The keyboard shortcuts are shown to the right of each option.

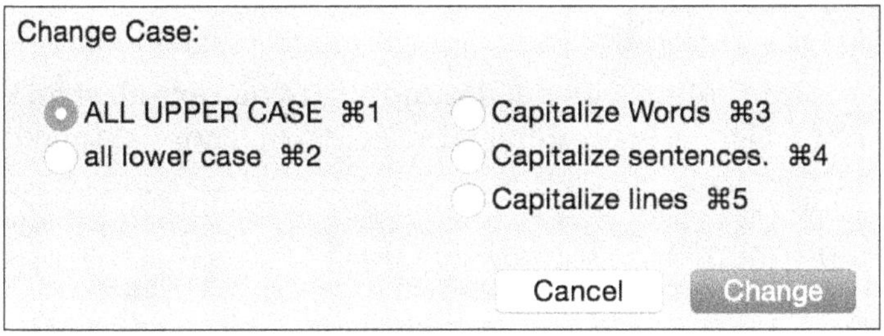

Options for case changes include uppercase and lowercase as well as capitalizing the first letter of each word, line, or the first word in a sentence.

Adding or removing prefixes or suffixes on each line in a selection is another common task. I needed to do this for a large amount of text lines the other day when I was building a text classifier. I needed to suffix each line with a comma and the name of what class (positive or negative) the line exemplified. Here is the prefix and suffix dialogue in Text Wrangler. Note how you can either insert or remove, but not both, in the same maneuver. If you need to perform both of these tasks, perform one, and then perform the other.

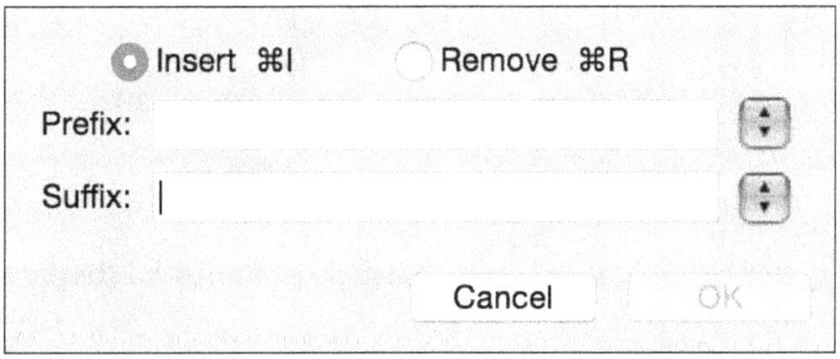

Zapping gremlins is another excellent task for your text editor. Both TextWrangler and Sublime Editor for Windows have this feature. In zapping gremlins, the editor can look for any characters that are outside of your desired character set, for example, control characters, NULL characters, and non-ASCII characters. It can either delete them or replace them with their character code. It could also replace the gremlins with any character that you specify. This makes them easier to find later.

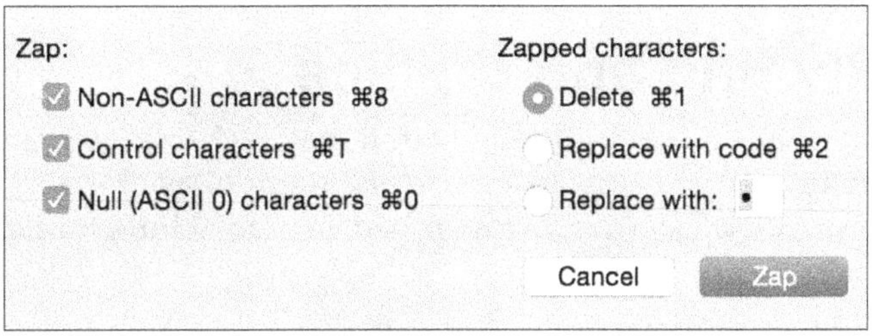

The column mode

When a text editor is in **column mode**, it means that you can select text in columns and not just in rows. Here is an example of selection in a normal (non-column) mode:

```
[2014-09-19 14:10:47] === #eurovision    4    Congratulations to Austria,
[2014-09-19 14:10:47] === #tinkerforge    3
[2014-09-19 14:10:47] === ##new    3    Welcome to ##NEW
[2014-09-19 14:10:47] === #postcyberpunk    3    Postcyberpunk related ma
[2014-09-19 14:10:47] === #osi    7    The Open Source Initiative
[2014-09-19 14:10:48] === #apg-dev    3    APG - latest version: 1.1.1 -
```

Here is an example of a selection in column mode. Hold down the **Option** key and select the text in columns. Once the text is selected, you can treat it just like you would treat any selected text: you can delete it, cut it or copy it onto the clipboard, or use any of the text tweaks we discussed in the preceding section as long as they work on a selection.

```
[2014-09-19 14:10:47] === #eurovision    4    Congratulations to Austria,
[2014-09-19 14:10:47] === #tinkerforge    3
[2014-09-19 14:10:47] === ##new    3    Welcome to ##NEW
[2014-09-19 14:10:47] === #postcyberpunk    3    Postcyberpunk related ma
[2014-09-19 14:10:47] === #osi    7    The Open Source Initiative
[2014-09-19 14:10:48] === #apg-dev    3    APG - latest version: 1.1.1 -
```

A few limitations of this feature include:

- Each character is one column, so characters should be displayed in a non-proportional, typewriter-style typeface.
- In Text Wrangler, the column mode only works when line wrapping is turned off. Turning off soft wrapping means your lines will extend to the right and not be wrapped.
- In Text Wrangler, the vertical height of the column you are drawing must be able to be drawn by you manually, so this is a technique for small amounts of data (hundreds or thousands of rows, but probably not hundreds *of* thousands of rows).

Heavy duty find and replace

Text editors really shine at manipulating text. It may feel strange to use a text editor in the column mode, as that seems like more of a natural task for a spreadsheet. Similarly, it may seem awkward to use a spreadsheet for **Find-Replace** after you see what a text editor can do.

The main portion of the **Find** dialogue window in Text Wrangler is shown as follows. The provided features include options for case-sensitive searches, wrapping around, searching in subselections of text, and looking for the given text pattern inside either a word or just a portion of a word. You can also paste special characters, whitespace (including tabs and line terminators), emojis, and so on, into the textbox. The little drop-down boxes to the right of the **Find** box provide additional functionality. The top one with the clock icon on it holds a list of recent searches and replacements. The bottom one with the letter **g** on it holds a list of built-in search patterns that might be useful, and at the bottom of this menu is an option to add your own patterns to the list.

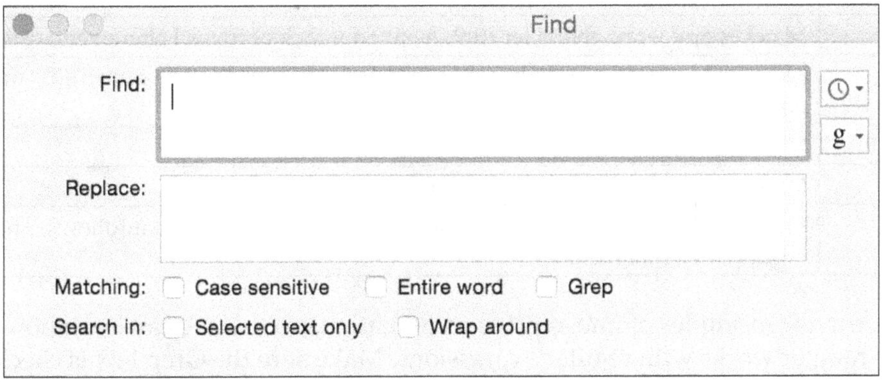

One of the most powerful find-replace features is enabled by the **Grep** checkbox. Checking this box allows us to use a regular expression pattern for our searches. In short, a **regular expression** (**regex**) is a pattern written in a special language, made up of symbols, and designed to match against some string text. A full treatment of regular expressions is beyond the scope of this book, but suffice it to say that they are enormously useful and we will be visiting them periodically when we need them to clean data.

> The reason the checkbox in the Text Wrangler interface says Grep—and not RegEx or Match—is that there are several slight variations on the regular expression pattern-matching language. Text Wrangler is signaling to us that it is using the one from Grep, a program originally written for Unix and the most common variant.

Here, we will outline a few of the indispensible regular expression symbols that we will use time and again to clean data. For more complicated patterns, it is worth consulting a special book or one of the myriad web pages that show all kinds of exotic regular expression syntaxes:

Symbol	What it does
`$`	Matches the end of the line
`^`	Matches the beginning of the line
`+`	Matches one or more of the specified characters
`*`	Matches 0 or more of the specified characters
`\w`	Matches any word character (0-9, A-z). To match nonword characters, use `\W`
`\s`	Matches any whitespace character (tab, line feed, or carriage return). To match non-whitespace characters, use `\S`
`\t`	Matches a tab character
`\r`	Matches a carriage return. Use `\n` for line feed.
`\`	This is the escape character. It matches the exact character that follows, not the regex pattern character.

Here are a few examples of find-replace combinations so that we can learn how Text Wrangler works with regular expressions. Make sure the Grep box is checked. If nothing is shown in the replace column, it means that the Replace field should be left empty.

Find	Replace	What it does
`\r`		Finds a line feed (line terminator) and replaces it with nothing. Another way to phrase this is "make multiple lines into one line".
`^\w+`	`-`	Matches the beginning of the line, followed by at least a one-word character. Adds a `-` character to the front of the line.
`\\r$`	`\[end\]`	Looks for all lines that end with the actual `\r` characters (backslash followed by r) and replaces them with the actual characters `[end]`. Note that [and] are special regex characters as well, so they will need to be escaped to use them as actual characters.

If regular expressions seem daunting, take heart. First, recall from the *Text tweaking* section earlier in this chapter that most text editors, Text Wrangler included, have many built-in search and replace features that are built on the most common regular expressions. So, you may find that you do not really have to write many regular expressions very often. Second, as regular expressions are so powerful and so useful, there are a lot of online resources that you can consult to learn how to build a complicated regex if you need it.

Two of my favorite resources for regex are Stack Overflow (`http://stackoverflow.com`) and regular-expresions.info (`http://regular-expressions.info`). There are also numerous regular expression testing websites available via a quick web search. These sites let you write and test the regular expressions on a sample text.

A word of caution

Be careful when using online regex testers, however, as they are usually designed to teach a particular flavor of regular expressions, such as for the regex parsers inside JavaScript, PHP, or Python. Some of the things you want to do may have the same regular expression syntax in your text editor as the one in these languages, or they may not. Depending on the complexity of what you are trying to do, it may be a better idea just to create a backup copy of your text data (or extract a small sample of the text in question into a new file) and experiment on it in your own text editor using its regular expression syntax.

Text sorting and processing duplicates

Once we have experimented with regex a little bit, we notice that our text editor will occasionally make these pattern-matching techniques available in other menu options, for example, in sorting and duplicate processing. Consider the following sorting dialogue to see how a regex can be applied to sorting multiple lines:

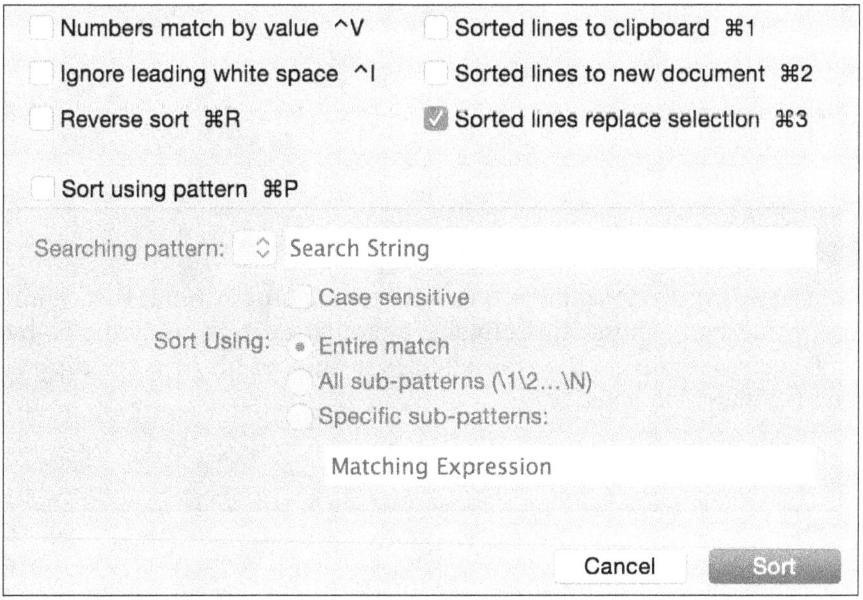

In this case, we can use the **Sort using pattern** checkbox to enter a regular expression pattern to sort by. The duplicate processing dialogue is similar. You can tell the editor whether to leave the original line or remove it. Interestingly, you can also remove the duplicates to another file or to the clipboard if you need to use them for something else, such as keeping a log of removed lines, perhaps.

> In data cleaning, it is a good idea to at least consider saving the removed lines into their own file in case you ever need them again.

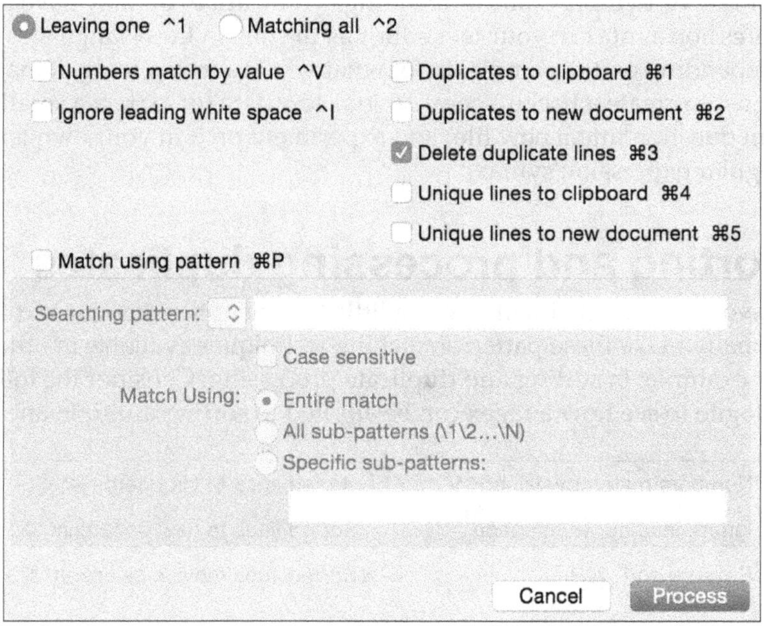

Process Lines Containing

One handy feature in Text Wrangler is called **Process Lines Containing**. It mixes searching (including the possibility of using a regular expression) with line-by-line processing, such as removing the affected lines to another file or to the clipboard, or deleting the matching lines.

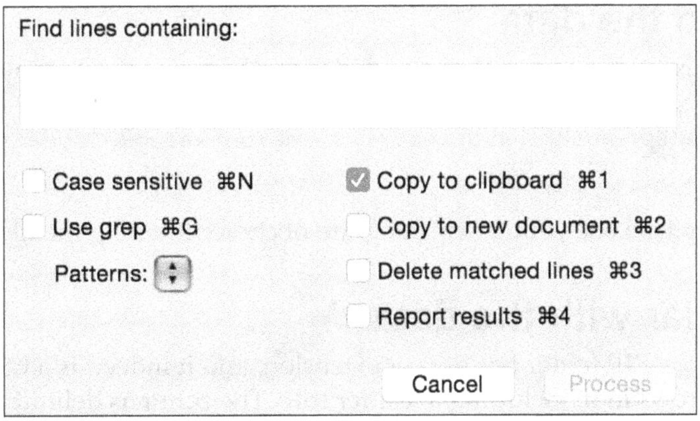

An example project

In this example project, we will download a spreadsheet, use Excel or a text editor to clean it, and then run some simple analyses on it.

Step one – state the problem

This project is inspired by some data made available by the Chronicle of Higher Education, a publication about college and university news and happenings. In 2012, they created an interactive feature called "Who does your college think its peers are?". In this feature, users can enter the name of any US-based college or university into a form and see an interactive visualization showing which other universities call that target school a **peer**. (Peers are universities that are similar in some way.) The original data came from U.S. government reports, but the Chronicle has made the data underlying this visualization free for anyone to use.

For this example, we are interested in a complimentary question: When University X appears on a list, which other universities are on these lists? To answer this question, we will need to find all the other universities that are listed with University X, and then we will have to count how many times each of their names occurs.

Step two – data collection

In this step, we will see the procedure to collect data and then clean it in a step-by-step manner. The upcoming sections discuss the actions we need to take in order to collect proper data for our project.

Download the data

The data for this project can be downloaded from the original article at `http://chronicle.com/article/Who-Does-Your-College-Think/134222/` or from the direct link to the spreadsheet at `https://s3.amazonaws.com/03peers/selected_peers.csv.zip`

The file is zipped, so use your unzip program of choice to unzip the file.

Get familiar with the data

The file inside the ZIP folder has a `.csv` extension, and it indeed is a CSV-delimited file with 1,686 rows in it, including a header row. The commas delimit two columns: the first column is the name of the university in question, and the second column is the list of all the universities that the original one listed as peers. These peers are themselves delimited by the pipe (|) character. Here is a sample row:

```
Harvard University,Yale University|Princeton University|Stanford
University
```

In this case, the first column states that Harvard University is the target university, and the second column shows that Yale, Princeton, and Stanford have been listed by Harvard as its peers.

Step three – data cleaning

As the goal of this example is to look at one particular university and all the times it is listed as some other university's peer, our first goal is to clean out any row that does *not* have the target university in it. We will then transform the file into a single long list of individual universities. At this point, our data will be clean and we will be ready to go to the analysis and visualization steps.

Extracting relevant lines

Let's compare two methods for extracting relevant lines: one using a spreadsheet and one using a text editor with the techniques outlined in this chapter.

Using a spreadsheet

Open the file in a spreadsheet program, highlight any row that has **Harvard** written in it (or your target university of choice) using conditional formatting, and delete the rest of the rows.

Using a text editor

Open the file in a text editor and use **Process Lines Containing** to find all lines that have the **Harvard University** phrase (or whatever your university of choice is) included, and then copy them to a new file.

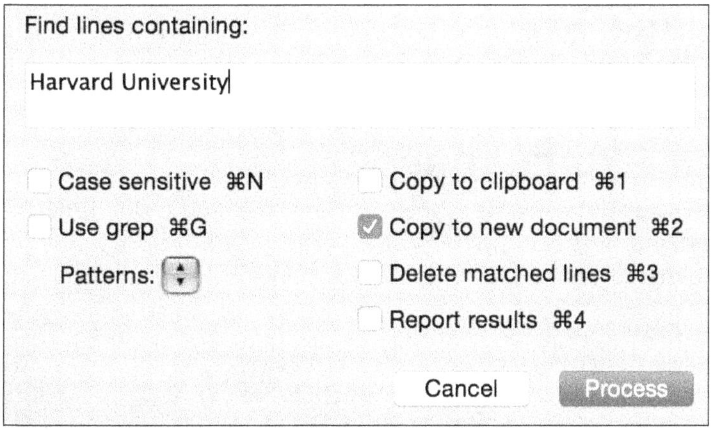

With either option, the result of this process is a new file with 26 lines in it, all of which include **Harvard University** somewhere in the line.

Transform the lines

Right now we have a file with 26 lines, each with multiple universities per line (wide data). We anticipate that we will probably be reading the file into Python at some point to perform a simple frequency count of universities. So, we decide that we want to change this to long data, with one university per line.

To transform the file so that there is one university per line, we will use a text editor and three instances of find and replace. First, we will find commas and replace them with `/r` (carriage return).

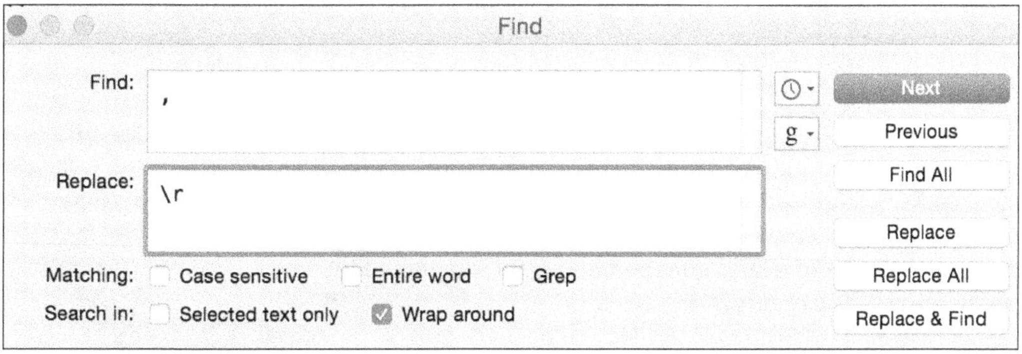

Next, find instances of the pipe character (|) and replace it with `\r`. At this point, the text file has 749 lines.

Finally, we need to remove all instances of **Harvard University**. (Remember, we are only interested in peers who are mentioned with Harvard, so we do not need Harvard itself in the count.) In Text Wrangler, we can put **Harvard University\r** in the **Find** box and leave the **Replace** box empty. This results in 26 lines deleted and a grand total of 723 lines in the file.

Step four – data analysis

As our main focus is data cleaning, we will not spend too much time on analysis or visualization, but here is a quick Python script to count how many times each of these peers are mentioned along with Harvard on some university's list:

```
from collections import Counter
with open('universities.txt') as infile:
    counted = Counter(filter(None,[line.strip() for line in
    infile]))
    sorted = counted.most_common()
    for key,value in sorted:
      print key, ",", value
```

The results show 232 unique universities and a count of how many times that university was mentioned. Here are the first few results. We can interpret these results as follows:

When Harvard is mentioned as a peer, Yale was also mentioned 26 times:

`Yale University , 26`

`Princeton University , 25`

`Cornell University , 24`

`Stanford University , 23`

`Columbia University in the City of New York , 22`

`Brown University , 21`

`University of Pennsylvania , 21`

At this point, you can take the list (or some portion of the longer list) and feed it into a bar graph or a word cloud or whatever type of visualization you think is persuasive or interesting. As the data is comma-delimited, you could even easily paste it into a spreadsheet program for further analysis. But at this point, we have answered our initial question about which peers are mentioned most, given a target university.

Summary

In this chapter, we learned some very practical tips for data cleaning using two easily accessible tools: text editors and spreadsheets. We outlined the available spreadsheet functions for splitting data, moving it around, finding and replacing parts, formatting it, and then putting it back together. Then, we learned how to get the most out of a simple text editor, including some of the built-in functions, and how to use find and replace and regular expressions most effectively.

In the next chapter, we will put together a variety of the techniques we have learned so far to perform some significant file conversions. Many of the techniques we will use will be based on what we have learned in the past two chapters about text editing, regular expressions, data types, and file formats, so get ready to solve some real-world data cleaning problems.

4

Speaking the Lingua Franca – Data Conversions

Last summer, I took a cheese-making class at a local cooking school. One of the first things we made was ricotta cheese. I was thrilled to learn that ricotta can be made in about an hour using just milk and buttermilk, and that buttermilk itself can be made from milk and lemon juice. In a kitchen, ingredients are constantly transformed into other ingredients, which will in turn be transformed into delicious meals. In our data science kitchen, we will routinely perform conversions from one data format to another. We might need to do this in order to perform various analyses, when we want to merge datasets together, or if we need to store a dataset in a new way.

A lingua franca is a language that is adopted as a common standard in a conversation between speakers of different languages. In converting data, there are several data formats that can serve as a common standard. We covered some of these in *Chapter 2, Fundamentals – Formats, Types, and Encodings*. JSON and CSV are two of the most common. In this chapter, we will spend some time learning:

- How to perform some quick conversions into JSON and CSV from software tools and languages (Excel, Google Spreadsheets, and phpMyAdmin).
- How to write Python and PHP programs to generate different text formats and convert between them.
- How to implement data conversions in order to accomplish a real-world task. In this project, we will download a friend network from Facebook using the netvizz software, and we will clean the data and convert it into the JSON format needed to build a visualization of your social network in D3. Then, we will clean the data in a different way, converting it into the Pajek format needed by the social network package called **networkx**.

Quick tool-based conversions

One of the quickest and easiest ways to convert a small to medium amount of data is just to ask whatever software tool you are using to do it for you. Sometimes, the application you are using will already have the option to convert the data into the format you want. Just as with the tips and tricks in *Chapter 3, Workhorses of Clean Data – Spreadsheets and Text Editors*, we want to take advantage of these hidden features in our tools, if at all possible. If you have too much data for an application-based conversion, or if the particular conversion you want is not available, we will cover programmatic solutions in the upcoming sections, *Converting with PHP* and *Converting with Python*.

Spreadsheet to CSV

Saving a spreadsheet as a delimited file is quite straightforward. Both Excel and Google spreadsheets have **File** menu options for **Save As**; in this option, select **CSV (MS DOS)**. Additionally, Google Spreadsheets has the options to save as an Excel file and save as a tab-delimited file. There are a few limitations with saving something as CSV:

- In both Excel and Google Spreadsheets, when you use the **Save As** feature, only the current sheet will be saved. This is because, by nature, a CSV file describes only one set of data; therefore, it cannot have multiple sheets in it. If you have a multiple-sheet spreadsheet, you will need to save each sheet as a separate CSV file.
- In both these tools, there are relatively few options for how to customize the CSV file, for example, Excel saves the data with commas as the separator (which makes sense as it is a CSV file) and gives no options to enclose data values in quotation marks or for different line terminators.

Spreadsheet to JSON

JSON is a little trickier to contend with than CSV. Excel does not have an easy JSON converter, though there are several converter tools online that purport to convert CSV files for you into JSON.

Google Spreadsheets, however, has a JSON converter available via a URL. There are a few downsides to this method, the first of which is that you have to publish your document to the Web (at least temporarily) in order to access the JSON version of it. You will also have to customize the URL with some very long numbers that identify your spreadsheet. It also produces a lot of information in the JSON dump—probably more than you will want or need. Nonetheless, here are some step-by-step instructions to convert a Google Spreadsheet into its JSON representation.

Step one – publish Google spreadsheet to the Web

After your Google spreadsheet is created and saved, select **Publish to the Web** from the **File** menu. Click through the subsequent dialogue boxes (I took all the default selections for mine). At this point, you will be ready to access the JSON for this file via a URL.

Step two – create the correct URL

The URL pattern to create JSON from a published Google spreadsheet looks like this:

```
http://spreadsheets.google.com/feeds/list/key/sheet/public/
basic?alt=json
```

There are three parts of this URL that you will need to alter to match your specific spreadsheet file:

- **list**: (optional) You can change `list` to, say, cells if you would prefer to see each cell listed separately with its reference (A1, A2, and so on) in the JSON file. If you want each row as an entity, leave `list` in the URL.
- **key**: Change `key` in this URL to match the long, unique number that Google internally uses to represent your file. In the URL of your spreadsheet, as you are looking at it in the browser, this key is shown as a long identifier between two slashes, just after the **/spreadsheets/d** portion of the URL, shown as follows:

- **sheet**: Change the word sheet in the sample URL to `od6` to indicate that you are interested in converting the first sheet.

> What does `od6` mean? Google uses a code to represent each of the sheets. However, the codes are not strictly in numeric order. There is a lengthy discussion about the numbering scheme on the question on this Stack Overflow post and its answers: `http://stackoverflow.com/questions/11290337/`

To test this procedure, we can create a Google spreadsheet for the universities and the counts that we generated from the exercise at the end of the example project in *Chapter 3, Workhorses of Clean Data – Spreadsheets and Text Editors*. The first three rows of this spreadsheet look like this:

Yale University	26
Princeton University	25
Cornell University	24

My URL to access this file via JSON looks like this:

```
http://spreadsheets.google.com/feeds/list/1mWIAk_5KNoQHr4vFgPHdm7GX8V
h22WjgAUYYHUyXSNM/od6/public/basic?alt=json
```

Pasting this URL into the browser yields a JSON representation of the data. It has 231 entries in it, each of which looks like the following snippet. I have formatted this entry with added line breaks for easier reading:


```
{
  "id":{
    "$t":"https://spreadsheets.google.com/feeds/list/1mWIAk_5KN
    oQHr4vFgPHdm7GX8Vh22WjgAUYYHUyXSNM/od6/public/basic/cokwr"
  },
  "updated":{"$t":"2014-12-17T20:02:57.196Z"},
  "category":[{
    "scheme":"http://schemas.google.com/spreadsheets/2006",
    "term"  :"http://schemas.google.com/spreadsheets/2006#list"
  }],
  "title":{
    "type":"text",
    "$t"  :"Yale University "
  },
  "content":{
    "type":"text",
    "$t"  :"_cokwr: 26"
  },
  "link": [{
    "rel" :"self",
    "type":"application/atom+xml",
    "href":"https://spreadsheets.google.com/feeds/list/1mWIAk_5KN
    oQHr4vFgPHdm7GX8Vh22WjgAUYYHUyXSNM/od6/public/basic/cokwr"
  }]
}
```

Even with my reformatting, this JSON is not very pretty, and many of these name-value pairs will be uninteresting to us. Nonetheless, we have successfully generated a functional JSON. If we are using a program to consume this JSON, we will ignore all the extraneous information about the spreadsheet itself and just go after the title and content entities and the `$t` values (`Yale University` and `_cokwr: 26`, in this case). These values are highlighted in the JSON shown in the preceding example. If you are wondering whether there is a way to go from a spreadsheet to CSV to JSON, the answer is yes. We will cover how to do exactly that in the *Converting with PHP* and *Converting with Python* sections later in this chapter.

SQL to CSV or JSON using phpMyAdmin

In this section, we'll discuss two options for writing JSON and CSV directly from a database, MySQL in our case, without using any programming.

First, phpMyAdmin is a very common web-based frontend for MySQL databases. If you are using a modern version of this tool, you will be able to export an entire table or the results of a query as a CSV or JSON file. Using the same enron database we first visited in *Chapter 1, Why Do You Need Clean Data?*, consider the following screenshot of the **Export** tab, with **JSON** selected as the target format for the entire **employeelist** table (CSV is also available in this select box):

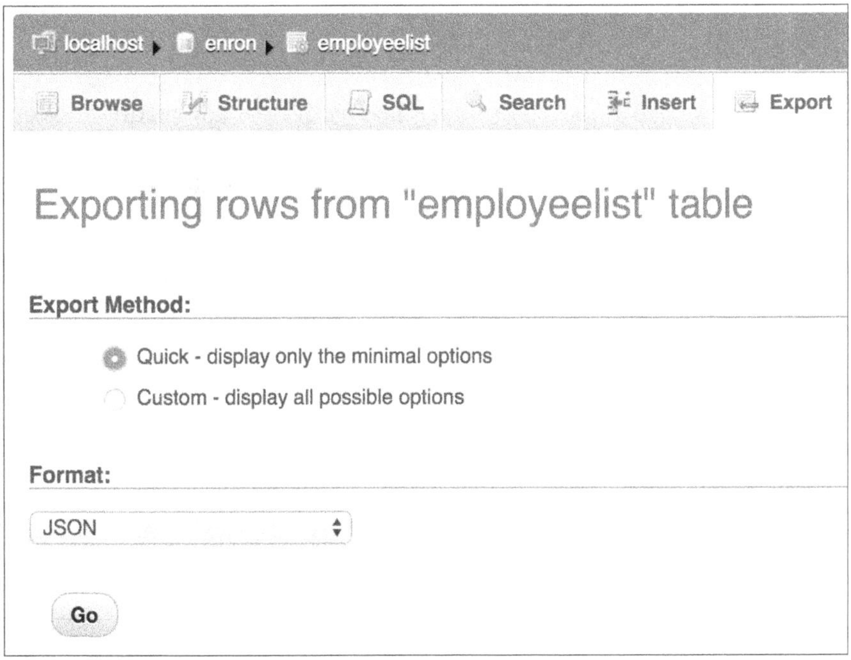

PhpMyAdmin JSON export for entire tables

The process to export the results of a query is very similar, except that instead of using the **Export** tab on the top of the screen, run the SQL query and then use the **Export** option under **Query results operations** at the bottom of the page, shown as follows:

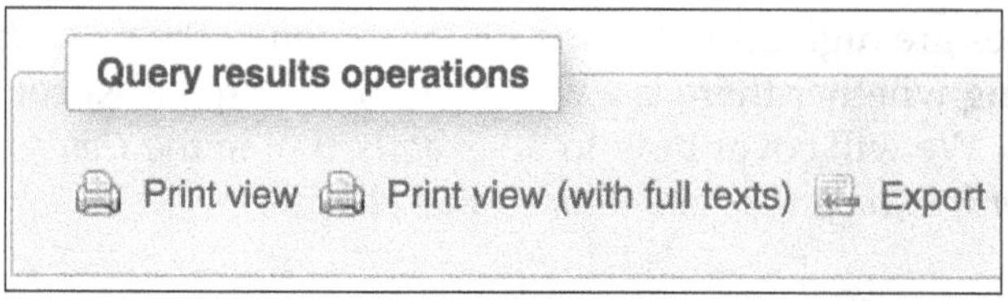

PhpMyAdmin can export the results of a query as well

Here is a simple query we can run on the `employeelist` table to test this process:

```
SELECT concat(firstName,  " ", lastName) as name, email_id
FROM employeelist
ORDER BY lastName;
```

When we export the results as JSON, phpMyAdmin shows us 151 values formatted like this:

```
{
  "name": "Lysa Akin",
  "email_id": "lysa.akin@enron.com"
}
```

The phpMyAdmin tool is a good one, and it is effective for converting moderate amounts of data stored in MySQL, especially as the results of a query. If you are using a different RDBMS, your SQL interface will likely have a few formatting options of its own that you should explore.

Another strategy is to bypass phpMyAdmin entirely and just use your MySQL command line to write out a CSV file that is formatted the way you want:

```
SELECT concat(firstName,  " ", lastName) as name, email_id
INTO OUTFILE 'enronEmployees.csv'
FIELDS TERMINATED BY ',' OPTIONALLY ENCLOSED BY '"'
LINES TERMINATED BY '\n'
FROM employeelist;
```

This will write a comma-delimited file with the name specified (`employees.csv`). It will be written into the current directory.

What about JSON? There is no very clean way to output JSON with this strategy, so you should either use the phpMyAdmin solution shown previously, or use a more robust solution written in PHP or Python. These programmatic solutions are covered in further sections, so keep reading.

Converting with PHP

In our *Chapter 2, Fundamentals – Formats, Types, and Encodings*, in a discussion on JSON numeric formatting, we briefly showed how to use PHP to connect to a database, run a query, build a PHP array from the results, and then print the JSON results to the screen. Here, we will first extend this example to write a file rather than print to the screen and also to write a CSV file. Next, we will show how to use PHP to read in JSON files and convert to CSV files, and vice versa.

SQL to JSON using PHP

In this section, we will write a PHP script to connect to the `enron` database, run a SQL query, and export is as a JSON-formatted file. Why write a PHP script for this instead of using phpMyAdmin? Well, this strategy will be useful in cases where we need to perform additional processing on the data before exporting it or where we suspect that we have more data than what a web-based application (such as phpMyAdmin) can run:

```
<?php
// connect to db, set up query, run the query
$dbc = mysqli_connect('localhost','username','password','enron')
or die('Error connecting to database!' . mysqli_error());

$select_query = "SELECT concat(firstName,  \" \", lastName) as
  name, email_id FROM  employeelist ORDER BY lastName";

$select_result = mysqli_query($dbc, $select_query);

if (!$select_result)
    die ("SELECT failed! [$select_query]" .  mysqli_error());

// ----JSON output----
// build a new array, suitable for json
$counts = array();
while($row = mysqli_fetch_array($select_result))
{
```

```
// add onto the json array
    array_push($counts, array('name'      => $row['name'],
    'email_id' => $row['email_id']));
}
// encode query results array as json
$json_formatted = json_encode($counts);

// write out the json file
file_put_contents("enronEmail.json", $json_formatted);
?>
```

This code writes a JSON-formatted output file to the location you specify in the `file_put_contents()` line.

SQL to CSV using PHP

The following code snippet shows how to use the PHP file output stream to create a CSV-formatted file of the results of a SQL query. Save this code as a `.php` file in the script-capable directory on your web server, and then request the file in the browser. It will automatically download a CSV file with the correct values in it:

```
<?php
// connect to db, set up query, run the query
  $dbc = mysqli_connect('localhost','username','password','enron')
  or die('Error connecting to database!' . mysqli_error());

$select_query = "SELECT concat(firstName,  \" \", lastName) as
  name, email_id FROM  employeelist ORDER BY lastName";

$select_result = mysqli_query($dbc, $select_query);

if (!$select_result)
    die ("SELECT failed! [$select_query]" .  mysqli_error());

// ----CSV output----
// set up a file stream
$file = fopen('php://output', 'w');
if ($file && $select_result)
{
    header('Content-Type: text/csv');
    header('Content-Disposition: attachment;
    filename="enronEmail.csv"');
    // write each result row to the file in csv format
```

```
        while($row = mysqli_fetch_assoc($select_result))
        {
          fputcsv($file, array_values($row));
        }
    }
    ?>
```

The results are formatted as follows (these are the first three lines only):

```
"Lysa Akin",lysa.akin@enron.com
"Phillip Allen",k..allen@enron.com
"Harry Arora",harry.arora@enron.com
```

If you are wondering whether Phillip's e-mail is really supposed to have two dots in it, we can run a quick query to find out how many of Enron's e-mails are formatted like that:

```
SELECT CONCAT(firstName,  " ", lastName) AS name, email_id
FROM employeelist
WHERE email_id LIKE "%..%"
ORDER BY name ASC;
```

It turns out that 24 of the e-mail addresses have double dots like that.

JSON to CSV using PHP

Here, we will use PHP to read in a JSON file and convert it to CSV and output a file:

```
<?php
// read in the file
$json = file_get_contents("outfile.json");
// convert JSON to an associative array
$array = json_decode ($json, true);
// open the file stream
$file = fopen('php://output', 'w');
header('Content-Type: text/csv');
header('Content-Disposition: attachment;
filename="enronEmail.csv"');
// loop through the array and write each item to the file
foreach ($array as $line)
{
    fputcsv($file, $line);
}
?>
```

This code will create a CSV with each line in it, just like the previous example. We should be aware that the `file_get_contents()` function reads the file into the memory as a string, so you may find that for extremely large files, you will need to use a combination of the `fread()`, `fgets()`, and `fclose()` PHP functions instead.

CSV to JSON using PHP

Another common task is to read in a CSV file and write it out as a JSON file. Most of the time, we have a CSV in which the first row is a header row. The header row lists the column name for each column in the file, and we would like each item in the header row to become the keys for the JSON-formatted version of the file:

```
<?php
$file = fopen('enronEmail.csv', 'r');
$headers = fgetcsv($file, 0, ',');
$complete = array();

while ($row = fgetcsv($file, 0, ','))
{
    $complete[] = array_combine($headers, $row);
}
fclose($file);
$json_formatted = json_encode($complete);
file_put_contents('enronEmail.json',$json_formatted);
?>
```

The result of this code on the `enronEmail.csv` file created earlier, with a header row, is as follows:

```
[{"name":"Lysa Akin","email_id":"lysa.akin@enron.com"},
{"name":"Phillip Allen","email_id":"k..allen@enron.com"},
{"name":"Harry Arora","email_id":"harry.arora@enron.com"}…]
```

For this example, of the 151 results in the actual CSV file, only the first three rows are shown.

Converting with Python

In this section, we describe a variety of ways to manipulate CSV into JSON, and vice versa, using Python. In these examples, we will explore different ways to accomplish this goal, both using specially installed libraries and using more plain-vanilla Python code.

CSV to JSON using Python

We have found several ways to convert CSV files to JSON using Python. The first of these uses the built-in `csv` and `json` libraries. Suppose we have a CSV file that has rows like this (only the first three rows shown):

```
name,email_id
"Lysa Akin",lysa.akin@enron.com
"Phillip Allen",k..allen@enron.com
"Harry Arora",harry.arora@enron.com
```

We can write a Python program to read these rows and convert them to JSON:

```
import json
import csv

# read in the CSV file
with open('enronEmail.csv') as file:
    file_csv = csv.DictReader(file)
    output = '['
    # process each dictionary row
    for row in file_csv:
      # put a comma between the entities
      output += json.dumps(row) + ','
    output = output.rstrip(',') + ']'
# write out a new file to disk
f = open('enronEmailPy.json','w')
f.write(output)
f.close()
```

The resulting JSON will look like this (only the first two rows are shown):

```
[{"email_id": "lysa.akin@enron.com", "name": "Lysa Akin"},
{"email_id": "k..allen@enron.com", "name": "Phillip Allen"},…]
```

One nice thing about using this method is that it does not require any special installations of libraries or any command-line access, apart from getting and putting the files you are reading (CSV) and writing (JSON).

CSV to JSON using csvkit

The second method of changing CSV into JSON relies on a very interesting Python toolkit called **csvkit**. To install csvkit using Canopy, simply launch the Canopy terminal window (you can find it inside Canopy by navigating to **Tools | Canopy Terminal**) and then run the `pip install csvkit` command. All the dependencies for using csvkit will be installed for you. At this point, you have the option of accessing csvkit via a Python program as a library using `import csvkit` or via the command line, as we will do in the following snippet:

```
csvjson enronEmail.csv > enronEmail.json
```

This command takes a `enronEmail.csv` CSV file and transforms it to a JSON `enronEmail.csvkit.json` file quickly and painlessly.

There are several other extremely useful command-line programs that come with the csvkit package, including `csvcut`, which can extract an arbitrary list of columns from a CSV file, and `csvformat`, which can perform delimiter exchanges on CSV files or alter line endings or similar cleaning procedures. The `csvcut` program is particularly helpful if you want to extract just a few columns for processing. For any of these command-line tools, you can redirect its output to a new file. The following command line takes a file called `bigFile.csv`, cuts out the first and third column, and saves the result as a new CSV file:

```
csvcut bigFile.csv -c 1,3 > firstThirdCols.csv
```

> Additional information about csvkit, including full documentation, downloads, and examples, is available at `http://csvkit.rtfd.org/`.

Python JSON to CSV

It is quite straightforward to use Python to read in a JSON file and convert it to CSV for processing:

```
import json
import csv

with open('enronEmailPy.json', 'r') as f:
    dicts = json.load(f)
out = open('enronEmailPy.csv', 'w')
writer = csv.DictWriter(out, dicts[0].keys())
writer.writeheader()
writer.writerows(dicts)
out.close()
```

This program takes a JSON file called `enronEmailPy.json` and exports a CSV-formatted version of this file using the keys for the JSON as the header row new file, called `enronEmailPy.csv`.

The example project

In this chapter, we have focused on converting data from one format to another, which is a common data cleaning task that will need to be done time and again before the rest of the data analysis project can be completed. We focused on some very common text formats (CSV and JSON) and common locations for data (files and SQL databases). Now, we are ready to extend our basic knowledge of data conversions with a sample project that will ask us to make conversions between some less standardized— but still text-based—data formats.

In this project, we want to investigate our Facebook social network. We will:

1. Download our Facebook social network (friends and relationships between them) using netvizz into a text-based file format called **Graph Description Format** (**GDF**).
2. Build a graphical representation of a Facebook social network showing the people in our network as nodes and their friendships as connecting lines (called *edges*) between these nodes. To do this, we will use the D3 JavaScript graphing library. This library expects a JSON representation of the data in the network.
3. Calculate some metrics about the social network, such as the size of the network (known as the *degree* of the network) and the shortest path between two people our network. To do this, we will use the `networkx` package in Python. This package expects data in a text-based format, called the **Pajek** format.

The primary goal of this project will be to show how to reconcile all these different expected formats (GDF, Pajek, and JSON) and perform conversions from one format to another. Our secondary goal will be to actually provide enough sample code and guidance to perform a small analysis of our social network.

Step one – download Facebook data as GDF

For this step, you will need to be logged into your Facebook account. Use Facebook's search box to find the netvizz app, or use this URL to directly link to the netvizz app: `https://apps.facebook.com/netvizz/`.

Once on the netvizz page, click on **personal network**. The page that follows explains that clicking on the **start** button will provide a downloadable file with two items in it: a GDF format file that lists all your friends and the connections between them and a tab-delimited **Tab Separated Values** (**TSV**) stats file. We are primarily interested in the GDF file for this project. Click on the **start** button, and on the subsequent page, right-click on the GDF file to save it to your local disk, as shown in the following screenshot:

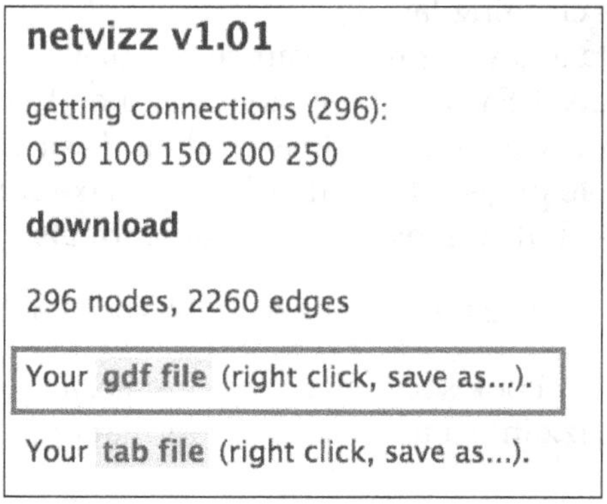

The netvizz Facebook app allows us to download our social network as a GDF file

It may be helpful to also give the file a shorter name at this point. (I called my file `personal.gdf` and saved it in a directory created just for this project.)

Step two – look at the GDF file format in a text editor

Open the file in your text editor (I am using Text Wrangler for this), and note a few things about the format of this file:

1. The file is divided into two parts: nodes and edges.
2. The nodes are found in the first part of the file, preceded by the word `nodedef`. The list of nodes is a list of all my friends and some basic facts about them (their gender and their internal Facebook identification number). The nodes are listed in the order of the date when the person joined Facebook.
3. The second part of the file shows the edges or connections between my friends. Sometimes, these are also called links. This section of the file is preceded by the word `edgedef`. The edges describe which of my friends are linked to which other friends.

Here is an excerpt of what a nodes section looks like:

```
nodedef>name VARCHAR,label VARCHAR,sex VARCHAR,locale
  VARCHAR,agerank INT
  1234,Bugs Bunny,male,en_US,296
  2345,Daffy Duck,male,en_US,295
  3456,Minnie Mouse,female,en_US,294
```

Here is an excerpt of what an edges section looks like. It shows that `Bugs` (`1234`) and `Daffy` (`2345`) are friends, and `Bugs` is also friends with `Minnie` (`3456`):

```
edgedef>node1 VARCHAR,node2 VARCHAR
1234,2345
1234,3456
3456,9876
```

Step three – convert the GDF file into JSON

The task we want to perform is to build a representation of this data as a social network in D3. First, we need to look at the dozens of available examples of D3 to build a social network, such as those available in the D3 galleries of examples, `https://github.com/mbostock/d3/wiki/Gallery` and `http://christopheviau.com/d3list/`.

These examples of social network diagrams rely on JSON files. Each JSON file shows nodes and the edges between them. Here is an example of what one of these JSON files should look like:

```
{"nodes": [
  {"name":"Bugs Bunny"},
  {"name":"Daffy Duck"},
  {"name":"Minnie Mouse"}],
  "edges": [
  {"source": 0,"target": 2},
  {"source": 1,"target": 3},
  {"source": 2,"target": 3}]}
```

The most important thing about this JSON code is to note that it has the same two main chunks as the GDF file did: nodes and edges. The nodes are simply the person's name. The edges are a list of number pairs representing friendship relations. Instead of using the Facebook identification number, though, these pairs use an index for each item in the nodes list, starting with `0`.

We do not have a JSON file at this point. We only have a GDF file. How will we build this JSON file? When we look closely at the GDF file, we can see that it looks a lot like two CSV files stacked on top of one another. From earlier in this chapter, we know we have several different strategies to convert from CSV to JSON.

Therefore, we decide to convert GDF to CSV and then CSV to JSON.

> Wait; what if that JSON example doesn't look like the JSON files I found online to perform a social network diagram in D3?
>
> Some of the examples of D3 social network visualizations that you may find online will show many additional values for each node or link, for example, they may include extra attributes that can be used to signify a difference in size, a hover feature, or a color change, as shown in this sample: `http://bl.ocks.org/christophermanning/1625629`. This visualization shows relationships between paid political lobbyists in Chicago. In this example, the code takes into account information in the JSON file to determine the size of the circles for the nodes and the text that is displayed when you hover over the nodes. It makes a really nice diagram, but it is complicated. As our primary goal is to learn how to clean the data, we will work with a pared down, simple example here that does not have many of these extras. Do not worry, though; our example will still build a nifty D3 diagram!

To convert the GDF file to JSON in the format we want, we can follow these steps:

1. Use a text editor to split the `personal.gdf` file into two files, `nodes.gdf` and `links.gdf`.
2. Alter the header row in each file to match the column names we eventually want in the JSON file:

```
id,name,gender,lang,num
1234,Bugs Bunny,male,en_US,296
2345,Daffy Duck,male,en_US,295
9876,Minnie Mouse,female,en_US,294

source,target
1234,2345
1234,9876
2345,9876
```

3. Use the `csvcut` utility (part of csvkit discussed previously) to extract the first and second columns from the `nodes.gdf` file and redirect the output to a new file called `nodesCut.gdf`:

```
csvcut -c 1,2 nodes.gdf > nodesCut.gdf
```

4. Now, we need to give each edge pair an indexed value rather than their full Facebook ID value. The index just identifies this node by its position in the node list. We need to perform this transformation so that the data will easily feed into the D3 force network code examples that we have, with as little refactoring as possible. We need to convert this:

```
source,target
1234,2345
1234,9876
2345,9876
```

into this:

```
source,target
0,1
0,2
1,2
```

Here is a small Python script that will create these index values automatically:

```
import csv

# read in the nodes
with open('nodesCut.gdf', 'r') as nodefile:
    nodereader = csv.reader(nodefile)
    nodeid, name = zip(*nodereader)

# read in the source and target of the edges
with open('edges.gdf', 'r') as edgefile:
    edgereader = csv.reader(edgefile)
    sourcearray, targetarray = zip(*edgereader)
slist = list(sourcearray)
tlist = list(targetarray)

# find the node index value for each source and target
for n,i in enumerate(nodeid):
    for j,s in enumerate(slist):
        if s == i:
            slist[j]=n-1
    for k,t in enumerate(tlist):
        if t == i:
            tlist[k]=n-1
# write out the new edge list with index values
with open('edgelistIndex.csv', 'wb') as indexfile:
    iwriter = csv.writer(indexfile)
    for c in range(len(slist)):
        iwriter.writerow([ slist[c], tlist[c]])
```

5. Now, go back to the `nodesCut.csv` file and remove the `id` column:

   ```
   csvcut -c 2 nodesCut.gdf > nodesCutName.gdf
   ```

6. Construct a small Python script that takes each of these files and writes them out to a complete JSON file, ready for D3 processing:

```
import csv
import json

# read in the nodes file
with open('nodesCutName.gdf') as nodefile:
    nodefile_csv = csv.DictReader(nodefile)
    noutput = '['
    ncounter = 0;

    # process each dictionary row
    for nrow in nodefile_csv:
        # look for ' in node names, like O'Connor
        nrow["name"] = \
        str(nrow["name"]).replace("'","")
        # put a comma between the entities
        if ncounter > 0:
            noutput += ','
        noutput += json.dumps(nrow)
        ncounter += 1
    noutput += ']'
    # write out a new file to disk
    f = open('complete.json','w')
    f.write('{')
    f.write('\"nodes\":' )
    f.write(noutput)

# read in the edge file
with open('edgelistIndex.csv') as edgefile:
    edgefile_csv = csv.DictReader(edgefile)
    eoutput = '['
    ecounter = 0;
    # process each dictionary row
    for erow in edgefile_csv:
        # make sure numeric data is coded as number not
        # string
        for ekey in erow:
            try:
                erow[ekey] = int(erow[ekey])
```

```
            except ValueError:
                # not an int
                pass
        # put a comma between the entities
        if ecounter > 0:
            eoutput += ','
        eoutput += json.dumps(erow)
        ecounter += 1
    eoutput += ']'

    # write out a new file to disk
    f.write(',')
    f.write('\"links\":')
    f.write(eoutput)
    f.write('}')
    f.close()
```

Step four – build a D3 diagram

This section shows how to feed our JSON file of nodes and links into a boilerplate example of building a force-directed graph in D3. This code example came from the D3 website and builds a simple graph using the JSON file provided. Each node is shown as a circle, and when you hover your mouse over the node, the person's name shows up as a tooltip:

```
<!DOCTYPE html>
<!-- this code is based on the force-directed graph D3 example given
at : https://gist.github.com/mbostock/4062045 -->

<meta charset="utf-8">
<style>

.node {
  stroke: #fff;
  stroke-width: 1.5px;
}

.link {
  stroke: #999;
  stroke-opacity: .6;
}

</style>
```

```
<body>
<!-- make sure you have downloaded the D3 libraries and stored them
locally -->
<script src="d3.min.js"></script>
<script>

var width = 960, height = 500;
var color = d3.scale.category20();
var force = d3.layout.force()
    .charge(-25)
    .linkDistance(30)
    .size([width, height]);

var svg = d3.select("body").append("svg")
    .attr("width", width)
    .attr("height", height);

d3.json("complete.json", function(error, graph) {
  force
      .nodes(graph.nodes)
      .links(graph.links)
      .start();

  var link = svg.selectAll(".link")
      .data(graph.links)
    .enter().append("line")
      .attr("class", "link")
      .style("stroke-width", function(d) { return Math.sqrt(d.value);
});

  var node = svg.selectAll(".node")
      .data(graph.nodes)
    .enter().append("circle")
      .attr("class", "node")
      .attr("r", 5)
      .style("fill", function(d) { return color(d.group); })
      .call(force.drag);

  node.append("title")
      .text(function(d) { return d.name; });

  force.on("tick", function() {
    link.attr("x1", function(d) { return d.source.x; })
      .attr("y1", function(d) { return d.source.y; })
```

```
        .attr("x2", function(d) { return d.target.x; })
        .attr("y2", function(d) { return d.target.y; });

      node.attr("cx", function(d) { return d.x; })
        .attr("cy", function(d) { return d.y; });
    });
  });
  </script>
```

The following screenshot shows an example of this social network. One of the nodes has been hovered over, showing the tooltip (name) of that node.

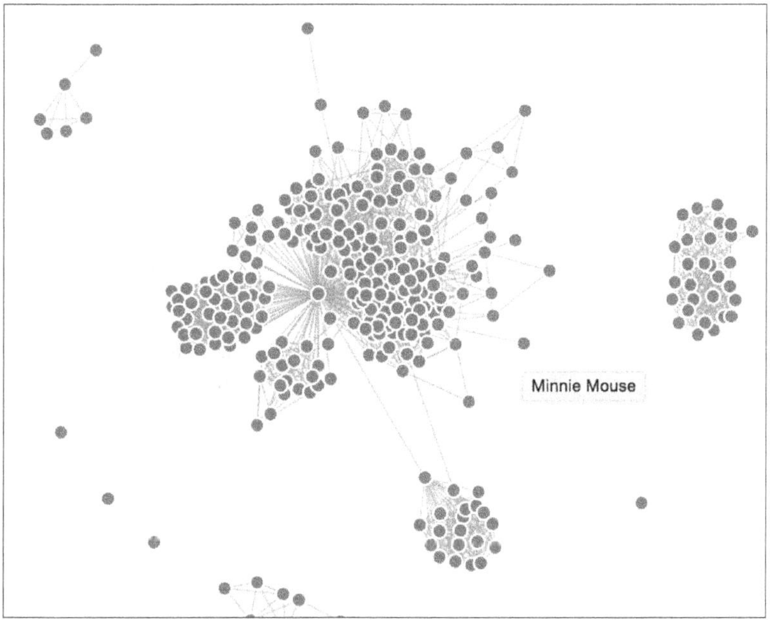

Social network built with D3

Step five – convert data to the Pajek file format

So far, we have converted a GDF file to CSV, and then to JSON, and built a D3 diagram of it. In the next two steps, we will continue to pursue our goal of getting the data in such a format that we can calculate some social network metrics on it.

For this step, we will take the original GDF file and tweak it to become a valid `Pajek` file, which is the format that is needed by the social network tool called networkx.

> The word *pajek* means *spider* in Slovenian. A social network can be thought of as a web made up of nodes and the links between them.

The format of our Facebook GDF file converted to a Pajek file looks like this:

```
*vertices 296
1234 Bugs_Bunny male en_US 296
2456 Daffy_Duck male en_US 295
9876 Minnie_Mouse female en_US 294
*edges
1234 2456
2456 9876
2456 3456
```

Here are a few important things to notice right away about this Pajek file format:

- It is space-delimited, not comma-delimited.
- Just like in the GDF file, there are two main sections of data, and these are labeled, starting with an asterisk `*`. The two sections are the vertices (another word for nodes) and the edges.
- There is a count of how many total vertices (nodes) there are in the file, and this count goes next to the word vertices on the top line.
- Each person's name has spaces removed and replaced with underscores.
- The other columns are optional in the node section.

To convert our GDF file into Pajek format, let's use the text editor, as these changes are fairly straightforward and our file is not very large. We will perform the data cleaning tasks as follows:

1. Save a copy of your GDF file as a new file and call it something like `fbPajek.net` (the `.net` extension is commonly used for Pajek network files).
2. Replace the top line in your file. Currently, it looks like this:

   ```
   nodedef>name VARCHAR,label VARCHAR,sex VARCHAR,locale
   VARCHAR,agerank INT
   ```

   You will need to change it to something like this:

   ```
   *vertices 296
   ```

   Make sure the number of vertices matches the number you have in your actual file. This is the count of nodes. There should be one per line in your GDF file.

3. Replace the edges line in your file. Currently, it looks like this:

   ```
   edgedef>node1 VARCHAR,node2 VARCHAR
   ```

   You will need to change it to look like this:

   ```
   *edges
   ```

4. Starting at line 2, replace every instance of a space with an underscore. This works because the only spaces in this file are in the names. Take a look at this:

   ```
   1234,Bugs Bunny,male,en_US,296
   2456,Daffy Duck,male,en_US,295
   3456,Minnie Mouse,female,en_US,294
   ```

   This action will turn the preceding into this:

   ```
   1234,Bugs_Bunny,male,en_US,296
   2456,Daffy_Duck,male,en_US,295
   3456,Minnie_Mouse,female,en_US,294
   ```

5. Now, use find and replace to replace all the instances of a comma with a space. The result for the nodes section will be:

   ```
   *vertices 296
   1234 Bugs_Bunny male en_US 296
   2456 Daffy_Duck male en_US 295
   3456 Minnie_Mouse female en_US 294
   ```

   The result for the edges section will be:

   ```
   *edqes
   1234 2456
   2456 9876
   2456 3456
   ```

6. One last thing; use the find feature of the text editor to locate any of your Facebook friends who have an apostrophe in their name. Replace this apostrophe with nothing. Thus, `Cap'n_Crunch` becomes:

   ```
   1998988 Capn_Crunch male en_US 137
   ```

   This is now a fully cleaned, Pajek-formatted file.

Step six – calculate simple network metrics

At this point, we are ready to run some simple social network metrics using a Python package like networkx. Even though **Social Network Analysis (SNA)** is beyond the scope of this book, we can still perform a few calculations quite easily without delving too deeply into the mysteries of SNA.

First, we should make sure that we have the `networkx` package installed. I am using Canopy for my Python editor, so I will use the Package Manager to search for networkx and install it.

Then, once networkx is installed, we can write some quick Python code to read our Pajek file and output a few interesting facts about the structure of my Facebook network:

```
import networkx as net

# read in the file
g = net.read_pajek('fb_pajek.net')

# how many nodes are in the graph?
# print len(g)

# create a degree map: a set of name-value pairs linking nodes
# to the number of edges in my network
deg = net.degree(g)
# sort the degree map and print the top ten nodes with the
# highest degree (highest number of edges in the network)
print sorted(deg.iteritems(), key=lambda(k,v): (-v,k))[0:9]
```

The result for my network looks like the following output. The top ten nodes are listed, along with a count of how many of my other nodes each of these links to:

```
[(u'Bambi', 134), (u'Cinderella', 56), (u'Capn_Crunch', 50),
  (u'Bugs_Bunny', 47), (u'Minnie_Mouse', 47), (u'Cruella_Deville',
  46), (u'Alice_Wonderland', 44), (u'Prince_Charming', 42),
  (u'Daffy_Duck', 42)]
```

This shows that `Bambi` is connected to `134` of my other friends, but `Prince_Charming` is only connected to `42` of my other friends.

> If you get any Python errors about missing quotations, double-check your Pajek format file to ensure that all node labels are free of spaces and other special characters. In the cleaning procedure explained in the preceding example, we removed spaces and the quotation character, but your friends may have more exotic characters in their names!

Of course, there are many more interesting things you can do with networkx and D3 visualizations, but this sample project was designed to give us a sense of how critical data-cleaning processes are to the successful outcome of any larger analysis effort.

Summary

In this chapter, we learned many different ways to convert data from one format to another. Some of these techniques are simple, such as just saving a file in the format you want or looking for a menu option to output the correct format. At other times, we will need to write our own programmatic solution.

Many projects, such as the sample project we implemented in this chapter, will require several different cleaning steps, and we will have to carefully plan out our cleaning steps and write down what we did. Both networkx and D3 are really nifty tools, but they do require data to be in a certain format before we are ready to use them. Likewise, Facebook data is easily available through netvizz, but it too has its own data format. Finding easy ways to convert from one file format to the other is a critical skill in data science.

In this chapter, we performed a lot of conversions between structured and semistructured data. But what about cleaning messy data, such as unstructured text?

In *Chapter 5, Collecting and Cleaning Data from the Web*, we will continue to fill up our data science cleaning toolbox by learning some of the ways in which we can clean pages that we find on the Web.

5
Collecting and Cleaning Data from the Web

One of the most common and useful kitchen tools is a strainer, also called a sieve, a colander, or chinois, the purpose of which is to separate solids from liquids during cooking. In this chapter, we will be building strainers for the data we find on the Web. We will learn how to create several types of programs that can help us find and keep the data we want, while discarding the parts we do not want.

In this chapter, we will:

- Understand two options to envision the structure of an HTML page, either (a) as a collection of lines that we can look for patterns in, or (b) as a tree structure containing nodes for which we can identify and collect values.
- Try out three methods to parse web pages, one that uses the line-by-line approach (regular expressions-based HTML parsing), and two that use the tree structure approach (Python's BeautifulSoup library and the Chrome browser tool called Scraper).
- Implement all three of these techniques on some real-world data; we will practice scraping out the date and time from messages posted to a web forum.

Understanding the HTML page structure

A web page is just a text file that contains some special markup **elements** (sometimes called HTML **tags**) intended to indicate to a web browser how the page should look when displayed to the user, for example, if we want a particular word to be displayed in a way that indicates emphasis, we can surround it with `<em>` tags like this:

It is `<em>very important</em>` that you follow these instructions.

All web pages have these same features; they are made up of text and the text may include tags. There are two main mental models we can employ to extract data from web pages. Both models have their useful aspects. In this section, we will describe the two structural models, and then in the next section, we will use three different tools for extracting data.

The line-by-line delimiter model

In the simplest way of thinking about web pages, we concentrate on the fact that there are many dozens of HTML elements/tags that are used to organize and display pages on the Web. If we want to extract interesting data from web pages in this simple model, we can use the page text and the embedded HTML elements themselves as **delimiters**. For instance, in case of the preceding example, we may decide we want to collect everything inside the `<em>` tags, or maybe we want to collect everything before an `<em>` tag or after an `</em>` tag.

In this model, we conceive the web page as a collection of largely unstructured text, and the HTML tags (or other features of the text, such as recurring words) help to provide structure which we can use to delimit the parts that we want. Once we have delimiters, we have the ability to strain out the interesting data from the junk.

For example, here is an excerpt from a real-world HTML page, a chat log from the Django IRC channel. Let's consider how we can use its HTML elements as delimiters to extract the interesting data:

```
<div id="content">
<h2>Sep 13, 2014</h2>

<a href="/2014/sep/14/">← next day</a> Sep 13, 2014  <a
  href="/2014/sep/12/">previous day →</a>

<ul id="ll">
<li class="le" rel="petisnnake"><a href="#1574618"
  name="1574618">#</a> <span style="color:#b78a0f;8"
  class="username" rel="petisnnake">&lt;petisnnake&gt;</span> i
  didnt know that </li>
```

```
...
</ul>
...
</div>
```

Given this example text, we could use the `<h2></h2>` tags as delimiters to extract the date of this particular chat log. We could use the `<li></li>` tags as delimiters for a line of text, and within that line, we can see that `rel=""` can be used to extract the username of the chatter. Finally, it appears that all the text extending from the end of `</span>` to the beginning of `</li>` is the actual line message sent to the chat channel by the user.

> These chat logs are all available online at the Django IRC log website, `http://django-irc-logs.com`. This website also provides a keyword search interface to the logs. The ellipses (...) in the preceding code represent text that has been removed for brevity in this example.

From this messy text, we are able to use the delimiter concept to extract three clean pieces of data (the date of log, user, and line message).

The tree structure model

Another way to imagine the textual web page is as a tree structure made up of HTML elements/tags, each of which is related to the other tags on the page. Each tag is shown as a **node**, and a tree is made up of all the different nodes in a particular page. A tag that shows up within another tag in the HTML is considered a **child**, and the enclosing tag is the **parent**. In the previous example of IRC chat, the HTML excerpt can be shown in a tree diagram that looks like this:

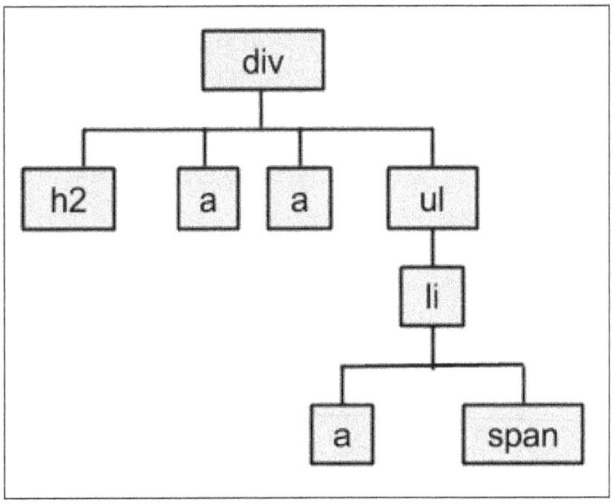

If we are able to envision our HTML text as a tree structure, we can use a programming language to build a tree for us. This allows us to pull out our desired text values based on their element name or position in the element list. For example:

- We may want the value of a tag by name (give me the text from the `<h2>` node)
- We may want all the nodes of a particular type (give me all the `<li>` nodes which are inside `<ul>` which are inside `<div>`)
- We may want all the attributes of a given element (give me a list of `rel` attributes from the `<li>` elements)

In the rest of the chapter, we will put both of these mental models—the line-by-line and the tree structure—into practice with some examples. We will walk through three different methods to extract and clean the data out of HTML pages.

Method one – Python and regular expressions

In this section, we will use a simple method to extract the data we want from an HTML page. This method is based on the concept of identifying delimiters in the page and using pattern matching via regular expressions to pull out the data we want.

You may remember that we experimented a little bit with regular expressions (regex) in *Chapter 3, Workhorses of Clean Data - Spreadsheets and Text Editors*, when we were learning about text editors. In this chapter, some of the concepts will be similar, except we will write a Python program to find matching text and extract it instead of using a text editor for replacements like we did in that chapter.

One final note before we start the example, although this regex method is fairly easy to understand, it does have some limitations which could be significant, depending on your particular project. We will describe the limitations of this method in detail at the end of the section.

Step one – find and save a Web file for experimenting

For this example, we are going to grab one of the IRC chat logs previously mentioned, from the Django project. These are publicly available files with a fairly regular structure, so they make a nice target for this project. Go to the Django IRC log archive at `http://django-irc-logs.com/` and find a date that looks appealing to you. Navigate to the target page for one of the dates and save it to your working directory. You should have a single `.html` file when you are done.

Step two – look into the file and decide what is worth extracting

Since we learned in *Chapter 2, Fundamentals – Formats, Types, and Encodings*, that `.html` files are just text, and *Chapter 3, Workhorses of Clean Data – Spreadsheets and Text Editors*, made us very comfortable with viewing text files in a text editor, this step should be easy. Just open the HTML file in a text editor and look at it. What looks ripe for extracting?

When I look in my file, I see several things I want to extract. Right away I see that for each chat comment, there is a line number, a username, and the comment itself. Let's plan on extracting these three things from each chat line.

The following figure shows the HTML file open in my text editor. I have turned on soft wrapping since some of the lines are quite long (in TextWrangler this option is located in the menu under **View** | **Text Display** | **Soft Wrap Text**). Around line **29** we see the beginning of a list of chat lines, each of which has the three items we are interested in:

```
29 <ul id="ll">
30 <li class="le" rel="petisnnake"><a href="#1574618" name="1574618">#</a> <span style="color:#b78a0f;8" class="username" rel="petisnnake">&lt;petisnnake&gt;</span> i didnt know that </li>
31 <li class="le" rel="dshap"><a href="#1574619" name="1574619">#</a> <span style="color:#b93d98;8" class="username" rel="dshap">&lt;dshap&gt;</span> FunkyBob: ahh, hmm, i wonder if there's a way to do it in my QuerySet subclass so i'm not creating a new manager subclass *only* for get_queryset to do the intiial filtering </li>
```

Our job is therefore to find the features of each line that look the same so we can predictably pull out the same three items from each chat line. Looking at the text, here are some possible rules we can follow to extract each data item accurately and with minimal tweaking:

- It appears that all three items we want are found within the `<li>` tags, which are themselves found inside the `<ul id="ll">` tag. Each `<li>` represents one chat message.
- Within that message, the line number is located in two places: it follows the string `<a href="#` and it is found within the quotation marks following the `name` attribute. In the example text shown, the first line number is `1574618`.
- The `username` attribute is found in three places, the first of which is as the value of the `rel` attribute of the `li class="le"`. Within the `span` tag, the `username` attribute is found again as the value of the `rel` attribute, and it is also found between the `<` and `>` symbols. In the example text, the first `username` is `petisnnake`.
- The line message is found following the `</span>` tag and before the `</li>` tag. In the example shown, the first line message is `i didnt know that`.

Now that we have the rules about where to find the data items, we can write our program.

Step three – write a Python program to pull out the interesting pieces and save them to a CSV file

Here is a short bit of code to open a given IRC log file in the format shown previously, parse out the three pieces we are interested in, and print them to a new CSV file:

```
import re
import io

row = []

infile  = io.open('django13-sept-2014.html', 'r', encoding='utf8')
outfile = io.open('django13-sept-2014.csv', 'a+', encoding='utf8')
for line in infile:
    pattern = re.compile(ur'<li class=\"le\" rel=\"(.+?)\"><a
href=\"#(.+?)\" name=\"(.+?)<\/span> (.+?)</li>', re.UNICODE)
    if pattern.search(line):
```

```
            username = pattern.search(line).group(1)
            linenum = pattern.search(line).group(2)
            message = pattern.search(line).group(4)
            row.append(linenum)
            row.append(username)
            row.append(message)
            outfile.write(', '.join(row))
            outfile.write(u'\n')
            row = []
    infile.close()
```

The trickiest bit of this code is the `pattern` line. This line builds the pattern match against which each line of the file will be compared.

> Be vigilant. Any time the website developers change the HTML in the page, we run the risk that our carefully constructed regular expression pattern will no longer work. In fact, in the months spent writing this book, the HTML for this page changed at least once!

Each matching target group looks like this: `.+?`. There are five of them. Three of these are the items we are interested in (`username`, `linenum`, and `message`), while the other two groups are just junk that we can discard. We will also discard the rest of the web page contents, since that did not match our pattern at all. Our program is like a sieve with exactly three functional holes in it. The good stuff will flow through the holes, leaving the junk behind.

Step four – view the file and make sure it is clean

When we open the new CSV file in a text editor, we can see that the first few lines now look like this:

```
1574618, petisnnake, i didnt know that
1574619, dshap, FunkyBob: ahh, hmm, i wonder if there's a way to do
it in my QuerySet subclass so i'm not creating a new manager subclass
*only* for get_queryset to do the intiial filtering
1574620, petisnnake, haven used Django since 1.5
```

That looks like a solid result. One thing you may notice is that there is no encapsulation character surrounding the text in the third column. This could prove to be a problem since we have used commas as a delimiter. What if we have commas in our third column? If this worries you, you can either add quotation marks around the third column, or you can use tabs to delimit the columns. To do this, change the first `outfile.write()` line to have `\t` (tab) as the join character instead of comma. You can also add some whitespace trimming to the message via `ltrim()` to remove any stray characters.

The limitations of parsing HTML using regular expressions

This regular expressions method seems pretty straightforward at first, but it has some limitations. First, for new data cleaners, regular expressions can be kind of a pain in the neck to design and perfect. You should definitely plan on spending a lot of time debugging and writing yourself copious documentation. To assist in the generation of regular expressions, I would definitely recommend using a regular expression tester, such as `http://Pythex.org`, or just use your favorite search engine to find one. Make sure you specify that you want a Python regex tester if that is the language you are using.

Next, you should know in advance that regular expressions are completely dependent on the structure of the web page staying the same in the future. So, if you plan to collect data from a website on a schedule, the regular expressions you write today may not work tomorrow. They will only work if the layout of the page does not change. A single space added between two tags will cause the entire regex to fail and will be extremely difficult to troubleshoot. Keep in mind too that most of the time you have little or no control over website changes, since it is usually not your own website that you are collecting data from!

Finally, there are many, many cases where it is next-to-impossible to accurately write a regular expression to match a given HTML construct. Regex is powerful but not perfect or infallible. For an amusing take on this issue, I refer you to the famous Stack Overflow answer that has been upvoted over 4000 times: `http://stackoverflow.com/questions/1732348/`. In this answer, the author humorously expresses the frustration of so many programmers who try over and over to explain why regex is not a perfect solution to parsing irregular and ever-changing HTML found in web pages.

Method two – Python and BeautifulSoup

Since regular expressions have some limitations, we will definitely need more tools in our data cleaning toolkit. Here, we describe how to extract data from HTML pages using a parse tree-based Python library called **BeautifulSoup**.

Step one – find and save a file for experimenting

For this step, we will use the same file as we did for Method 1: the file from the Django IRC channel. We will search for the same three items. Doing this will make it easy to compare the two methods to each other.

Step two – install BeautifulSoup

BeautifulSoup is currently in version 4. This version will work for both Python 2.7 and Python 3.

> If you are using the Enthought Canopy Python environment, simply run `pip install beautifulsoup4` in the Canopy Terminal.

Step three – write a Python program to extract the data

The three items we are interested in are found within the set of `li` tags, specifically those with `class="le"`. There are not any other `li` tags in this particular file, but let's be specific just in case. Here are the items we want and where to find them in the parse tree:

- We can extract the username from the `li` tag underneath the `rel` attribute.
- We can get the `linenum` value from the `name` attribute in the `a` tag. The `a` tag is also the first item in the contents of the `li` tag.

  > Remember that arrays are zero-based so we need to ask for item 0.

  In BeautifulSoup, the **contents** of a tag are the items underneath that tag in the parse tree. Some other packages will call them **child** items.

- We can extract the message as the fourth content item in the `li` tag (referenced as array item [3]). We also notice that there is a leading space at the front of every message, so we want to strip that off before saving the data.

Here is the Python code that corresponds to the outline of what we want from the parse tree:

```
from bs4 import BeautifulSoup
import io

infile  = io.open('django13-sept-2014.html', 'r', encoding='utf8')
outfile = io.open('django13-sept-2014.csv', 'a+', encoding='utf8')
soup = BeautifulSoup(infile)

row = []
allLines = soup.findAll("li","le")
for line in allLines:
    username = line['rel']
    linenum = line.contents[0]['name']
    message = line.contents[3].lstrip()
    row.append(linenum)
    row.append(username)
    row.append(message)
    outfile.write(', '.join(row))
    outfile.write(u'\n')
    row = []
infile.close()
```

Step four – view the file and make sure it is clean

When we open the new CSV file in a text editor, we can see that the first few lines now look identical to the ones from Method 1:

```
1574618, petisnnake, i didnt know that
1574619, dshap, FunkyBob: ahh, hmm, i wonder if there's a way to do
it in my QuerySet subclass so i'm not creating a new manager subclass
*only* for get_queryset to do the intiial filtering
1574620, petisnnake, haven used Django since 1.5
```

Just like with the regular expressions method, if you are worried about commas embedded within the last column, you can encapsulate the column text in quotes or just use tabs to delimit the columns instead.

Method three – Chrome Scraper

If you really do not want to write a program to parse out data, there are several browser-based tools that use a tree structure to allow you to identify and extract the data you are interested in. I think the easiest to use with minimum work is a Chrome extension called **Scraper**, created by a developer called **mnmldave** (real name: **Dave Heaton**).

Step one – install the Scraper Chrome extension

Download the Chrome browser if you do not already have that running. Make sure that you get the correct Scraper extension; there are several extensions that have very similar names. I recommend using the developer's own GitHub site for this product, available at `http://mnmldave.github.io/scraper/`. This way you will be able to have the correct scraper tool, rather than trying to search using the Chrome store. From the `http://mmldave.github.io/scraper` site, click the link to install the extension from the Google Store, and restart your browser.

Step two – collect data from the website

Point your browser to the same web URL we have been using to get the data for the other two web data extraction experiments, one of the Django IRC logs. I have been using the September 13, 2014 log for the examples and screenshots here, so I will go to `http://django-irc-logs.com/2014/sep/13/`.

In my browser, at the time of writing, this page looks like this:

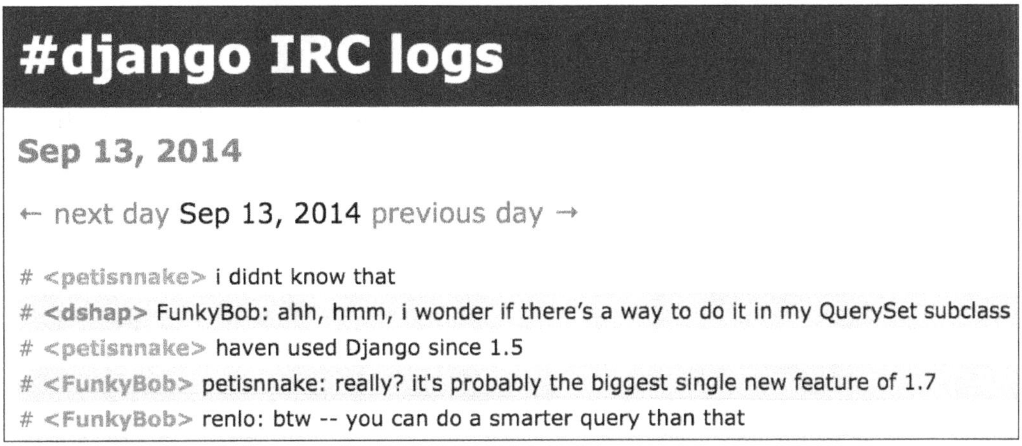
#django IRC logs
Sep 13, 2014
← next day Sep 13, 2014 previous day →
<petisnnake> i didnt know that
<dshap> FunkyBob: ahh, hmm, i wonder if there's a way to do it in my QuerySet subclass
<petisnnake> haven used Django since 1.5
<FunkyBob> petisnnake: really? it's probably the biggest single new feature of 1.7
<FunkyBob> renlo: btw -- you can do a smarter query than that

We have three items from this IRC log that we are interested in:

- The line number (we know from our previous two experiments that this is part of the link underneath the # sign)
- The username (located between the < and > symbols)
- The actual line message

Scraper allows us to highlight each of these three items in turn and export the values to a Google Spreadsheet, where we can then reassemble them into a single sheet and export as CSV (or do whatever else we want with them). Here is how to do it:

1. Use your mouse to highlight the item you want to scrape.
2. Right-click and choose **Scrape similar...** from the menu. In the following example, I have selected the username **petisnnake** as the one that I want Scraper to use:

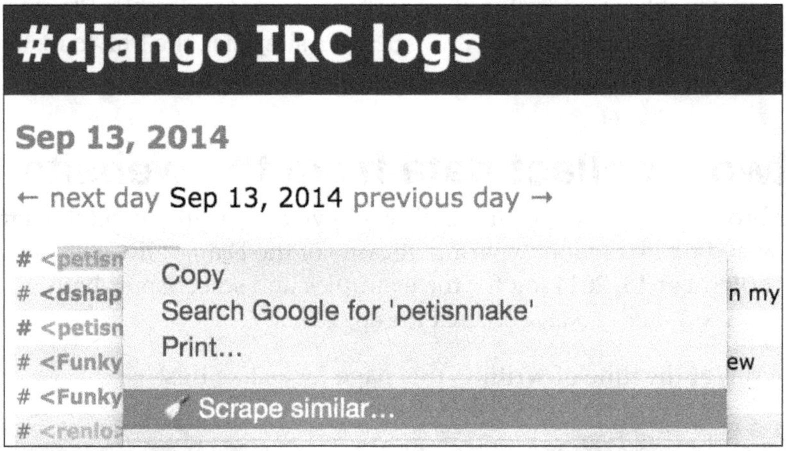

3. After selecting **Scrape similar**, the tool will show you a new window with a collection of all the similar items from the page. The following screenshot shows the entire list of usernames that Scraper found:

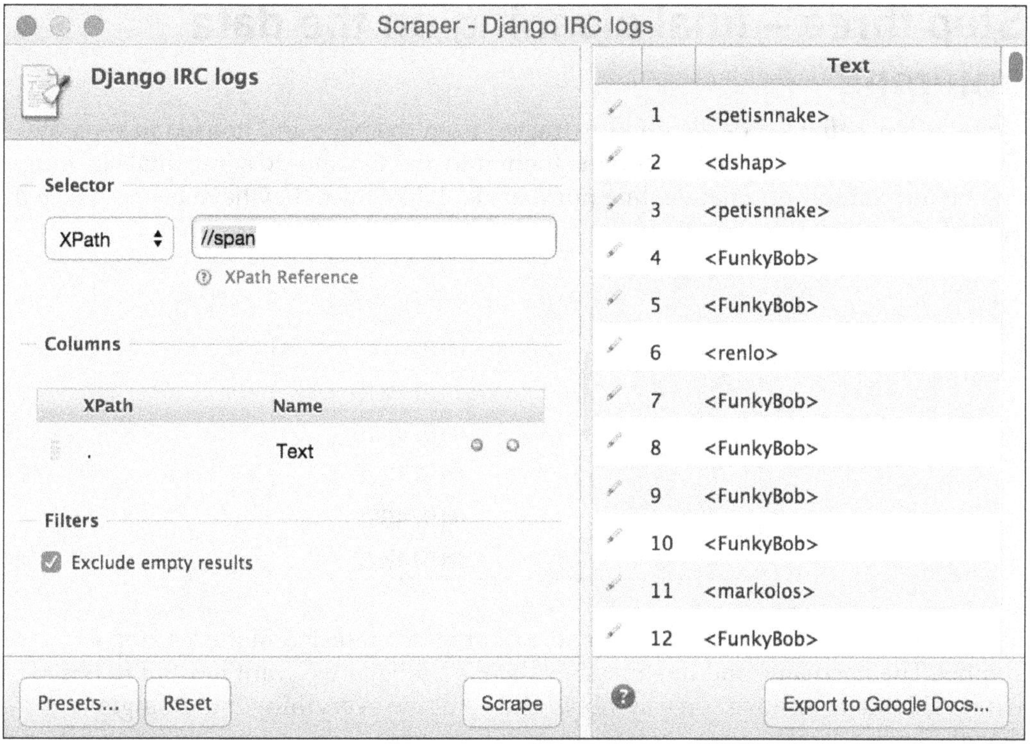

Scraper finds all the similar items based on one sample username.

4. At the bottom of the window, there is a button labeled **Export to Google Docs...**. Note that depending on your settings, you may have to click to agree to allow access to Google Docs from within Scraper.

Step three – final cleaning on the data columns

Once we have all the data elements extracted from the page and housed in separate Google Docs, we will need to combine them into one file and do some final cleaning. Here is an example of what the line numbers look like once they have been extracted, but before we have cleaned them:

	A	B
1	Link	URL
2	#	#1574618
3	#	#1574619
4	#	#1574620
5	#	#1574621
6	#	#1574622

We are not interested in column **A** at all, nor are we interested in the leading **#** symbol. The username and line message data is similar—we want most of it, but we would like to remove some symbols and combine everything into a single Google Spreadsheet.

Using our find-and-replace techniques from *Chapter 3, Workhorses of Clean Data – Spreadsheets and Text Editors* (namely removing the **#**, **<**, and **>** symbols and pasting the rows into a single sheet), we end up with a single clean dataset that looks like this:

	A	B	C
1	1574618	petisnnake	i didnt know that
2	1574619	dshap	FunkyBob: ahh, hmm, i wonder if there's a way to do it in my QuerySet
3	1574620	petisnnake	haven used Django since 1.5
4	1574621	FunkyBob	petisnnake: really? it's probably the biggest single new feature of 1.7
5	1574622	FunkyBob	renlo: btw -- you can do a smarter query than that

Scraper is a nice tool for extracting small amounts of data from web pages. It has a handy Google Spreadsheets interface, and can be a quick solution if you do not feel like writing a program to do this work. In the next section, we will tackle a larger project. It may be complicated enough that we will have to implement a few of the concepts from this chapter into a single solution.

Example project – Extracting data from e-mail and web forums

The Django IRC logs project was pretty simple. It was designed to show you the differences between three solid techniques that are commonly used to extract clean data from within HTML pages. The data we extracted included the line number, the username, and the IRC chat message, all of which were easy to find and required almost no additional cleaning. In this new example project, we will consider a case that is conceptually similar, but that will require us to extend the idea of data extraction beyond HTML to two other types of semi-structured text found on the Web: e-mail messages hosted on the Web and web-based discussion forums.

The background of the project

I was recently working on a research study about how social media can be used to provide software technical support. Specifically, I was trying to discover whether certain types of software development organizations that make APIs and frameworks should move their technical support for developers to Stack Overflow or whether they should continue to use older media, such as e-mail and web forums. To complete this study, I compared (among other things) how long it took developers to get an answer to their API question via Stack Overflow versus how long it took on older social media such as web forums and e-mail groups.

In this project, we will work on a small piece of this question. We will download two types of raw data representing the older social media: HTML files from a web forum and e-mail messages from Google Groups. We will write Python code to extract the dates and time of the messages sent to these two support forums. We will then figure out which messages were sent in reply to the others and calculate some basic summary statistics about how long it took each message to get a reply.

> If you are wondering why we aren't extracting data for the Stack Overflow portion of the question in this example project, just wait until *Chapter 9, Stack Overflow Project*. That entire chapter is devoted to creating and cleaning a Stack Overflow database.

This project will be divided into two parts. In Part one, we will extract data from the e-mail archive from a project hosted on Google Groups, and in Part two, we will extract our data from the HTML files of a different project.

Part one – cleaning data from Google Groups e-mail

Many software companies have traditionally used e-mail mailing lists or hybrid e-mail-web forums to provide technical support for their products. Google Groups is a popular choice for this service. Users can either send e-mails to the group, or they can read and search the messages in a web browser. However, some companies have moved away from providing technical support to developers via Google Groups (including Google products themselves), and are instead using Stack Overflow. The database product Google BigQuery is one such group that now uses Stack Overflow.

Step one – collect the Google Groups messages

To study the response times for questions on the BigQuery Google Group, I first created a list of the URLs for all the postings in that group. You can find my complete list of URLs on my GitHub site: `https://github.com/megansquire/stackpaper2015/blob/master/BigQueryGGurls.txt`.

Once we have a list of target URLs, we can write a Python program to download all the e-mails residing in those URLs, and save them to disk. In the following program, my list of URLs has been saved as the file called `GGurls.txt`. The `time` library is included, so we can take a short `sleep()` method in between requests to the Google Groups server:

```
import urllib2
import time

with open('GGurls.txt', 'r') as f:
    urls = []
    for url in f:
        urls.append(url.strip())

currentFileNum = 1
for url in urls:
    print("Downloading: {0} Number: {1}".format(url, currentFileNum))
    time.sleep(2)
    htmlFile = urllib2.urlopen(url)
    urlFile = open("msg%d.txt" %currentFileNum,'wb')
    urlFile.write(htmlFile.read())
    urlFile.close()
    currentFileNum = currentFileNum +1
```

This program results in 667 files being written to disk.

Step two – extract data from the Google Groups messages

We now have 667 e-mail messages in separate files. Our task is to write a program to read these in one at a time and use one of the techniques from this chapter to extract the pieces of information we need. If we peek inside one of the e-mail messages, we see lots of **headers**, which store information about the e-mail, or its **metadata**. We can quickly see the three headers that identify the metadata elements that we need:

```
In-Reply-To: <ab71b72a-ef9b-4484-b0cc-a72ecb2a3b85@r9g2000yqd.
googlegroups.com>
Date: Mon, 30 Apr 2012 10:33:18 -0700
Message-ID: <CA+qSDkQ4JB+Cn7HNjmtLOqqkbJnyBu=Z1Ocs5-dTe5cN9UEPyA@mail.
gmail.com>
```

All messages have `Message-ID` and `Date`, but the `In-Reply-To` header will only appear in a message that is a reply to another message. An `In-Reply-To` value must be the `Message-ID` value of another message.

The following code shows a regular expression-based solution to extract the `Date`, `Message-ID`, and `In-Reply-To` (if available) values and to create some lists of original and reply messages. Then, the code attempts to calculate the time differences between a message and its replies:

```
import os
import re
import email.utils
import time
import datetime
import numpy

originals = {}
replies = {}
timelist = []

for filename in os.listdir(os.getcwd()):
    if filename.endswith(".txt"):
        f=open(filename, 'r')
        i=''
        m=''
        d=''
        for line in f:
            irt = re.search('(In\-Reply\-To: <)(.+?)@', line)
            mid = re.search('(Message\-ID: <)(.+?)@', line)
```

```
            dt = re.search('(Date: )(.+?)\r', line)
            if irt:
                i= irt.group(2)
            if mid:
                m= mid.group(2)
            if dt:
                d= dt.group(2)
        f.close()
        if i and d:
            replies[i] = d
        if m and d:
            originals[m] = d

for (messageid, origdate) in originals.items():
    try:
        if replies[messageid]:
            replydate = replies[messageid]
            try:
                parseddate = email.utils.parsedate(origdate)
                parsedreply = email.utils.parsedate(replydate)
            except:
                pass
            try:
                # this still creates some malformed (error) times
                timeddate = time.mktime(parseddate)
                timedreply = time.mktime(parsedreply)
            except:
                pass
            try:
                dtdate = datetime.datetime.fromtimestamp(timeddate)
                dtreply = datetime.datetime.fromtimestamp(timedreply)
            except:
                pass
            try:
                difference = dtreply - dtdate
                totalseconds = difference.total_seconds()
                timeinhours =  (difference.days*86400+difference.
seconds)/3600
                # this is a hack to take care of negative times
                # I should probably handle this with timezones but
alas
                if timeinhours > 1:
                    #print timeinhours
```

```
                    timelist.append(timeinhours)
            except:
                pass
    except:
        pass

print numpy.mean(timelist)
print numpy.std(timelist)
print numpy.median(timelist)
```

In this code, the initial `for` loop zips through each message and extracts the three pieces of data we are interested in. (This program does not store these to a separate file or to disk, but you could add this functionality if you wish to.) This portion of the code also creates two important lists:

- `originals[]` is a list of original messages. We make the assumption that these are primarily questions being asked of the list members.
- `replies[]` is a list of reply messages. We assume that these are primarily answers to questions asked in another message.

The second `for` loop processes each message in the list of original messages, doing the following, if there is a reply to the original message, try to figure out how long that reply took to be sent. We then keep a list of reply times.

Extraction code

For this chapter, we are mostly interested in the cleaning and extraction portion of the code, so let's look closely at those lines. Here, we process each line of the e-mail file looking for three e-mail headers: `In-Reply-To`, `Message-ID`, and `Date`. We use regex searching and grouping, just like we did in Method 1 earlier in this chapter, to delimit the headers and easily extract the values that follow:

```
for line in f:
    irt = re.search('(In\-Reply\-To: <)(.+?)@', line)
    mid = re.search('(Message\-ID: <)(.+?)@', line)
    dt = re.search('(Date: )(.+?)\r', line)
    if irt:
        i = irt.group(2)
    if mid:
        m = mid.group(2)
    if dt:
        d = dt.group(2)
```

Why did we decide to use regex here instead of a tree-based parser? There are two main reasons:

1. Because the e-mails we downloaded are not HTML, they cannot easily be described as a tree of nodes with parents and children. Therefore, a parse tree-based solution such as BeautifulSoup is not the best choice.
2. Because e-mail headers are structured and very predictable (especially the three headers we are looking for here), a regex solution is acceptable.

Program output

The output of this program is to print three numbers that estimate the mean, standard deviation, and median time in hours for replies to messages on this Google Group. When I run this code, my results are as follows:

```
178.911877395
876.102630872
18.0
```

This means that the median response time to a message posted to the BigQuery Google Group was about 18 hours. Now let's consider how to extract similar data from a different source: web forums. Do you think responses to questions in a web forum will be faster, slower, or about the same as a Google Group?

Part two – cleaning data from web forums

The web forums we will study for this project are from a company called **DocuSign**. They also moved their developer support to Stack Overflow, but they have an archive of their older web-based developer forum still online. I poked around on their website until I found out how to download some of the messages from those old forums. The process shown here is more involved than the Google Groups example, but you will learn a lot about how to collect data automatically.

Step one – collect some RSS that points us to HTML files

The DocuSign developer forum has thousands of messages on it. We would like to have a list of the URLs for all those messages or discussion threads so that we can write some code to download them all automatically, and extract the reply times efficiently.

To do this, first we will need a list of all the URLs for the discussions. I found that the archive of DocuSign's old Dev-Zone developer site is located at `https://community.docusign.com/t5/DevZone-Archives-Read-Only/ct-p/dev_zone`.

The site looks like this in the browser:

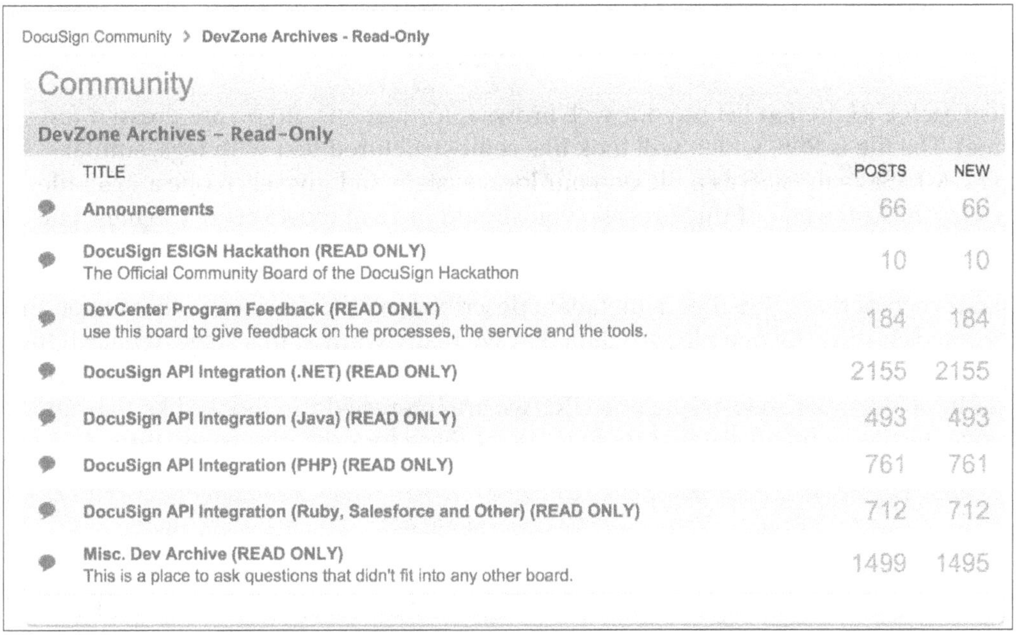

DocuSign Community > DevZone Archives - Read-Only
Community
DevZone Archives - Read-Only
TITLE
POSTS
NEW
Announcements
66 66
DocuSign ESIGN Hackathon (READ ONLY)
The Official Community Board of the DocuSign Hackathon
10 10
DevCenter Program Feedback (READ ONLY)
use this board to give feedback on the processes, the service and the tools.
184 184
DocuSign API Integration (.NET) (READ ONLY)
2155 2155
DocuSign API Integration (Java) (READ ONLY)
493 493
DocuSign API Integration (PHP) (READ ONLY)
761 761
DocuSign API Integration (Ruby, Salesforce and Other) (READ ONLY)
712 712
Misc. Dev Archive (READ ONLY)
This is a place to ask questions that didn't fit into any other board.
1499 1495

We definitely do not want to click through each one of those forums and then click into each message and save it manually. That would take forever, and it would be extremely boring. Is there a better way?

The DocuSign website's **Help** pages indicate that it is possible to download a **Really Simple Syndication** (**RSS**) file showing the newest threads and messages in each forum. We can use the RSS files to automatically collect the URLs for many of the discussions on the site. The RSS files we are interested in are the ones relating to the developer support forums only (not the announcements or sales forums). These RSS files are available from the following URLs:

- `https://community.docusign.com/docusign/rss/board?board.id=upcoming_releases`
- `https://community.docusign.com/docusign/rss/board?board.id=DocuSign_Developer_Connection`
- `https://community.docusign.com/docusign/rss/board?board.id=Electronic_Signature_API`

- `https://community.docusign.com/docusign/rss/board?board.id=Java`
- `https://community.docusign.com/docusign/rss/board?board.id=php_api`
- `https://community.docusign.com/docusign/rss/board?board.id=dev_other`
- `https://community.docusign.com/docusign/rss/board?board.id=Ask_A_Development_Question_Board`

Visit each URL in that list in your web browser (or just one, if you are pressed for time). The file is RSS, which will look like semi-structured text with tags, similar to HTML. Save the RSS as a file on your local system and give each one a `.rss` file extension. At the end of this process, you should have at most seven RSS files, one for each preceding URL shown.

Inside each of these RSS files is metadata describing all the discussion threads on the forum, including the one piece of data that we really want at this stage: the URL for each particular discussion thread. Open one of the RSS files in a text editor and you will be able to spot an example of a URL we are interested in. It looks like this, and inside the file, you will see that there is one of these for each discussion thread:

```
<guid>http://community.docusign.com/t5/Misc-Dev-Archive-READ-ONLY/
Re-Custom-CheckBox-Tabs-not-marked-when-setting-value-to-quot-X/m-
p/28884#M1674</guid>
```

Now, we can write a program to loop through each RSS file, look for these URLs, visit them, and then extract the reply times we are interested in. The next section breaks this down into a series of smaller steps, and then shows a program that does the entire job.

Step two – Extract URLs from RSS; collect and parse HTML

In this step, we will write a program that will do the following:

1. Open each RSS file that we saved in Step 1.
2. Every time we see a `<guid>` and `</guid>` tag pair, extract the URL inside and add it to a list.
3. For each URL in the list, download whatever HTML file is at that location.
4. Read that HTML file and extract the original post time and the reply time from each message.
5. Calculate how long it took to send a reply with mean, median, and standard deviation, like we did in Part 1.

Here is some Python code to handle all these steps. We will go over the extraction parts in detail at the end of the code listing:

```
import os
import re
import urllib2
import datetime
import numpy

alllinks = []
timelist = []
for filename in os.listdir(os.getcwd()):
    if filename.endswith('.rss'):
        f = open(filename, 'r')
        linktext = ''
        linkurl = ''
        for line in f:
            # find the URLs for discussion threads
            linktext = re.search('(<guid>)(.+?)(<\/guid>)', line)

            if linktext:
                linkurl= linktext.group(2)
                alllinks.append(linkurl)
        f.close()

mainmessage = ''
reply = ''
maindateobj = datetime.datetime.today()
replydateobj = datetime.datetime.today()
for item in alllinks:
    print "==="
    print "working on thread\n" + item
    response = urllib2.urlopen(item)
    html = response.read()
    # this is the regex needed to match the timestamp
    tuples = re.findall('lia-message-posted-on\">\s+<span
class=\"local-date\">\\xe2\\x80\\x8e(.*?)<\/span>\s+<span
class=\"local-time\">([\w:\sAM|PM]+)<\/span>', html)
    mainmessage = tuples[0]
    if len(tuples) > 1:
        reply = tuples[1]
    if mainmessage:
        print "main: "
        maindateasstr = mainmessage[0] + " " + mainmessage[1]
        print maindateasstr
        maindateobj = datetime.datetime.strptime(maindateasstr,
'%m-%d-%Y %I:%M %p')
    if reply:
        print "reply: "
        replydateasstr = reply[0] + " " + reply[1]
```

```
        print replydateasstr
        replydateobj = datetime.datetime.strptime(replydateasstr,
'%m-%d-%Y %I:%M %p')

        # only calculate difference if there was a reply
        difference = replydateobj - maindateobj
        totalseconds = difference.total_seconds()
        timeinhours =  (difference.days*86400+difference.seconds)/3600
        if timeinhours > 1:
            print timeinhours
            timelist.append(timeinhours)

print "when all is said and done, in hours:"
print numpy.mean(timelist)
print numpy.std(timelist)
print numpy.median(timelist)
```

Program status

As the program works, it prints out status messages so we know what it is working on. The status messages look like this, and there is one of these for each URL that is found in the RSS feed(s):

```
===
working on thread
http://community.docusign.com/t5/Misc-Dev-Archive-READ-ONLY/Can-you-disable-the-Echosign-notification-in-Adobe-Reader/m-p/21473#M1156
main:
06-21-2013 08:09 AM
reply:
06-24-2013 10:34 AM
74
```

In this display, 74 represents the rounded number of hours between the posted time of the first message in the thread and the first reply in the thread (about three days, plus two hours).

Program output

At its conclusion, this program prints out the mean, standard deviation, and median reply times in hours, just like the Part 1 program did for Google Groups:

```
when all is said and done, in hours:
695.009009009
2506.66701108
20.0
```

It looks like reply time in the DocuSign forum is a tiny bit slower than Google Groups. It is reporting 20 hours compared to Google Groups, which took 18 hours, but at least both numbers are in the same approximate range. Your results might change, since new messages are getting added all the time.

Extraction code

Since we are mostly interested in data extraction, let's look closely at the part of the code where that happens. Here is the most relevant line of code:

```
tuples = re.findall('lia-message-posted-on\">\s+<span class=\"local-
date\">\\xe2\\x80\\x8e(.*?)<\/span>\s+<span class=\"local-
time\">([\w:\sAM|PM]+)<\/span>', html)
```

Just like with some of our previous examples, this code also relies on regular expressions to do its work. However, this regex is pretty messy. Maybe we should have written this with BeautifulSoup? Let's take a look at the original HTML that we are trying to match so that we can understand more about what this code is trying to do and whether we should have done this a different way. What follows is a screenshot of how the page looks in the browser. The times we are interested in have been annotated on the screenshot:

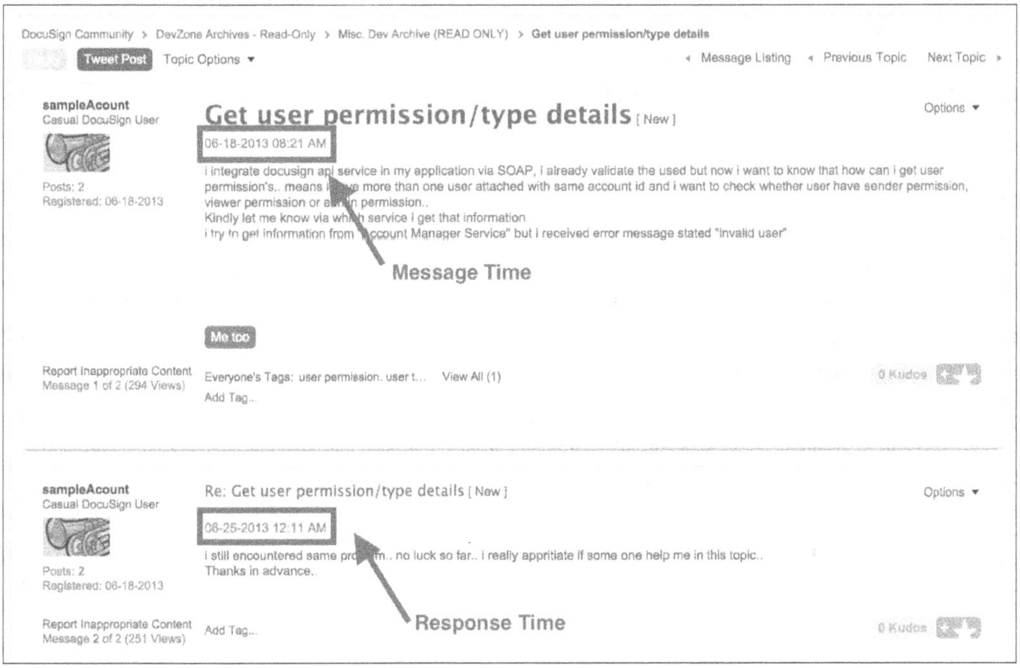

What does the underlying HTML look like though? That is the part that our program will need to be able to parse. It turns out that the date of the original message is printed in several places on the HTML page, but the date and time combination is only printed once for the original and once for the reply. Here is the HTML showing how these look (the HTML has been condensed and newlines removed for easier viewing):

```
<p class="lia-message-dates lia-message-post-date lia-component-post-
date-last-edited" class="lia-message-dates lia-message-post-date">
<span class="DateTime lia-message-posted-on lia-component-common-
widget-date" class="DateTime lia-message-posted-on">
<span class="local-date">⊠06-18-2013</span>
<span class="local-time">08:21 AM</span>

<p class="lia-message-dates lia-message-post-date lia-component-post-
date-last-edited" class="lia-message-dates lia-message-post-date">
<span class="DateTime lia-message-posted-on lia-component-common-
widget-date" class="DateTime lia-message-posted-on">
<span class="local-date">⊠06-25-2013</span>
<span class="local-time">12:11 AM</span>
```

This turns out to be a pretty straightforward problem for regex to solve, since we can write a single regular expression and find all the instances of it for both types of messages. In the code, we state that the first instance we find becomes the original message, and the next one becomes the reply, as follows:

```
mainmessage = tuples[0]
if len(tuples) > 1:
    reply = tuples[1]
```

We could have used a parse tree-based solution such as BeautifulSoup, but we would have to contend with the fact that the span class values are identical for both sets of dates, and even the parent element (the <p> tag) turns out to have the same class. So, this parse tree is substantially more complex than the one shown in Method 2 earlier in the chapter.

If you really wanted to try to use BeautifulSoup for this extraction, my recommendation would be first to look at the structure of the page using your browser's Developer Tools, for example, in the Chrome browser, you can select the element you are interested in—the date and time in this case—and right-click it, and then choose **Inspect Element**. This will open a Developer Tools panel showing where this piece of data is found in the overall document tree. Little arrows to the left of each HTML element indicate if there are child nodes. You can then decide how to proceed through locating your target element in the parse tree programmatically, and you could make a plan to differentiate it from the other nodes. Since this task is well beyond the scope of this introductory book, I will leave that as an exercise for the reader.

Summary

In this chapter, we discovered a few tried-and-true techniques for separating interesting data from unwanted data. When we make broth in our chef's kitchen, we use a strainer to catch the bones and vegetable husks that we do not want, while allowing the delicious liquid that we *do* want to flow through the holes in the sieve into our container. The same idea applies when we are extracting data from web pages in our data science kitchen. We want to devise a cleaning plan that allows us to extract what we want, while leaving the rest of the HTML behind.

Along the way, we reviewed the two main mental models used in extracting data from HTML, namely a line-by-line delimiter approach and the parse tree/nodes model. We then looked into three solid, proven methods to parse HTML pages to extract the data we want: regular expressions, BeautifulSoup, and a Chrome-based point-and-click Scraper tool. Finally, we put together a project that collected and extracted useful data from real-world e-mail and HTML pages.

Text data such as e-mail and HTML turned out to not be very difficult to clean, but what about binary files? In the next chapter, we will explore how to extract clean data from a much more difficult target: PDF files.

6
Cleaning Data in PDF Files

In the last chapter, we discovered different ways of separating the data we want from the data we do not want. We imagined that the data cleaning process was a little like making chicken stock, in which our goal was to keep the broth but strain out the bones. But what happens if the data we want is not so easily distinguishable from the data we do not want?

Consider a fine, older wine with considerable sediment. At first glance, we might not be able to see the sediment suspended in the liquid. But after the wine spends some time in a decanter, the sediment falls to the bottom, and we are able to pour out a cleaner, more aromatic wine. A simple strainer would not have been able to separate the wine from the sediment in this case—a special-purpose tool would have been needed.

In this chapter, we will experiment with several data decanters to extract all the good stuff hidden inside inscrutable PDF files. We will explore the following topics:

- What PDF files are for and why it is difficult to extract data from them
- How to copy and paste from PDF files, and what to do when this does not work
- How to shrink a PDF file by saving only the pages that we need
- How to extract text and numbers from a PDF file using the tools inside a Python package called **pdfMiner**
- How to extract tabular data from within a PDF file using a browser-based Java application called **Tabula**
- How to use the full, paid version of Adobe Acrobat to extract a table of data

Why is cleaning PDF files difficult?

Files saved in **Portable Document Format** (**PDF**) are a little more complicated than the text files we have looked at so far in this book. PDF is a binary format that was invented by Adobe Systems, which later evolved into an open standard so that multiple applications could create PDF versions of their documents. The purpose of a PDF file is to provide a way of viewing the text and graphics in a document independent of the software that did the original layout.

In the early 1990s, the heyday of desktop publishing, each graphic design software package had a different proprietary format for its files, and the packages were quite expensive. In those days, in order to view a document created in Word, Pagemaker, or Quark, you would have to open the document using the same software that had created it. This was especially problematic in the early days of the Web, since there were not many available techniques in HTML to create sophisticated layouts, but people still wanted to share files with each other. PDF was meant to be a vendor-neutral layout format. Adobe made its Acrobat Reader software free for anyone to download, and subsequently the PDF format became widely used.

> Here is a fun fact about the early days of Acrobat Reader. The words `click here` when entered into Google search engine still bring up *Adobe's Acrobat PDF Reader download website* as the first result, and have done so for years. This is because so many websites distribute PDF files along with a message saying something like, "To view this file you must have Acrobat Reader installed. Click here to download it." Since Google's search algorithm uses the link text to learn what sites go with what keywords, the keyword click here is now associated with Adobe Acrobat's download site.

PDF is still used to make vendor- and application-neutral versions of files that have layouts that are more complicated than what could be achieved with plain text. For example, viewing the same document in the various versions of Microsoft Word still sometimes causes documents with lots of embedded tables, styles, images, forms, and fonts to look different from one another. This can be due to a number of factors, such as differences in operating systems or versions of the installed Word software itself. Even with applications that are intended to be compatible between software packages or versions, subtle differences can result in incompatibilities. PDF was created to solve some of this.

Right away we can tell that PDF is going to be more difficult to deal with than a text file, because it is a binary format, and because it has embedded fonts, images, and so on. So most of the tools in our trusty data cleaning toolbox, such as text editors and command-line tools (`less`) are largely useless with PDF files. Fortunately there are still a few tricks we can use to get the data out of a PDF file.

Try simple solutions first – copying

Suppose that on your way to decant your bottle of fine red wine, you spill the bottle on the floor. Your first thought might be that this is a complete disaster and you will have to replace the whole carpet. But before you start ripping out the entire floor, it is probably worth trying to clean the mess with an old bartender's trick: club soda and a damp cloth. In this section, we outline a few things to try first, before getting involved in an expensive file renovation project. They might not work, but they are worth a try.

Our experimental file

Let's practice cleaning PDF data by using a real PDF file. We also do not want this experiment to be too easy, so let's choose a very complicated file. Suppose we are interested in pulling the data out of a file we found on the Pew Research Center's website called "Is College Worth It?". Published in 2011, this PDF file is 159 pages long and contains numerous data tables showing various ways of measuring if attaining a college education in the United States is worth the investment. We would like to find a way to quickly extract the data within these numerous tables so that we can run some additional statistics on it. For example, here is what one of the tables in the report looks like:

Q.23/Q.24, **BASED ON TOTAL**[31]

Which of these would you say is the most important role colleges and universities play in society?

All		*4-year Private*	*4-year Public*	*2-year Private/Public*	*For profit*
38	Prepare students to be productive members of the workforce	23	28	47	63
27	Prepare young people to be responsible citizens	48	31	14	8
21	Ensure that all qualified students have equal access to a college education	16	24	25	20
4	Contribute to the economic development of their region or locality	2	5	8	2
4	Conduct research to help solve medical, scientific, social, and other national problems	5	8	3	1
2	Provide continuing education for adults of all ages	2	1	1	3
3	None is "very important"/No answer	4	4	3	2

This table is fairly complicated. It only has six columns and eight rows, but several of the rows take up two lines, and the header row text is only shown on five of the columns.

[The complete report can be found at the PewResearch website at `http://www.pewsocialtrends.org/2011/05/15/is-college-worth-it/`, and the particular file we are using is labeled Complete Report: `http://www.pewsocialtrends.org/files/2011/05/higher-ed-report.pdf`.]

Step one – try copying out the data we want

The data we will experiment on in this example is found on page 149 of the PDF file (labeled page 143 in their document). If we open the file in a PDF viewer, such as Preview on Mac OSX, and attempt to select just the data in the table, we already see that some strange things are happening. For example, even though we did not mean to select the page number (143); it got selected anyway. This does not bode well for our experiment, but let's continue. Copy the data out by using Command-C or select **Edit | Copy**.

143

Q.23/Q.24, **BASED ON TOTAL**[31]

Which of these would you say is the most important role colleges and universities play in society?

All		*4-year Private*	*4-year Public*	*2-year Private/Public*	*For profit*
38	Prepare students to be productive members of the workforce	23	28	47	63
27	Prepare young people to be responsible citizens	48	31	14	8
21	Ensure that all qualified students have equal access to a college education	16	24	25	20
4	Contribute to the economic development of their region or locality	2	5	8	2
4	Conduct research to help solve medical, scientific, social, and other national problems	5	8	3	1
2	Provide continuing education for adults of all ages	2	1	1	3
3	None is "very important"/No answer	4	4	3	2

How text looks when selected in this PDF from within Preview

Step two – try pasting the copied data into a text editor

The following screenshot shows how the copied text looks when it is pasted into Text Wrangler, our text editor:

```
38 Prepare students to be productive
members of the workforce
27 Prepare young people to be responsible
citizens
21 Ensure that all qualified students have
4-year 4-year 2-year Private Public Private/Public
23 28 47 48 31 14 16 24 25
For profit
63 8 20
143
     equal access to a college education
4 Contribute to the economic development 2582
of their region or locality
4 Conduct research to help solve medical, 5831
scientific, social, and other national
problems
2 Provide continuing education for adults 2113
of all ages
3 None is "very important"/No answer 4432
```

Clearly, this data is not in any sensible order after copying and pasting it. The page number is included, the numbers are horizontal instead of vertical, and the column headers are out of order. Even some of the numbers have been combined; for example, the final row contains the numbers 4,4,3,2; but in the pasted version, this becomes a single number **4432**. It would probably take longer to clean up this data manually at this point than it would have taken just to retype the original table. We can conclude that with this particular PDF file, we are going to have to take stronger measures to clean it.

> We should note at this point that the other areas of this PDF file *do* clean up nicely. For example, the Preface, a text-only section located on page 3 of the file, copies out just fine using the preceding technique. With this file, it is only the actual tabular data that is a problem. You should experiment with all parts of a PDF file—including text and tabular data—before deciding on an extraction technique.

Step three – make a smaller version of the file

Our copying and pasting procedures have not worked, so we have resigned ourselves to the fact that we are going to need to prepare for more invasive measures. Perhaps if we are not interested in extracting data from all 159 pages of this PDF file, we can identify just the area of the PDF that we want to operate on, and save that section to a separate file.

To do this in **Preview** on MacOSX, launch the **File | Print...** dialog box. In the **Pages** area, we will enter the range of pages we actually want to copy. For the purpose of this experiment, we are only interested in page 149; so enter `149` in both the **From:** and **to:** boxes as shown in the following screenshot.

Then from the **PDF** dropdown box at the bottom, select **Open PDF in Preview**. You will see your single-page PDF in a new window. From here, we can save this as a new file and give it a new name, such as `report149.pdf` or the like.

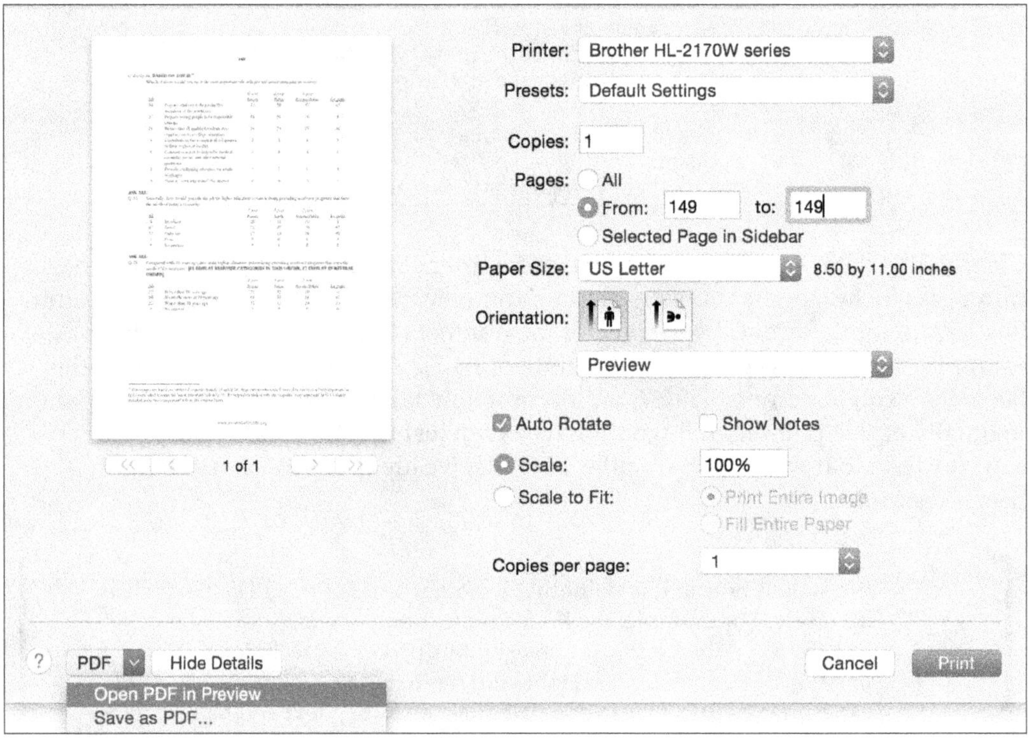

Another technique to try – pdfMiner

Now that we have a smaller file to experiment with, let's try some programmatic solutions to extract the text and see if we fare any better. pdfMiner is a Python package with two embedded tools to operate on PDF files. We are particularly interested in experimenting with one of these tools, a command-line program called `pdf2txt` that is designed to extract text from within a PDF document. Maybe this will be able to help us get those tables of numbers out of the file correctly.

Step one – install pdfMiner

Launch the Canopy Python environment. From the Canopy Terminal Window, run the following command:

```
pip install pdfminer
```

This will install the entire pdfMiner package and all its associated command-line tools.

> The documentation for pdfMiner and the two tools that come with it, `pdf2txt` and `dumpPDF`, is located at `http://www.unixuser.org/~euske/python/pdfminer/`.

Step two – pull text from the PDF file

We can extract all text from a PDF file using the command-line tool called `pdf2txt.py`. To do this, use the Canopy Terminal and navigate to the directory where the file is located. The basic format of the command is `pdf2txt.py <filename>`. If you have a larger file that has multiple pages (or you did not already break the PDF into smaller ones), you can also run `pdf2txt.py -p149 <filename>` to specify that you only want page 149.

Just as with the preceding copy-and-paste experiment, we will try this technique not only on the tables located on page 149, but also on the Preface on page 3. To extract just the text from page 3, we run the following command:

```
pdf2txt.py -p3 pewReport.pdf
```

After running this command, the extracted preface of the Pew Research report appears in our command-line window:

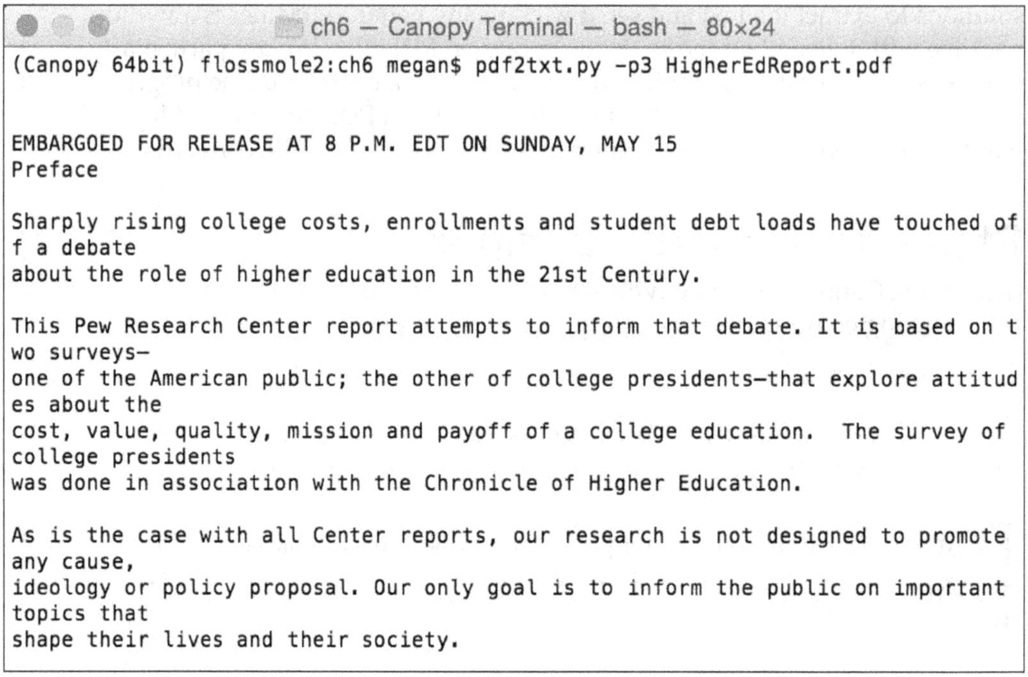
ch6 — Canopy Terminal — bash — 80×24
(Canopy 64bit) flossmole2:ch6 megan$ pdf2txt.py -p3 HigherEdReport.pdf
EMBARGOED FOR RELEASE AT 8 P.M. EDT ON SUNDAY, MAY 15
Preface
Sharply rising college costs, enrollments and student debt loads have touched of
f a debate
about the role of higher education in the 21st Century.
This Pew Research Center report attempts to inform that debate. It is based on t
wo surveys–
one of the American public; the other of college presidents–that explore attitud
es about the
cost, value, quality, mission and payoff of a college education. The survey of
college presidents
was done in association with the Chronicle of Higher Education.
As is the case with all Center reports, our research is not designed to promote
any cause,
ideology or policy proposal. Our only goal is to inform the public on important
topics that
shape their lives and their society.

To save this text to a file called `pewPreface.txt`, we can simply add a redirect to our command line as follows:

```
pdf2txt.py -p3 pewReport.pdf > pewPreface.txt
```

But what about those troublesome data tables located on page 149? What happens when we use `pdf2txt` on those? We can run the following command:

```
pdf2txt.py pewReport149.pdf
```

The results are slightly better than copy and paste, but not by much. The actual data output section is shown in the following screenshot. The column headers and data are mixed together, and the data from different columns are shown out of order.

```
ch6 — Canopy Terminal — bash — 80×24
4-year
Private

23

4-year
Public
28

48

16

2

5

2

4

31

24
```

We will have to declare the tabular data extraction portion of this experiment a failure, though pdfMiner worked reasonably well on line-by-line text-only extraction.

> Remember that your success with each of these tools may vary. Much of it depends on the particular characteristics of the original PDF file.

It looks like we chose a very tricky PDF for this example, but let's not get disheartened. Instead, we will move on to another tool and see how we fare with it.

Third choice – Tabula

Tabula is a Java-based program to extract data within tables in PDF files. We will download the Tabula software and put it to work on the tricky tables in our page 149 file.

Step one – download Tabula

Tabula is available to be downloaded from its website at `http://tabula.technology/`. The site includes some simple download instructions.

> On Mac OSX version 10.10.1, I had to download the legacy Java 6 application before I was able to run Tabula. The process was straightforward and required only following the on-screen instructions.

Step two – run Tabula

Launch Tabula from inside the downloaded `.zip` archive. On the Mac, the Tabula application file is called simply `Tabula.app`. You can copy this to your `Applications` folder if you like.

When Tabula starts, it launches a tab or window within your default web browser at the address `http://127.0.0.1:8080/`. The initial action portion of the screen looks like this:

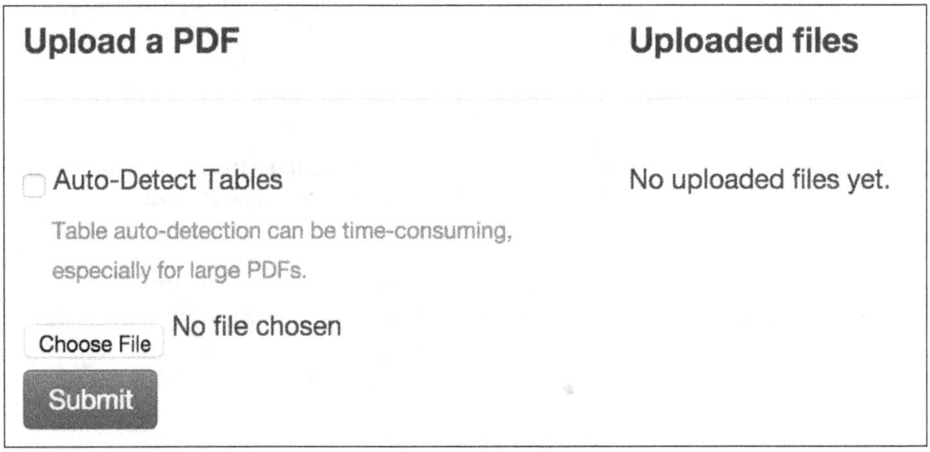

The warning that auto-detecting tables takes a long time is true. For the single-page `perResearch149.pdf` file, with three tables in it, table auto-detection took two full minutes and resulted in an error message about an incorrectly formatted PDF file.

Step three – direct Tabula to extract the data

Once Tabula reads in the file, it is time to direct it where the tables are. Using your mouse cursor, select the table you are interested in. I drew a box around the entire first table.

Tabula took about 30 seconds to read in the table, and the results are shown as follows:

Extracted tabular data

		4-year	4-year	2-year	
All		Private	Public	Private/Public	For profit
38	Prepare students to be productive	23	28	47	63
	members of the workforce				
27	Prepare young people to be responsible	48	31	14	8
	citizens				
21	Ensure that all qualified students have	16	24	25	20
	equal access to a college education				
4	Contribute to the economic development	2	5	8	2
	of their region or locality				
4	Conduct research to help solve medical,	5	8	3	1
	scientific, social, and other national				
	problems				
2	Provide continuing education for adults	2	1	1	3

Compared to the way the data was read with copy and paste and `pdf2txt`, this data looks great. But if you are not happy with the way Tabula reads in the table, you can repeat this process by clearing your selection and redrawing the rectangle.

Step four – copy the data out

We can use the **Download Data** button within Tabula to save the data to a friendlier file format, such as CSV or TSV. As we know from our work in previous chapters, these are formats that can be cleaned, if necessary, in a spreadsheet or text editor. Right on cue, we are ready for our next step.

Step five – more cleaning

Open the CSV file in Excel or a text editor and take a look at it. At this stage, we have had a lot of failures in getting this PDF data extracted, so it is very tempting to just quit now. However, if you have made it this far in a book about data cleaning, you can probably guess that this data could be made even cleaner. Here are some simple data cleaning tasks that we know how to do already from earlier chapters:

1. We can combine all the two-line text cells into a single cell. For example, in column **B**, many of the phrases take up more than one row. **Prepare students to be productive** and **members of the workforce** should be in one cell as a single phrase. The same is true for the headers in Rows **1** and **2** (**4-year** and **Private** should be in a single cell). To clean this in Excel, create a new column between columns **B** and **C**. Use the `concatenate()` function to join B3:B4, B5:B6, and so on. Use **Paste-Special** to add the new concatenated values into a new column. Then remove the two columns you no longer need. Do the same for rows **1** and **2**.
2. Remove blank lines between rows.

   When these procedures are finished, the data looks like this:

	A	B	C	D	E	F
1	All		4-year Private	4-year Public	2-year Private/Public	For profit
2	38	Prepare students to be productive members of the workforce	23	28	47	63
3	27	Prepare young people to be responsible citizens	48	31	14	8
4	21	Ensure that all qualified students have equal access to a college education	16	24	25	20
5	4	Contribute to the economic development of their region or locality	2	5	8	2
6	4	Conduct research to help solve medical, scientific, social, and other national problems	5	8	3	1
7	2	Provide continuing education for adults of all ages	2	1	1	3
8	3	None is "very important" /No answer	4	4	3	2

> Tabula might seem like a lot of work compared to cutting and pasting data or running a simple command-line tool. That is true, unless your PDF file turns out to be finicky like this one was. Remember that specialty tools are there for a reason—but do not use them unless you really need them. Start with a simple solution first and only proceed to a more difficult tool when you really need it.

When all else fails – the fourth technique

Adobe Systems sells a paid, commercial version of their Acrobat software that has some additional features above and beyond just allowing you to read PDF files. With the full version of Acrobat, you can create complex PDF files and manipulate existing files in various ways. One of the features that is relevant here is the **Export Selection As...** option found within Acrobat.

To get started using this feature, launch Acrobat and use the **File Open** dialog to open the PDF file. Within the file, navigate to the table holding the data you want to export. The following screenshot shows how to select the data from the page 149 PDF we have been operating on. Use your mouse to select the data, then right-click and choose **Export Selection As...**

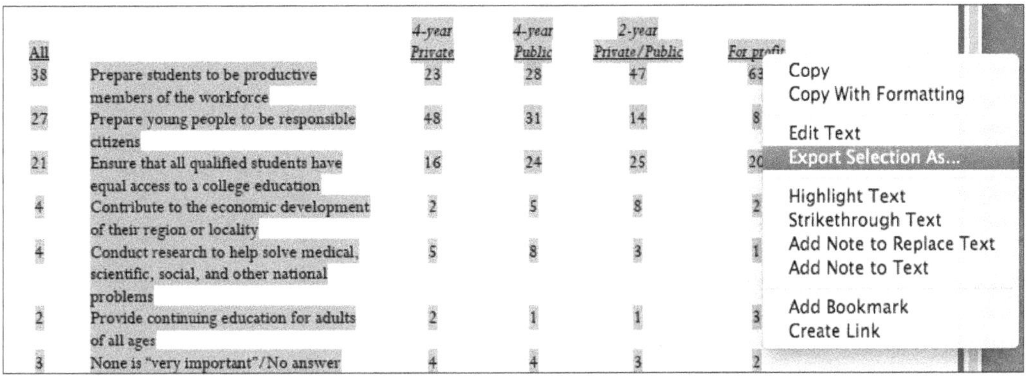

At this point, Acrobat will ask you how you want the data exported. CSV is one of the choices. Excel Workbook (`.xlsx`) would also be a fine choice if you are sure you will not want to also edit the file in a text editor. Since I know that Excel can also open CSV files, I decided to save my file in that format so I would have the most flexibility between editing in Excel and my text editor.

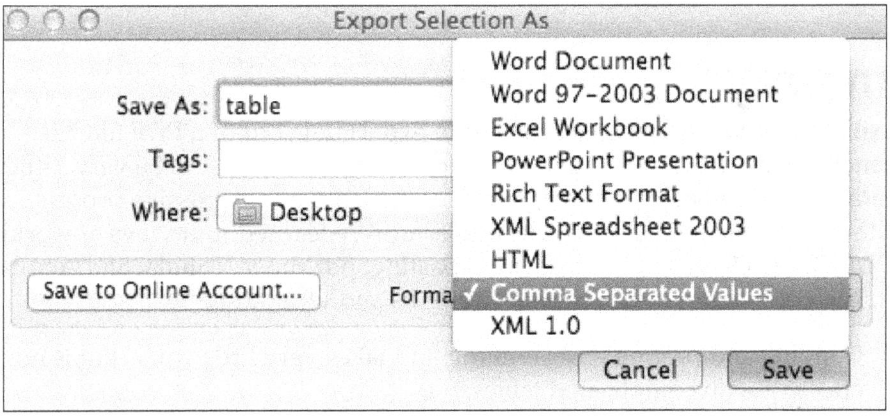

After choosing the format for the file, we will be prompted for a filename and location for where to save the file. When we launch the resulting file, either in a text editor or in Excel, we can see that it looks a lot like the Tabula version we saw in the previous section. Here is how our CSV file will look when opened in Excel:

	A	B	C	D	E	F
1	All		4-year Privat	4-year Public	2-year Privat	For profit
2	38	Prepare stud	23	28	47	63
3		members of the workforce				
4	27	Prepare your	48	31	14	8
5		citizens				
6	21	Ensure that a	16	24	25	20
7		equal access to a college education				
8	4	Contribute to	2	5	8	2
9		of their region or locality				
10	4	Conduct rese	5	8	3	1
11		scientific, social, and other national				
12		problems				
13	2	Provide cont	2	1	1	3
14		of all ages				
15	3	None is Òver	4	4	3	2

At this point, we can use the exact same cleaning routine we used with the Tabula data, where we concatenated the B2:B3 cells into a single cell and then removed the empty rows.

Summary

The goal of this chapter was to learn how to export data out of a PDF file. Like sediment in a fine wine, the data in PDF files can appear at first to be very difficult to separate. Unlike decanting wine, however, which is a very passive process, separating PDF data took a lot of trial and error. We learned four ways of working with PDF files to clean data: copying and pasting, pdfMiner, Tabula, and Acrobat export. Each of these tools has certain strengths and weaknesses:

- Copying and pasting costs nothing and takes very little work, but is not as effective with complicated tables.
- pdfMiner/Pdf2txt is also free, and as a command-line tool, it could be automated. It also works on large amounts of data. But like copying and pasting, it is easily confused by certain types of tables.

- Tabula takes some work to set up, and since it is a product undergoing development, it does occasionally give strange warnings. It is also a little slower than the other options. However, its output is very clean, even with complicated tables.
- Acrobat gives similar output to Tabula, but with almost no setup and very little effort. It is a paid product.

By the end, we had a clean dataset that was ready for analysis or long-term storage.

In the next chapter, we will focus on data that has been placed into long-term storage in a **Relational Database Management System** (**RDBMS**). We will learn about the challenges of cleaning data stored this way, as well as some of the common data anomalies and how to fix them.

7
RDBMS Cleaning Techniques

Home refrigerators all come with shelves and most have one or two drawers for vegetables. But if you ever visit a home organization store or talk to a professional organizer, you will learn that there are also numerous additional storage options, including egg containers, cheese boxes, soda can dispensers, wine bottle holders, labeling systems for leftovers, and stackable, color-coded bins in a variety of sizes. But do we really need all these extras? To answer this, ask yourself these questions, are my frequently used foods easy to find? Are food items taking up more space than they should? Are leftovers clearly labeled so I remember what they are and when I made them? If our answers are *no*, organization experts say that containers and labels can help us optimize storage, reduce waste, and make our lives easier.

The same is true in our **Relational Database Management System** (**RDBMS**). As the classic long-term data storage solution, RDBMS is a standard part of the modern data science toolkit. But all too often, we are guilty of just depositing data in the database, with little thought about the details. In this chapter, we will learn how to design an RDBMS that goes beyond *two shelves and a drawer*. We will learn a few techniques that will ensure our RDBMS is optimizing storage, reducing waste, and making our lives easier. Specifically, we will:

- Learn how to find anomalies in our RDBMS data
- Learn several strategies to clean different types of problematic data
- Learn when and how to create new tables for your cleaned data, including creating both child tables and lookup tables
- Learn how to document the rules governing the changes you made

Getting ready

To set up the examples in this chapter, we will be working with a popular dataset called **Sentiment140**. This dataset was created to help learn about the positive and negative sentiments in messages on Twitter. We are not really concerned with sentiment analysis in this book, but we are going to use this dataset to practice cleaning data after it has already been imported into a relational database.

To get started with the Sentiment140 dataset, you will need a MySQL server set up and ready to go, just like in the earlier Enron examples.

Step one – download and examine Sentiment140

The version of the Sentiment140 data that we want to use is the original set of two files available directly from the Sentiment140 project at `http://help.sentiment140.com/for-students`. This ZIP file of tweets and their positive and negative polarity (or sentiment, on a scale of 0, 2, or 4) was created by some graduate students at Stanford University. Since this file was made publicly available, the original Sentiment140 files have been added by other websites and made available as part of many larger collections of tweets. For this chapter, we will use the original Sentiment140 text file, which is either available as a link from the preceding site or by following the precise path to `http://cs.stanford.edu/people/alecmgo/trainingandtestdata.zip`.

Download the ZIP file, extract it, and take a look at the two CSV files inside using your text editor. Right away, you will notice that one file has many more lines than the other, but both these files have the same number of columns in them. The data is comma-delimited, and each column has been enclosed in double quotes. The description of each column can be found on the `for-students` page linked in the preceding section.

Step two – clean for database import

For our purposes—learning how to clean data—it will be sufficient to load the smaller of these files into a single MySQL database table. Everything we need to do to learn, we can accomplish with the smaller file, the one called `testdata.manual.2009.06.14.csv`.

As we are looking at the data, we may notice a few areas that will trip us up if we try to import this file directly into MySQL. One of the trouble spots is located at line 28 in the file:

```
"4","46","Thu May 14 02:58:07 UTC 2009","""booz allen""",
```

Do you see the triple quotation marks `"""` right before the `booz` keyword and after the word `allen`? The same issue comes up later on line 41 with double quotation marks around the song title `P.Y.T`:

```
"4","131","Sun May 17 15:05:03 UTC 2009","Danny
Gokey","VickyTigger","I'm listening to ""P.Y.T"" by Danny Gokey…"
```

The problem with these extra quotation marks is that the MySQL import routine will use the quotation marks to delimit the column text. This will produce an error, as MySQL will think that the line has more columns than there really are.

To fix this, in our text editor, we can use **Find and Replace** to replace all instances of `"""` with `"` (double quote) and all instances of `""` with `'` (single quote).

> These `""` could also probably be removed entirely with very little negative effect on this cleaning exercise. To do this, we would simply search for `""` and replace it with nothing. But if you want to stick close to the original intent of the tweet, a single quote (or even an escaped double quote like this `\"`) is a safe choice for a replacement character.

Save this cleaned file to a new filename, something like `cleanedTestData.csv`. We are now ready to import it into MySQL.

Step three – import the data into MySQL in a single table

To load our somewhat cleaner data file into MySQL, we will need to revisit the CSV-to-SQL techniques from the *Importing spreadsheet data into MySQL* section in *Chapter 3, Workhorses of Clean Data – Spreadsheets and Text Editors*:

1. From the command line, navigate to the directory where you have saved the file you created in step two. This is the file we are going to import into MySQL.
2. Then, launch your MySQL client, and connect to your database server:

   ```
   user@machine:~/sentiment140$ mysql -hlocalhost -umsquire -p
   Enter password:
   ```

3. Enter your password, and after you are logged in, create a database within MySQL to hold the table, as follows:

```
mysql> CREATE DATABASE sentiment140;
mysql> USE sentiment140;
```

4. Next, we need to create a table to hold the data. The data type and lengths for each column should represent our best attempt to match the data we have. Some of the columns will be varchars, and each of them will need a length. As we might not know what those lengths should be, we can use our cleaning tools to discern an appropriate range.

5. If we open our CSV file in Excel (Google Spreadsheets will work just fine for this as well), we can run some simple functions to find the maximum lengths of some of our text fields. The `len()` function, for example, gives the length of a text string in characters, and the `max()` function can tell us the highest number in a range. With our CSV file open, we can apply these functions to see how long our varchar columns in MySQL should be.

   The following screenshot shows a method to use functions to solve this problem. It shows the `length()` function applied to column **G**, and the `max()` function used in column **H** but applied to column **G**.

	A	B	C	D	E	F	G	H
1	4	3	Mon May 11 03:17:40 UT(	kindle2	tpryan	@stellargirl I looooooooov	=LEN(F1)	=MAX(G1:G498)
2	4	4	Mon May 11 03:18:03 UT(	kindle2	vcu451	Reading my kindle2... Lov	=LEN(F2)	
3	4	5	Mon May 11 03:18:54 UT(	kindle2	chadfu	Ok, first assesment of the	=LEN(F3)	

   Columns **G** and **H** show how to get the length of a text column in Excel and then get the maximum value.

6. To calculate these maximum lengths more quickly, we can also take an Excel shortcut. The following array formula can work to quickly combine the maximum value with the length of a text column in a single cell—just make sure you press *Ctrl* + *Shift* + *Enter* after typing this nested function rather than just *Enter*:

```
=max(len(f1:f498))
```

   This nested function can be applied to any text column to get the maximum length of the text in that column, and it only uses a single cell to do this without requiring any intermediate length calculations.

After we run these functions, it turns out that the maximum length for any of our tweets is 144 characters.

Detecting and cleaning abnormalities

You might be wondering how a tweet in this dataset could possibly be 144 characters long as Twitter limits all tweets to a maximum length of 140 characters. It turns out that in the sentiment140 dataset, the **&** character was sometimes translated to the HTML equivalent code, `&amp`, but not always. Some other HTML code was used too, for instance, sometimes, the **<** character became `<` and **>** became `>`. So, for a few very long tweets, this addition of just a few more characters can easily push this tweet over the length limit of 140. As we know that these HTML-coded characters were not what the original person tweeted, and because we see that they happen sometimes but not all the time, we call these **data abnormalities**.

To clean these, we have two choices. We can either go ahead and import the messy data into the database and try to clean it there, or we can attempt to clean it first in Excel or a text editor. To show the difference in these two techniques, we will do both here. First, we will use find and replace in our spreadsheet or text editor to try to convert the characters shown in the following table. We can import the CSV file into Excel and see how much cleaning we can do there:

HTML code	Replace with	The count of instances	The Excel function used to find count
`<`	`<`	6	`=COUNTIF(F1:F498,"*&lt*")`
`>`	`>`	5	`=COUNTIF(F1:F498,"*&gt*")`
`&`	`&`	24	`=COUNTIF(F1:F498,"*&amp*")`

The first two character swaps work fine with **Find and Replace** in Excel. The `<` and `>` HTML-encoded characters are changed. Take a look at the text like this:

```
I'm listening to 'P.Y.T' by Danny Gokey &lt;3 &lt;3 &lt;3 Aww,
  he's so amazing. I &lt;3 him so much :)
```

The preceding becomes text like this:

```
I'm listening to 'P.Y.T' by Danny Gokey <3 <3 <3 Aww, he's so
  amazing. I <3 him so much :)
```

However, when we attempt to use Excel to find `&` and replace it with `&`, you may run into an error, as shown:

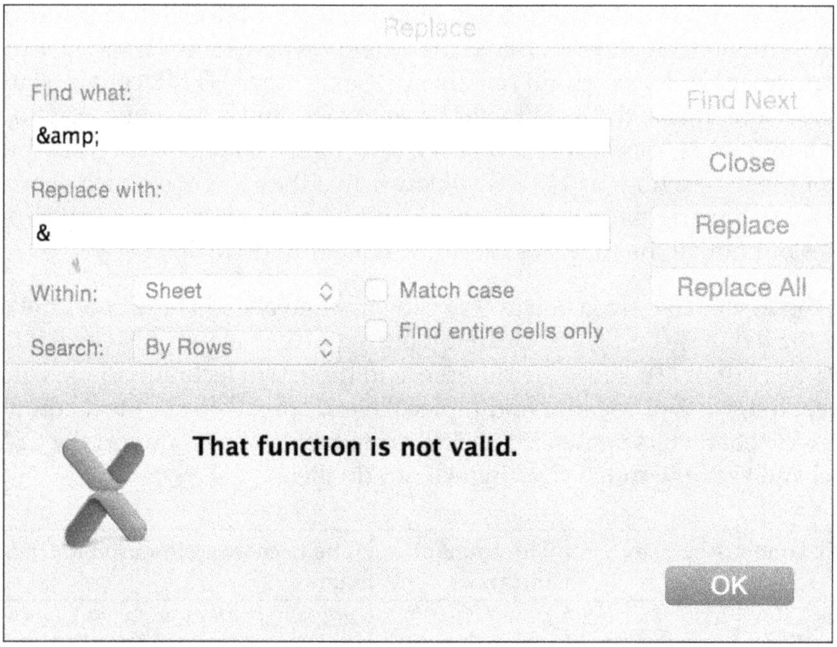

Some operating systems and versions of Excel have a problem with our selection of the & character as a replacement. At this point, if we run into this error, we could take a few different approaches:

- We could use our search engine of choice to attempt to find an Excel solution to this error
- We could move our CSV text data into a text editor and perform the find and replace function in there
- We could forge ahead and throw the data into the database despite it having the weird `&` characters in it and then attempt to clean it inside the database

Normally, I would be in favor of not moving dirty data into the database if it is even remotely possible to clean it outside of the database. However, as this is a chapter about cleaning inside a database, let's go ahead and import the half-cleaned data into the database, and we will work on cleaning the `&` issue once the data is inside the table.

Creating our table

To move our half-cleaned data into the database, we will first write our `CREATE` statement and then run it on our MySQL database. The `CREATE` statement is shown as follows:

```
mysql> CREATE TABLE sentiment140 (
    ->   polarity enum('0','2','4') DEFAULT NULL,
    ->   id int(11) PRIMARY KEY,
    ->   date_of_tweet varchar(28) DEFAULT NULL,
    ->   query_phrase varchar(10) DEFAULT NULL,
    ->   user varchar(10) DEFAULT NULL,
    ->   tweet_text varchar(144) DEFAULT NULL
    -> ) ENGINE=MyISAM DEFAULT CHARSET=utf8;
```

> This statement uses the simple and fast MyISAM engine as we do not anticipate needing any InnoDB features such as row-level locking or transactions. For more on the difference between MyISAM and InnoDB, there is a handy discussion of when to use each storage engine located here: `http://stackoverflow.com/questions/20148/myisam-versus-innodb`.

You might notice that the code still requires 144 for the length of the `tweet_text` column. This is because we were unable to clean these columns with the `&` code in them. However, this does not bother me too much because I know that varchar columns will not use their extra space unless they need it. After all, this is why they are called varchar, or variable character, columns. But if this extra length really bothers you, you can alter the table later to only have 140 characters for that column.

Next, we will use the MySQL command line to run the following import statement from the location:

```
mysql> LOAD DATA LOCAL INFILE 'cleanedTestData.csv'
    ->   INTO TABLE sentiment140
    ->   FIELDS TERMINATED BY ',' ENCLOSED BY '"' ESCAPED BY '\'
    ->   (polarity, id, date_of_tweet, query_phrase, user,
         tweet_text);
```

This command loads the data from our cleaned CSV file into the new table we created. A success message will look like this, indicating that all 498 rows were loaded into the table:

```
Query OK, 498 rows affected (0.00 sec)
Records: 498  Deleted: 0  Skipped: 0  Warnings: 0
```

> If you have access to a browser-based interface such as phpMyAdmin (or a desktop application such as MySQL Workbench or Toad for MySQL), all of these SQL commands can be completed inside these tools very easily and without having to type on the command line, for example, in phpMyAdmin, you can use the Import tab and upload the CSV file there. Just make sure that the data file is cleaned following the procedures in *Step two - clean for database import*, or you may get errors about having too many columns in your file. This error is caused by quotation mark problems.

Step four – clean the & character

In the last step, we decided to postpone cleaning the `&` character because Excel was giving a weird error about it. Now that we have finished *Step three - import the data into MySQL in a single table* and our data is imported into MySQL, we can very easily clean the data using an `UPDATE` statement and the `replace()` string function. Here is the SQL query needed to take all instances of `&` and replace them with `&`:

```
UPDATE sentiment140 SET tweet_text = replace(tweet_text,'&amp;',
  '&');
```

The `replace()` function works just like find and replace in Excel or in a text editor. We can see that tweet ID 594, which used to say `#at&t is complete fail`, now reads `#at&t is complete fail`.

Step five – clean other mystery characters

As we are perusing the `tweet_text` column, we may have noticed a few odd tweets, such as tweet IDs 613 and 2086:

```
613, Talk is Cheap: Bing that, I?ll stick with Google
2086, Stanford University?s Facebook Profile
```

The `?` character is what we should be concerned about. As with the HTML-encoded characters we saw earlier, this character issue is also very likely an artifact of a prior conversion between character sets. In this case, there was probably some kind of high-ASCII or Unicode apostrophe (sometimes called a **smart quote**) in the original tweet, but when the data was converted into a lower-order character set, such as plain ASCII, that particular flavor of apostrophe was simply changed to a `?`.

Depending on what we plan to do with the data, we might not want to leave out the `?` character, for example, if we are performing word counting or text mining, it may be very important that we convert `I?ll` to `I'll` and `University?s` to `University's`. If we decide that this is important, then our job is to detect the tweets, where this error happened, and then devise a strategy to convert the question mark back to a single quote. The trick, of course, is that we cannot just replace every question mark in the `tweet_text` column with a single quote character, because some tweets have question marks in them that should be left alone.

To locate the problem characters, we can run some SQL queries that attempts to locate the problems using a regular expression. We are interested in question marks that appear in odd places, such as with an alphabetic character immediately following them. Here is an initial pass at a regular SQL expression using the MySQL `REGEXP` feature. Running this will give us a rough idea of where the problem question marks might reside:

```
SELECT id, tweet_text
FROM sentiment140
WHERE tweet_text
REGEXP '\\?[[:alpha:]]+';
```

This SQL regular expression asks for any question mark characters that are immediately followed by one or more alphabetic characters. The SQL query yields six rows, four of which turn out to have odd question marks and two of which are **false positives**. False positives are tweets that matched our pattern but that should not actually be changed. The two false positives are tweets with IDs **234** and **2204**. These two included question marks as part of a legitimate URL. Tweets **139**, **224**, **613**, and **2086** are **true positives**, which means tweets that were correctly detected as anomalous and should be changed. All the results are shown in the following phpMyAdmin screenshot:

id	tweet_text
139	?Obama Administration Must Stop Bonuses to AIG Ponzi Schemers ... http://bit.ly/2CUlg
224	Life?s a bitch? and so is Dick Cheney. #p2 #bipart #tlot #tcot #hhrs #GOP #DNC http://is.gd/DjyQ
234	jQuery UI 1.6 Book Review - http://cfbloggers.org/?c=30631
613	Talk is Cheap: Bing that, I?ll stick with Google. http://bit.ly/XC3C8
2086	Stanford University?s Facebook Profile is One of the Most Popular Official University Pages - http://tinyurl.com/p5b3fl
2204	Learning jQuery 1.3 Book Review - http://cfbloggers.org/?c=30629

Tweet **139** is strange, though. It has a question mark before the word **Obama**, as if the name of a news article was being quoted, but there is no matching quote (or missing quote) at the end of the string. Was this supposed to be some other character? This might actually be a false positive too, or at least not enough of a true positive to actually make us fix it. While we are looking at the tweets closely, **224** also has an extra strange question mark in a place where it does not seem to belong.

If we are going to write a `replace()` function to change problematic question marks to single quotes, we will somehow need to write a regular expression that matches only the true positives and does not match any of the false positives. However, as this dataset is small, and there are only four true positives—or three if we decide **139** does not need to be cleaned—then we could just clean the true positives by hand. This is especially a good idea as we have a few questions about other possible issues such as the extra question mark in tweet **224**.

In this case, as we only have three problem rows, it will be faster to simply run three small `UPDATE` commands on the data rather than attempting to craft the perfect regular expression. Here is the SQL query to take care of tweets **224** (first issue only), **613**, and **2086**:

```
UPDATE sentiment140 SET tweet_text = 'Life''s a bitch? and so is
  Dick Cheney. #p2 #bipart #tlot #tcot #hhrs #GOP #DNC
  http://is.gd/DjyQ' WHERE id = 224;

UPDATE sentiment140 SET tweet_text = 'Talk is Cheap: Bing that,
  I''ll stick with Google. http://bit.ly/XC3C8' WHERE id = 613;

UPDATE sentiment140 SET tweet_text = 'Stanford University''s
  Facebook Profile is One of the Most Popular Official University
  Pages - http://tinyurl.com/p5b3fl' WHERE id = 2086;
```

> Note that we had to escape our single quotes in these update statements. In MySQL, the escape character is either the backslash or single quote itself. These examples show the single quote as the escape character.

Step six – clean the dates

If we take a look at the `date_of_tweet` column, we see that we created it as a simple variable character field, `varchar(30)`. What is so wrong with that? Well, suppose we want to put the tweets in order from earliest to latest. Right now, we cannot use a simple SQL `ORDER BY` clause and get the proper date order, because we will get an alphabetical order instead. All Fridays will come before any Mondays, and May will always come after June. We can test this with the following SQL query:

```
SELECT id, date_of_tweet
FROM sentiment140
ORDER BY date_of_tweet;
```

The first few rows are in order but down near row 28, we start to see a problem:

```
2018  Fri May 15 06:45:54 UTC 2009
2544  Mon Jun 08 00:01:27 UTC 2009
…
3  Mon May 11 03:17:40 UTC 2009
```

`May 11` does not come after `May 15` or `June 8`. To fix this, we will need to create a new column that cleans these date strings and turns them into proper MySQL datetime data types. We learned in the *Converting between data types* section in *Chapter 2, Fundamentals – Formats, Types, and Encodings*, that MySQL works best when dates and time are stored as native **date**, **time**, or **datetime** types. The format to insert a datetime type looks like this: `YYYY-MM-DD HH:MM:SS`. But this is not what our data looks like in the `date_of_tweet` column.

There are numerous built-in MySQL functions that can help us format our messy date string into the preferred format. By doing this, we will be able to take advantage of MySQL's ability to perform math on the dates and time, for example, finding the difference between two dates or times or sorting items properly in the order of their dates or times.

To get our string into a MySQL-friendly datetime type, we will perform the following procedure:

1. Alter the table to include a new column, the purpose of which is to hold the new datetime information. We can call this new column `date_of_tweet_new` or `date_clean` or some other name that clearly differentiates it from the original `date_of_tweet` column. The SQL query to perform this task is as follows:

   ```
   ALTER TABLE sentiment140
   ADD date_clean DATETIME NULL
   AFTER date_of_tweet;
   ```

2. Perform an update on each row, during which we format the old date string into a properly formatted datetime type instead of a string and add the new value into the newly created `date_clean` column. The SQL to perform this task is as follows:

```
UPDATE sentiment140
SET date_clean = str_to_date(date_of_tweet,
   '%a %b %d %H:%i:%s UTC %Y');
```

At this point, we have a new column that has been populated with the clean datetime. Recall that the old `date_of_tweet` column was flawed in that it was not sorting dates properly. To test whether the dates are being sorted correctly now, we can select our data in the order of the new column:

```
SELECT id, date_of_tweet
FROM sentiment140
ORDER BY date_clean;
```

We see that the rows are now perfectly sorted, with the May 11 date coming first, and no dates are out of order.

Should we remove the old `date` column? This is up to you. If you are worried that you may have made a mistake or that you might need to have the original data for some reason, then by all means, keep it. But if you feel like removing it, simply drop the column, as shown:

```
ALTER TABLE sentiment140
DROP date_of_tweet;
```

You could also create a copy of the Sentiment140 table that has the original columns in it as a backup.

Step seven – separate user mentions, hashtags, and URLs

Another problem with this data right now is that there are lots of interesting pieces of information hidden inside the `tweet_text` column, for example, consider all the times that a person directs a tweet to the attention of another person using the `@` symbol before their username. This is called a **mention** on Twitter. It might be interesting to count how many times a particular person is mentioned or how many times they are mentioned in conjunction with a particular keyword. Another interesting piece of data hidden in some of the tweets is **hashtags**; for example, the tweet with ID 2165 discusses the concepts of jobs and babysitting using the `#jobs` and `#sittercity` hashtags.

This same tweet also includes an external, non-Twitter **URL**. We can extract each of these mentions, hashtags, and URLs and save them separately in the database.

This task will be similar to how we cleaned the dates, but with one important difference. In the case of the dates, we only had one possible corrected version of the date, so it was sufficient to add a single new column to hold the new, cleaned version. With mentions, hashtags, and URLs, however, we may have zero or more in a single `tweet_text` value, for example, the tweet we looked at earlier (ID 2165) had two hashtags in it, as does this tweet (ID 2223):

```
HTML 5 Demos! Lots of great stuff to come! Yes, I'm excited. :)
  http://htmlfive.appspot.com #io2009 #googleio
```

This tweet has zero mentions, one URL, and two hashtags. Tweet 13078 includes three mentions but no hashtags or URLs:

```
Monday already. Iran may implode. Kitchen is a disaster. @annagoss
  seems happy. @sebulous had a nice weekend and @goldpanda is
  great. whoop.
```

We will need to change our database structure to hold these new pieces of information—hashtags, URLs, and mentions—all the while keeping in mind that a given tweet can have a lot of these in it.

Create some new tables

Following relational database theory, we should avoid creating columns that will store multivalue attributes, for example, if a tweet has three hashtags, we should not just deposit all three hashtags into a single column. The impact of this rule for us is that we cannot just copy the `ALTER` procedure we used for the date cleaning problem earlier.

Instead, we need to create three new tables: `sentiment140_mentions`, `sentiment140_urls`, and `sentiment140_hashtags`. The primary key for each new table will be a synthetic ID column, and each table will include just two other columns: `tweet_id`, which ties this new table back to the original `sentiment140` table, and the actual extracted text of the hashtag, mention, or URL. Here are three `CREATE` statements to create the tables we need:

```
CREATE TABLE IF NOT EXISTS sentiment140_mentions (
  id int(11) NOT NULL AUTO_INCREMENT,
  tweet_id int(11) NOT NULL,
  mention varchar(144) NOT NULL,
  PRIMARY KEY (id)
) ENGINE=MyISAM DEFAULT CHARSET=utf8;
```

```
CREATE TABLE IF NOT EXISTS sentiment140_hashtags (
  id int(11) NOT NULL AUTO_INCREMENT,
  tweet_id int(11) NOT NULL,
  hashtag varchar(144) NOT NULL,
  PRIMARY KEY (id)
) ENGINE=MyISAM DEFAULT CHARSET=utf8;

CREATE TABLE IF NOT EXISTS sentiment140_urls (
  id int(11) NOT NULL AUTO_INCREMENT,
  tweet_id int(11) NOT NULL,
  url varchar(144) NOT NULL,
  PRIMARY KEY (id)
) ENGINE=MyISAM DEFAULT CHARSET=utf8;
```

> These tables do not use foreign keys back to the original `sentiment140` tweet table. If you would like to add these, that is certainly possible. For the purposes of learning how to clean this dataset, however, it is not necessary.

Now that our tables are created, it is time to fill them with the data that we have carefully extracted from `tweet_text column`. We will work on each extraction case separately, starting with user mentions.

Extract user mentions

To design a procedure that can handle the extraction of the user mentions, let's first review what we know about mentions in tweets:

- The user mention always starts with the @ sign
- The user mention is the word that immediately follows the @ sign
- If there is a space after @, it is not a user mention
- There are no spaces inside the user mention itself
- As e-mail addresses also use @, we should be mindful of them

Using these rules, we can construct some valid user mentions:

- @foo
- @foobar1
- @_1foobar_

We can construct some examples of invalid user mentions:

- @ foo (the space following the @ invalidates it)
- foo@bar.com (bar.com is not recognized)
- @foo bar (only @foo will be recognized)
- @foo.bar (only @foo will be recognized)

> In this example, we assume that we do not care about the difference between a regular `@mention` and.`@mention`, sometimes called a dot-mention. These are tweets with a period in front of the `@` sign. They are designed to push a tweet to all of the user's followers.

As this rule set is more complicated than what we can execute efficiently in SQL, it is preferable to write a simple little script to clean these tweets using some regular expressions. We can write this type of script in any language that can connect to our database, such as Python or PHP. As we used PHP to connect to the database in *Chapter 2, Fundamentals – Formats, Types, and Encodings*, let's use a quick PHP script here as well. This script connects to the database, searches for user mentions in the `tweet_text` column, and moves any found mentions into the new `sentiment140_mentions` table:

```
<?php
// connect to db
$dbc = mysqli_connect('localhost', 'username', 'password',
  'sentiment140')
    or die('Error connecting to database!' . mysqli_error());
$dbc->set_charset("utf8");

// pull out the tweets
$select_query = "SELECT id, tweet_text FROM sentiment140";
$select_result = mysqli_query($dbc, $select_query);

// die if the query failed
if (!$select_result)
    die ("SELECT failed! [$select_query]" .  mysqli_error());

// pull out the mentions, if any
$mentions = array();
while($row = mysqli_fetch_array($select_result))
{
    if (preg_match_all(
        "/(?<!\pL)@(\pL+)/iu",
```

```
            $row["tweet_text"],
            $mentions
        ))
        {
            foreach ($mentions[0] as $name)
            {
                $insert_query = "INSERT into sentiment140_mentions (id,
    tweet_id, mention) VALUES (NULL," . $row["id"] . ",'$name')";
                echo "<br />$insert_query";
                $insert_result = mysqli_query($dbc, $insert_query);
                // die if the query failed
                if (!$insert_result)
                    die ("INSERT failed! [$insert_query]" .
                    mysqli_error());
            }
        }
    }
    ?>
```

After running this little script on the `sentiment140` table, we see that 124 unique user mentions have been extracted out of the 498 original tweets. A few interesting things about this script include that it will handle Unicode characters in usernames, even though this dataset does not happen to have any. We can test this by quickly inserting a test row at the end of the `sentiment140` table, for example:

```
INSERT INTO sentiment140 (id, tweet_text) VALUES(99999, "This is a @
Тест");
```

Then, run the script again; you will see that a row has been added to the `sentiment140_mentions` table, with the `@Тест` Unicode user mention successfully extracted. In the next section, we will build a similar script to extract hashtags.

Extract hashtags

Hashtags have their own rules, which are slightly different to user mentions. Here is a list of some of the rules we can use to determine whether something is a hashtag:

- Hashtags start with the # sign
- The hashtag is the word that immediately follows the # sign
- Hashtags can have underscores in them but no spaces and no other punctuation

The PHP code to extract hashtags into their own table is mostly identical to the user mentions code, with the exception of the regular expression in the middle of the code. We can simply change the `$mentions` variable to `$hashtags`, and then adjust the regular expression to look like this:

```
if (preg_match_all(
        "/(#\pL+)/iu",
        $row["tweet_text"],
        $hashtags
    ))
```

This regular expression says that we are interested in matching case-insensitive Unicode letter characters. Then, we need to change our `INSERT` line to use the correct table and column names like this:

```
$insert_query = "INSERT INTO sentiment140_hashtags (id, tweet_id,
  hashtag) VALUES (NULL," . $row["id"] . ",'$name')";
```

When we successfully run this script, we see that 54 hashtags have been added to the `sentiment140_hashtags` table. Many more of the tweets have multiple hashtags, even more than the tweets that had multiple user mentions, for example, we can see right away that tweets 174 and 224 both have several embedded hashtags.

Next, we will use this same skeleton script and modify it again to extract URLs.

Extract URLs

Pulling out the URLs from the text can be as simple as looking for any string that starts with *http://* or *https://*, or it could get a lot more complex depending on what types of URLs the text string includes, for example, some strings might include *file://* URLs or torrent links, such as magnet URLs, or other types of unusual links. In the case of our Twitter data, we have it somewhat easier, as the URLs that were included in our dataset all start with HTTP. So, we could be lazy and just design a simple regular expression to extract any string that follows http:// or https://. This regular expression would just look like this:

```
if (preg_match_all(
        "!https?://\S+!",
        $row["tweet_text"],
        $urls
    ))
```

However, if we do a bit of hunting on our favorite search engine, it turns out that we can easily find some pretty impressive and useful generic URL matching patterns that will handle more sophisticated link patterns. The reason that this is useful is that if we write our URL extraction to handle more sophisticated cases, then it will still work if our data changes in the future.

A very well-documented URL pattern matching routine is given on the `http://daringfireball.net/2010/07/improved_regex_for_matching_urls` website. The following code shows how to modify our PHP code to use this pattern for URL extraction in the Sentiment140 dataset:

```
<?php
// connect to db
$dbc = mysqli_connect('localhost', 'username', 'password',
  'sentiment140')
    or die('Error connecting to database!' . mysqli_error());
$dbc->set_charset("utf8");

// pull out the tweets
$select_query = "SELECT id, tweet_text FROM sentiment140";
$select_result = mysqli_query($dbc, $select_query);

// die if the query failed
if (!$select_result)
    die ("SELECT failed! [$select_query]" .  mysqli_error());

// pull out the URLS, if any
$urls = array();
$pattern  = '#\b(([\w-]+://?|www[.])[^\s()<>]+(?:\([\w\d]+\)|([^[:punc
t:]\s]|/)))#';

while($row = mysqli_fetch_array($select_result))
{
    echo "<br/>working on tweet id: " . $row["id"];
    if (preg_match_all(
        $pattern,
        $row["tweet_text"],
        $urls
    ))
    {
        foreach ($urls[0] as $name)
        {
            echo "<br/>----url: ".$name;
            $insert_query = "INSERT into sentiment140_urls (id,
            tweet_id, url)
```

```
                VALUES (NULL," . $row["id"] . ",'$name')";
            echo "<br />$insert_query";
            $insert_result = mysqli_query($dbc, $insert_query);
            // die if the query failed
            if (!$insert_result)
                die ("INSERT failed! [$insert_query]" .
                mysqli_error());
        }
    }
}
?>
```

This program is nearly identical to the mention extracting program we wrote earlier, with two exceptions. First, we stored the regular expression pattern in a variable called `$pattern`, as it was long and complicated. Second, we made small changes to our database `INSERT` command, just as we did for the hasthtag extraction.

A full line-by-line explanation of the regular expression pattern is available on its original website, but the short explanation is that the pattern shown will match any URL protocol, such as http:// or file://, and it also attempts to match valid domain name patterns as well and directory/file patterns a few levels deep. The source website provides its own test dataset too if you want to see the variety of patterns that it will match and a few known patterns that will definitely *not* match.

Step eight – cleaning for lookup tables

In the *Step seven – Separate user mentions, hashtags, and URLs* section, we created new tables to hold the extracted hashtags, user mentions, and URLs, and then provided a way to link each row back to the original table via the `id` column. We followed the rules of database normalization by creating new tables that represent the one-to-many relationship between a tweet and user mentions, between a tweet and hashtags, or between a tweet and URLs. In this step, we will continue optimizing this table for performance and efficiency.

The column we are concerned with now is the `query_phrase` column. Looking at the column data, we can see that it contains the same phrases repeated over and over. These were apparently the search phrases that were originally used to locate and select the tweets that now exist in this dataset. Of the 498 tweets in the `sentiment140` table, how many of the query phrases are repeated over and over? We can use the following SQL to detect this:

```
SELECT count(DISTINCT query_phrase)
FROM sentiment140;
```

The query result shows that there are only 80 distinct query phrases, but these are used over and over in the 498 rows.

This may not seem like a problem in a table of 498 rows, but if we had an extremely large table, such as with hundreds of millions of rows, we should be concerned with two things about this column. First, duplicating these strings over and over takes up unnecessary space in the database, and second, searching for distinct string values is very slow.

To solve this problem, we will create a **lookup table** of query values. Each query string will exist only once in this new table, and we will also create an ID number for each one. Then, we will change the original table to use these new numeric values rather than the string values that it is using now. Our procedure to accomplish this is as follows:

1. Create a new lookup table:

   ```
   CREATE TABLE sentiment140_queries (
     query_id int(11) NOT NULL AUTO_INCREMENT,
     query_phrase varchar(25) NOT NULL,
     PRIMARY KEY (query_id)
   ) ENGINE=MyISAM DEFAULT CHARSET=utf8 AUTO_INCREMENT=1;
   ```

2. Populate the lookup table with the distinct query phrases and automatically give each one a `query_id` number:

   ```
   INSERT INTO sentiment140_queries (query_phrase)
   SELECT DISTINCT query_phrase FROM sentiment140;
   ```

3. Create a new column in the original table to hold the query phrase number:

   ```
   ALTER TABLE sentiment140
   ADD query_id INT NOT NULL AFTER query_phrase;
   ```

4. Make a backup of the `sentiment140` table in case the next step goes wrong. Any time we perform `UPDATE` on a table, it is a good idea to make a backup. To create a copy of the `sentiment140` table, we can use a tool like phpMyAdmin to copy the table easily (use the **Operations** tab). Alternately, we can recreate a copy of the table and then import into it the rows from the original table, as shown in the following SQL:

   ```
   CREATE TABLE sentiment140_backup(
     polarity int(1) DEFAULT NULL,
     id int(5)NOT NULL,
     date_of_tweet varchar(30) CHARACTER SET utf8 DEFAULT NULL
     ,
     date_clean datetime DEFAULT NULL COMMENT 'holds clean,
     formatted date_of_tweet',
   ```

```
    query_id int(11) NOT  NULL,
    user varchar(25) CHARACTER SET utf8 DEFAULT NULL,
    tweet_text varchar(144) CHARACTER SET utf8 DEFAULT NULL ,
    PRIMARY KEY (id)) ENGINE=MyISAM DEFAULT CHARSET=utf8;

SET SQL_MODE='NO_AUTO_VALUE_ON_ZERO';
INSERT INTO sentiment140_backup SELECT * FROM sentiment140;
```

5. Populate the new column with the correct number. To do this, we join the two tables together on their text column, then look up to the correct number value from the lookup table, and insert it into the `sentiment140` table. In the following query, each table has been given an alias, `s` and `sq`:

```
UPDATE sentiment140 s
INNER JOIN sentiment140_queries sq
ON s.query_phrase = sq.query_phrase
SET s.query_id = sq.query_id;
```

6. Remove the old `query_phrase` column in the `sentiment140` table:

```
ALTER TABLE sentiment140
DROP query_phrase;
```

At this point, we have an effective way to create a list of phrases, as follows. These are shown in the alphabetical order:

```
SELECT query_phrase
FROM sentiment140_queries
ORDER BY 1;
```

We can also find out the tweets with a given phrase (`baseball`) by performing a join between the two tables:

```
SELECT s.id, s.tweet_text, sq.query_phrase
FROM sentiment140 s
INNER JOIN sentiment140_queries sq
  ON s.query_id = sq.query_id
WHERE sq.query_phrase = 'baseball';
```

At this point, we have a cleaned `sentiment140` table and four new tables to hold various extracted and cleaned values, including hashtags, user mentions, URLs, and query phrases. Our `tweet_text` and `date_clean` columns are clean, and we have a lookup table for query phrases.

Step nine – document what you did

With nine steps of cleaning and multiple languages and tools in use, there is no doubt there'll be a point at which we will make a mistake and have to repeat a step. If we had to describe to someone else what we did, we will almost certainly have trouble remembering the exact steps and all the reasons why we did each thing.

To save ourselves mistakes along the way, it is essential that we keep a log of our cleaning steps. At a minimum, the log should contain these in the order in which they were performed:

- Every SQL statement
- Every Excel function or text editor routine, including screenshots if necessary
- Every script
- Notes and comments about why you did each thing

Another excellent idea is to create a backup of the tables at each stage, for example, we created a backup just before we performed `UPDATE` on the `sentiment140` table, and we discussed performing backups after we created the new `date_clean` column. Backups are easy to do and you can always drop the backed-up table later if you decide you do not need it.

Summary

In this chapter, we used a sample dataset, a collection of tweets called Sentiment140, to learn how to clean and manipulate data in a relational database management system. We performed a few basic cleaning procedures in Excel, and then we reviewed how to get the data out of a CSV file and into the database. At this point, the rest of the cleaning procedures were performed inside the RDBMS itself. We learned how to manipulate strings into proper dates, and then we worked on extracting three kinds of data from within the tweet text, ultimately moving these extracted values to new, clean tables. Next, we learned how to create a lookup table of values that are currently stored inefficiently, thus allowing us to update the original table with efficient, numeric lookup values. Finally, because we performed a lot of steps and because there is always the potential for mistakes or miscommunication about what we did, we reviewed some strategies to document our cleaning procedures.

In the next chapter, we will switch our perspective away from cleaning what has been given to us toward preparing cleaned data for others to use. We will learn some best practices to create datasets that require the least amount of cleaning by others.

8
Best Practices for Sharing Your Clean Data

So far in this book, we have learned many different ways to clean and organize our datasets. Perhaps now it is time to consider letting our cleaned data be used by others. The goal of this chapter is to present a few best practices for inviting some friends into your data science kitchen. Sharing your data could mean providing it to other people, other teams, or even just some future version of yourself. What is the best way to package your data for consumption by others? How should you tell people about the cleaned data you have? How can you ensure that all your hard work is attributed to you?

In this chapter, we will learn:

- How to present and package your cleaned data
- How to provide clear documentation for what is included in your data
- How to protect and extend your hard work by licensing your cleaned data
- How to find and evaluate the options for publicizing your cleaned data

One thing we should state clearly before we begin this chapter is that we should only clean and share data that we have the right to share. Perhaps that seems obvious, but it is worth repeating. This entire chapter assumes that you are only cleaning, and subsequently sharing, data that you actually have the right to work with in this way. If you are wondering about this, read the *Setting terms and licenses for your data* section of this chapter, and make sure you follow the same guidelines that you would ask your users to follow.

Preparing a clean data package

In this section, we delve into the many important questions that need to be answered before you can release a data package for general consumption.

How do you want people to access your data? If it is in a database, do you want users to be able to log in and run SQL commands on it? Or do you want to create downloadable flat text files for them to use? Do you need to create an API for the data? How much data do you have anyway, and do you want different levels of access for different parts of the data?

The technical aspects of how you want to share your clean data are extremely important. In general, it is probably a good idea to start with the simple things and move to a more sophisticated distribution plan when and if you need to. The following are some options for distributing data, in the order of the least complicated to the most complicated. Of course, with greater sophistication comes greater benefits:

- **Compressed plain text** - This is a very low-stakes distribution method. As we learned in *Chapter 2, Fundamentals - Formats, Types, and Encodings*, plain text can be compressed down to create very small file sizes. A simple CSV or JSON file is universally useful and can be converted to many other formats easily. Some considerations include:
    - How will you let users download the files? An open link on a web page is extremely easy and convenient, but it does not allow you to require credentials such as usernames and passwords to access the files. If that is important to you, then you will have to consider other methods to distribute files; for example, by using an FTP server with a username and password or by using the access controls on your web server.
    - How big are your files? How much traffic are you expecting? How much traffic will your hosting provider allow before they start charging extra?
- **Compressed SQL files** - Distributing SQL files allows your users to recreate your database structure and data on their own system. Some considerations include:
    - Your user might be running a different database system than you are, so they will have to clean the data anyway. It may be more efficient just to give them plain text.
    - Your database system might have different server settings to theirs, so you will have to clarify these custom settings in advance.

  - You will also need to plan in advance for whether your datasets are designed to grow over time, for example, by deciding whether you will provide only `UPDATE` statements, or whether you will always provide enough `CREATE` and `INSERT` statements to recreate the entire database.

- **Live database access** - Providing your users with direct access into your database is a very nice way to let them interact with your data at a low level. Some considerations include:
  - Providing live access does require that you set up an individual username and password for each user, which means keeping track of the users.
  - Because you have identifiable users, you will need to provide a way to correspond with them about support issues, including lost credentials and how to use the system.
  - It is probably not a good idea to allow generic usernames and passwords unless you have also built a secure frontend onto the database and taken basic precautions like limiting the number of queries a user can execute and limiting the length of time a query can take. An ill-formed `OUTER JOIN` on a table of half a dozen terabytes will likely bring your database to a halt and affect the rest of the users.
  - Do you want your users to be able to build programs that access your data, for example, through the ODBC or JDBC middleware layer? If so, you will need to take this into account when planning access permissions and when configuring the server.

- **API** — Designing an **Application Programming Interface** (**API**) to your data will allow your end users to write their own programs that can access your data and receive result sets in a predictable way. The advantages of an API are that it will provide access over the Internet to your data in a known, limited way and your users do not have to parse data files or wrestle with translating data from one format to another. Some considerations include:
  - Building a good API is more expensive up front than the other choices listed here; however, if you have a lot of needy users and a very limited support staff, then building an API might actually save you money in the long run.
  - Using an API requires more technical knowledge on the part of your users than some of the other methods listed. You should be prepared to have plenty of documentation ready, with examples.

  - You will need a credentialing and security plan in place to keep track of who is allowed to access your data and what they can do with it. If you are planning multiple levels of access, for example, to monetize different layers of your data, things like users transitioning from one layer to another need to be clearly planned out in advance.
  - Just like with regular database access, overuse or misuse of the API by users is always a possibility. You will need to plan ahead and take precautions to spot and remove malicious or inattentive users who may—through willful or unintentional misuse—make the service inaccessible to everyone.

Choosing a distribution method will have a lot to do with your budget, including money and time, as well as the expectations of your users. The best advice I can give you is that I have had good luck following the open source software motto, *Release Early and Often*. This works for me because I have a small user community, and a limited budget, and not a lot of spare cycles to devote to exotic packaging plans that may or may not work.

A word of caution – Using GitHub to distribute data

GitHub is a cloud-based file repository designed for software developers to collaborate on software and host their code for others to download. It has exploded in popularity and currently hosts well over 16 million project repositories. For this reason, many data scientists I talk to immediately suggest storing their data on GitHub.

Unfortunately, GitHub has some limitations in its ability to store non-code data, and despite its ubiquity among technical people and its ease-of-use, you should be aware of a few policies it has that might affect your data. These policies are covered in the Help guide, available at `https://help.github.com/articles/what-is-my-disk-quota`, but we have summarized the important ones here:

- First, GitHub is a wrapper around the source code control system, Git, and that system is not designed to store SQL. The Help guide says, "Large SQL files do not play well with version control systems such as Git." I am not sure what "play well" means, but I am definitely sure I want to avoid learning that when my users' happiness is at stake.

- Second, GitHub has some serious file size limits. It lists 1GB per project (repository) as a limit and 100MB per file as a limit. Most of the data files I release are, as individuals, smaller than that limit, but since I release many of the time series files multiple times per year, I would have to create multiple repositories for them. Under this scheme, each time I released new files, I would have to assess whether I was bumping up against file size limits. This quickly becomes a big headache.

In short, GitHub itself recommends a web hosting solution to distribute files, especially if they are large or if they are database-oriented. If you do decide to host on GitHub, be very conscious about posting files with user credentials in them. This includes posting your usernames and passwords for database systems, your authentication keys and secrets for Twitter, or any other personal details. Since GitHub is a Git repository at heart, the mistakes are there forever, unless the repository itself is deleted. If you find that you did make a mistake and post personal details to GitHub, you must immediately deauthenticate all current accounts and recreate all keys and passwords.

Documenting your data

Once people have access to the data, and ideally even beforehand, they need to know what it is that they are getting. Documenting the data may feel like an afterthought to you, but it is extremely important for your users, since they are not as familiar with the data or all the things you did to it. In this section, we will review some of the things you can add to your data package to make it easier to understand.

README files

The simple `README` file has a long history in computing. It is just a text file that is distributed with a software package, or that lives in a directory containing other files, and the idea is that the user should read the `README` file first, before getting started with the rest of the software package or files. The `README` file will tell the user important information about the package, such as who wrote it and why, installation instructions, known bugs, and other basic instructions to use the file.

If you are constructing packages of data, for example, zipped files full of text or SQL files, it is quick and easy to add a `README` file to the file package before zipping it. If you are making a website or online directory for your files, adding a `README` file in a conspicuous place can be very helpful. The following screenshot shows one of the web directories I use to distribute files for a project I work on, called **FLOSSmole**. I have added a `README` directory to include all the files I want the users to read first. I prefaced this directory name with an underscore so that it will always show up at the top of the list, alphabetically:

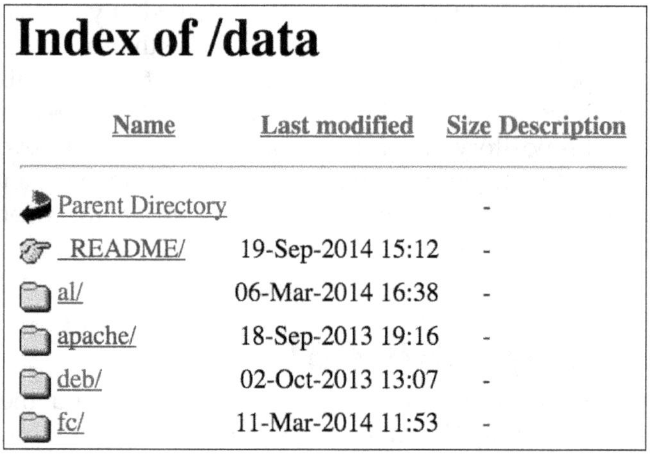

Index of /data
Name
Last modified
Size
Description
Parent Directory
-
_README/
19-Sep-2014 15:12
-
al/
06-Mar-2014 16:38
-
apache/
18-Sep-2013 19:16
-
deb/
02-Oct-2013 13:07
-
fc/
11-Mar-2014 11:53
-

A directory of files on a website showing the README file at the top.

Inside the `README.txt` file, I give both general and specific instructions to the user about the files. Here is an example of the `README` file I give for my data in this directory:

```
README for http://flossdata.syr.edu/data directory

What is this place?
This is a repository of flat files or data "dumps", from the FLOSSmole
project.

What is FLOSSmole?
Since 2004, FLOSSmole aims to:
    --freely provide data about free, libre, and open source software
(FLOSS) projects in multiple formats for anyone to download;
    --integrate donated data & scripts from other research teams;
    --provide a community for researchers to discuss public data about
FLOSS development.
```

```
FLOSSmole contains: Several terabytes (TB) of data covering the period
2004-now, and growing with data sets from nearly 10,000 web-based
collection operations, and growing each month. This includes data for
millions of open source projects and their developers.

If you use FLOSSmole data, please cite it accordingly:
Howison, J., Conklin, M., & Crowston, K. (2006). FLOSSmole: A
collaborative repository for FLOSS research data and analyses.
International Journal of Information Technology and Web Engineering,
1(3), 17-26.

What is included on this site?
Flat files, date and time-stamped, from various software forges &
projects. We have a lot of other data in our database that is not
available here in flat files. For example, IRC logs and email from
various projects. For those, see the following:

1. Direct database access. Please use this link for direct access to
our MySQL database: http://flossmole.org/content/direct-db-access-
flossmole-collection-available

2. FLOSSmole web site. Includes updates, visualizations, and examples.
http://flossmole.org/
```

This example `README` file is for an entire directory of files, but you can have a `README` file for each file, or for different directories. It is up to you.

File headers

Another effective way to communicate information to your users, especially if you are creating flat files of text or SQL commands, is to place a header at the top of each file explaining its format and usage. A common practice is to preface each line of the header with some type of comment-like character, such as `#` or `//`.

Some items that are commonly included in file headers include:

- The name of the file and the name of the package in which it was found
- The name of the person or people who were involved in creating it, and their organization and location
- The date it was released
- Its version number, or where to find earlier versions of the file
- The purpose of the file

- The place where the data originally came from, as well as any changes that were made to the data between now and then
- The format of the file and how it is organized, for example, listing the fields and what they mean
- The terms of use or a license for the file

The following example shows an example header from a TSV file distributed for one of my data projects. In it, I explain what the data is and how to interpret each column in the file. I also explain my policies for how to cite the data, as well as to share the data. We will discuss options to license and share later in this chapter:

```
# Author: Squire, M. & Gazda, R.
# License: Open Database License 1.0
# This data 2012LTinsultsLKML.tsv.txt is made available under the
# Open Database License: http://opendatacommons.org/licenses/
# odbl/1.0/.
#
# filename: 2012LTinsultsLKML.tsv.txt
# explanation: This data set is part of a larger group of data
# sets described in the paper below, and hosted on the
# FLOSSmole.org site. Contains insults gleaned from messages sent
# to the LKML mailing list by Linus Torvalds during the year 2012
#
# explanation of fields:
# date: this is the date the original email was sent
# markmail permalink: this is a permalink to the email on markmail
# (for easy reading)
# type: this is our code for what type of insult this is
# mail excerpt: this is the fragment of the email containing the
# insult(s). Ellipses (...) have been added where necessary.
#
# Please cite the paper and FLOSSmole as follows:
#
# Squire, M. & Gazda, R. (2015). FLOSS as a source for profanity
# and insults: Collecting the data. In Proceedings of 48th
# Hawai'i International Conference on System Sciences (HICSS-48).
# IEEE. Hawaii, USA. 5290-5298
#
# Howison, J., Conklin, M., & Crowston, K. (2006). FLOSSmole: A
# collaborative repository for FLOSS research data and analyses.
# International Journal of Information Technology and Web
# Engineering, 1(3), 17-26.
```

If you anticipate that your users will be regularly collecting your data files, you should be consistent in your use of a comment character for the header. In the preceding example, I used the # character. The reason for this is that your users may write a program to automatically download and parse your data, perhaps loading it in a database or using it in a program. Your consistent use of a comment character will allow the user to skip the headers and not process them.

Data models and diagrams

If you are distributing SQL files to build a database, or if you are providing live access to a database for querying, you might find that a visual diagram, such as an **entity-relationship diagram** (**ERD**), will really help your users.

In some of my own projects, I like to provide both a textual description of the tables, such as with the headers and README files previously described, but also a visual diagram of the tables and the relationships between them. Because the databases I distribute are extremely large, I also colorize my diagrams, and I annotate each part of the diagram to indicate what is inside that part of the database.

The following screenshot shows a high-level overview of what one of my large diagrams looks like. It is zoomed out to show the size of the ERD:

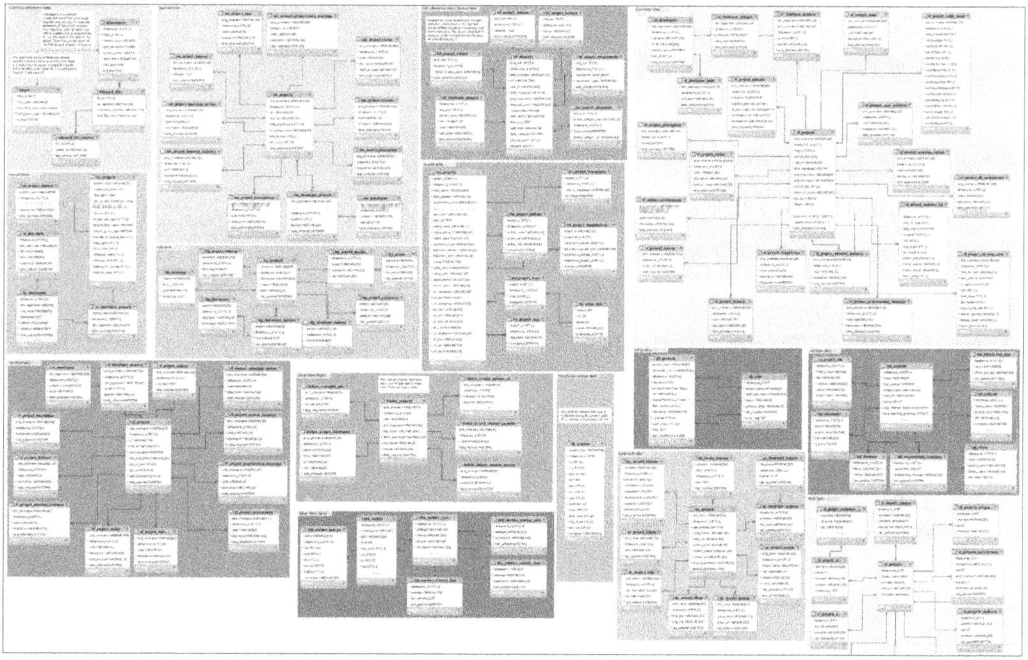

Since this ERD is a bit overwhelming and hard to read, even on a large monitor, I have colorized each separate section of the database and I have provided notes where needed. The following is a screenshot of a closer view of the orange section from the upper left of the big figure:

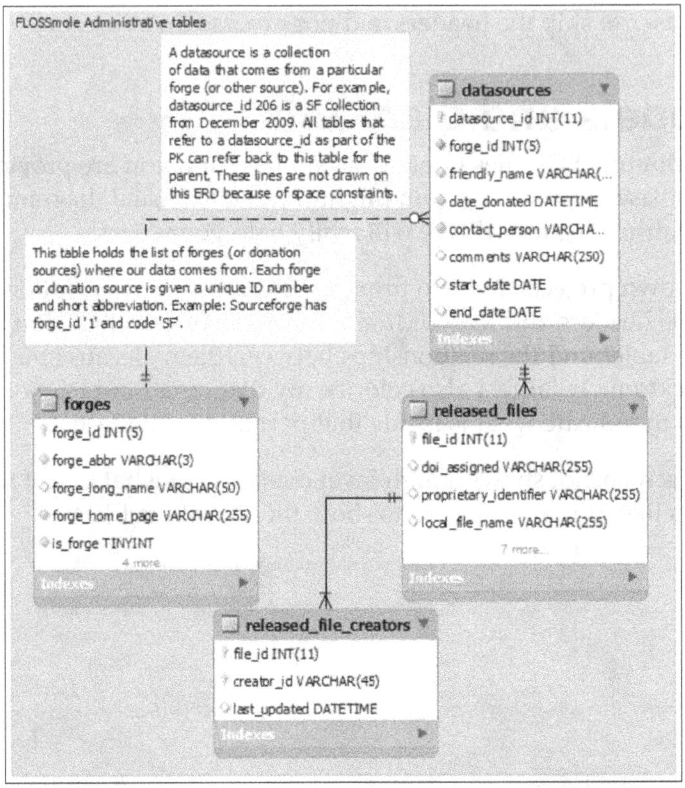

A close-up view of one of the database sections, including notes describing the purpose of the tables.

By reading this diagram, the user gets a nice overview of how the different sections of the database fit together. Importantly, high-level notes are shown directly on the diagram, and when the user wants more detailed information about a particular field, they can refer to the README file or the header inside that particular file.

To create an ERD, you can use any number of RDBMS tools, including MySQL Workbench (this is the one I used to create the colorized version you see here). Other popular tools include Microsoft Visio, Sparx Enterprise Architect, and draw.io. Many of these tools will allow you to connect to your RDBMS and reverse-engineer a diagram from an existing database, or forward-engineer SQL statements from a drawing. In either case, the ERD will certainly help your users understand the data model better.

Documentation wiki or CMS

Another way to keep all the documentation for a project organized is to publish it to a wiki or to a **content management system** (**CMS**). There are hundreds of CMS and wiki software packages available for this purpose, but popular options include MediaWiki, WordPress, Joomla!, and Drupal. GitHub also has a wiki service for projects hosted there, as do some of the other software hosting services, such as Sourceforge and Bitbucket.

You can use a CMS or wiki to provide the download links to your files themselves, and you can use the CMS to post documentation and explanations. I have also used a CMS in my own work to host a blog of updates, visualizations showing example graphs, charts built with the data, and also a repository for scripts that my users might find helpful to work with my data.

Here are some common sections that most data-oriented projects included in a documentation CMS or wiki:

- **About the project** — This tells the users what the purpose of the data project is and how to contact the project leaders. This section may also include ideas for how to get involved, how to join a mailing list or discussion area, or how to contact the project principals.
- **Getting the data** — This explains the different mechanisms to access the data. Common choices will include direct database access, file downloads, or an API. This section also explains any special signup or login procedures.
- **Using the data** — This includes starter queries, usage examples, graphics built with the data, and diagrams and ERDs. It provides links to things other people have done with the data. This section also explains, again if necessary, your expectations for the citation of the data and any licensing policies.

In this section, we discussed a variety of ways to document our data, including READMEs, file headers, ERDs, and web-based solutions. Throughout this discussion, we mentioned the concept of licensing the data and explaining your expectations to cite and share the data. In the next section, we delve deeper into the particulars of licensing your datasets.

Setting terms and licenses for your data

An important part of any plan for data distribution is deciding the expectations you have for how your users will cite, share, or remix your data. The list of expectations for how you want users to work with your data is called the data's **Terms of Use** (**ToU**). The ToU may also give the users specific rights, such as the ability to make changes or redistribute the data. This collection of rights that you grant to the users is called the **data license**. Users can choose to use your dataset—or not—based on whether they agree to abide by its ToU. They can also decide to use the data based on whether what they want to do with the data has been allowed by its license.

In this section, we will outline a few choices you can make for how to set expectations for how users should interact with your data. We will also review some of the most common items you may wish to include in the ToU, as well as some of the more common pre-made licenses that can be applied to your datasets.

Common terms of use

Not everyone has the same goals in sharing their data, for example, I am part of a project where the specific goal is to collect, clean, and redistribute data for the scientific community. Because I am a college professor, part of my work responsibility is to publish academic research papers, software, and datasets that are useful to others. Therefore, it is important to me that people cite my papers and published datasets when they are used. However, one of my other friends, who is not an academic, routinely publishes datasets completely anonymously, and with no expectation for citation or notification when that data is used.

Here is a list of common considerations when setting expectations for the use of your data:

- **Citations** - Do you want people who publish something based on your data to state clearly that they got the data from you? If so, what URL or reference should they use?
- **Privacy** - Do you have any rules about protecting the privacy of your users or their information? Do you want your users to abide by any particular privacy guidelines or research guidelines? For example, some people ask that users follow similar procedures to those they followed with their own **Institutional Research Boards** (**IRB**) or other research ethics groups (for example, the **Association of Internet Researchers** (**AOIR**)).

- **Appropriate uses for the data** - Do you suspect that your dataset could be misused in some way? Could the data be taken out of context? Could its contents be combined with other datasets in a harmful way? For some projects, it would be a very good idea to set expectations for your users for how they can use the data you are providing.
- **Contact** - Do you have a particular way that you want the users of the data to notify you if they are using the data? Do they need to notify you at all? Guidelines for how and why to contact you, as the dataset provider, are helpful if you anticipate users having questions or concerns about the data.

As we discussed earlier in the *Documenting your data* section of this chapter, the ToU for a dataset can be made available to the potential users inside a README file, inside file headers, or on a website. If you are providing live database access, you may also notify your potential users that, by accepting a username and password for the database system, they are agreeing to abide by your terms. A similar structure can be used for API access as well, where actively using an authentication token or access credentials indicates the user is in agreement with your ToU.

Of course, all of these best practices are subject to the laws and policies of various international states and organizations. It can be very complicated to try to get all of this correct without a little help. To assist data providers in setting expectations for their users, a few generic licensing schemes have emerged over time. We will discuss two of these now:

Creative Commons

Creative Commons (CC) licenses are prepackaged, generic sets of rules that providers of copyrighted, or copyrightable, materials can apply to their works. These licenses set out what the users of the works are allowed to do. By stating the license up front, the owner of the work can avoid having to grant individual licenses to every single person that wants to change or redistribute a particular work.

The issue with CC—and this might not be an issue for you at all, depending on what you are doing with it—is that CC licenses are intended to be applied to copyrightable work. Is your database or dataset copyrightable? Are you interested in licensing the contents of the database, or the database itself? To help you answer that question, we will point you to the Creative Commons wiki, which addresses all the considerations for this question in greater detail than we can hope to do here. This page even has a frequently asked questions section specifically about data and databases: `https://wiki.creativecommons.org/Data`.

ODbL and Open Data Commons

Another good choice to license data is the **Open Database License** (**ODbL**). This is a license that has been generically designed for databases. The **Open Knowledge Foundation** (**OKF**) has created a two-minute guide to deciding how to open your data, which you can find here: `http://OpenDataCommons.org/guide/`.

If you want even more choice, the `http://OpenDefinition.org` website, also part of the OKF, gives a selection of even more prepackaged licenses that you can apply to your dataset. These range from very open public domain-style licenses, all the way to licenses that require attribution and sharing of derivative works. In addition, they provide an Open Data Handbook, which is extremely helpful at walking you through the process of thinking about the intellectual property in your database or dataset and what you want to do with it. You can download the Open Data Handbook or browse it online here: `http://OpenDataHandbook.org`.

Publicizing your data

Once you have a complete data package, it is time to tell the world about it. Publicizing the existence of your data will ensure its use by the most people possible. If you already have a user community in mind for your data, publicizing it may be as simple as sending out a URL on a mailing list or to a specific research group. Sometimes, though, we create a dataset that we think might be interesting to a larger, more amorphous group.

Lists of datasets

There are many lists of data collections available on the Web, most of which are organized around some kind of theme. The publishers of these types of meta-collections (collections of collections) are usually more than happy to list new sources of data that fit into their niche. Meta-collection themes can include:

- Datasets related to the same topic, for example, music data, biological data, or collections of articles on news stories
- Datasets related to solving the same type of problem, for example, datasets that can be used to develop recommender systems or datasets used to train machine learning classifiers
- Datasets related to a particular technical issue, for example, datasets that are designed to benchmark or test a particular software or hardware design
- Datasets designed for use in particular systems, for example, datasets that are optimized for learning a programming language such as R, a data visualization service such as Tableau, or a cloud-based platform such as Amazon Web Services

- Datasets that all have the same type of license, for example, by listing only sets of public domain data or only data that has been cleared for academic research

If you find that your datasets are not well represented on any of these lists, or do not fit the requirements of the existing meta-collections, another option is to start your own data repository.

Open Data on Stack Exchange

The Open Data area on Stack Exchange, found at `http://opendata.stackexchange.com`, is a collection of questions and answers relevant to open datasets. There have been many instances where I have found interesting datasets here, and other times I have been able to show other people how to answer a question using one of my own datasets. This Q&A website is also a great way to learn what kinds of questions people have, and what kind of formats they like for the data they want to use.

Before advertising your data as a solution to someone's problem on Stack Exchange, be sure that your access methods, documentation, and licenses are up to standard using the guidelines we discussed previously in this chapter. This is especially important on Stack Exchange, since both questions and answers can be down-voted by users. The last thing you want to do is try to publicize your data with a bunch of broken links and confusing documentation.

Hackathons

Another fun way to get people involved with your data is to publicize it as a usable dataset for a hackathon. Data hackathons are usually day-long or multiday events where programmers and data scientists come together to practice different techniques on datasets, or to solve a particular class of problem using data.

A simple search engine query for data hackathon will show you what the focus of the current crop of hackathons is. Some of them are sponsored by companies, and some are designed to respond to social problems. Most of them have a wiki or some other method to add your URL and a brief description of the data to the list of datasets that can be used on the day of the hackathon. I hesitate to recommend a particular one, since the very nature of a hackathon is to happen once and then morph and change into something else. They also tend to be held at irregular times and be organized by ad hoc groups.

If your dataset is designed with an academic purpose in mind, for example, if it is a research dataset, you might consider hosting your own hackathon during the workshops or poster sessions of an academic conference. This is an excellent way to get people engaged in manipulating your data, and at the very least, you may get some good feedback from the people at the conference for ways to improve your data, or what datasets they think you should build next.

Summary

In this chapter, we looked at a wide variety of possibilities to share our cleaned data. We discussed various solutions and tradeoffs for different ways of packaging and distributing our data. We also reviewed the basics of providing documentation, including the most important things that your users need to know and how to communicate those items in a documentation file. We noticed that licenses and terms of use nearly always appear in documentation, but what do they mean and how should you choose one for your data? We reviewed some common terms of use for data projects, as well as the most common licensing schemes: Creative Commons, and ODbL. Finally, we brainstormed some ways for you to publicize your data, including data meta-collections, the Open Data Stack Exchange site, and data-centric hackathons.

At this point in the book, you have seen a complete beginning-to-end overview of data cleaning. The next two chapters consist of longer, more detailed projects that will give you some more practical exposure to data cleaning tasks using the skills we learned earlier in the book.

9
Stack Overflow Project

This is the first of two full, chapter-length projects where we will put everything we have learned about data cleaning into practice. We can think of each project as a dinner party where we show off our best skills from our data science kitchen. To host a successful dinner party, we should of course have our menu and guest list planned in advance. However, the mark of a true expert is how we react when things do not go exactly according to plan. We have all had that moment when we forget to buy an important ingredient, despite our carefully prepared recipes and shopping lists. Will we be able to adjust our plan to meet the new challenges we meet along the way?

In this chapter, we will tackle some data cleaning using the publicly-released Stack Overflow database dump. Stack Overflow is part of the Stack Exchange family of question-and-answer websites. On these sites, writing good questions and answers can earn a user points and badges that accumulate over time. To practice our data cleaning skills, we will use the same six-step method we introduced back in *Chapter 1, Why Do You Need Clean Data?*.

- Decide what kind of problem we are trying to solve — why are we looking at this data?
- Collect and store our data, which consists of downloading and extracting the data dump provided by Stack Overflow, creating a MySQL database to hold the data, and writing scripts to import the data into the MySQL database. Because the Stack Overflow dataset is so massive, we will also create some smaller test tables, filled with randomly selected rows.
- Perform some trial cleaning tasks on the test tables before attempting to clean the entire dataset.
- Analyze the data. Do we need to perform any calculations? Should we write some aggregate functions to count or sum the data? Do we need to transform the data in some way?

- Provide visualizations of the data, if possible.
- Resolve the problem we set out to investigate. Did our process work? Were we successful?

That is a lot of work, but the more we prepare in advance and the earlier we start, the more likely we will be able to call our data science dinner party a success.

Step one – posing a question about Stack Overflow

To start our project, we need to pose a reasonably interesting question that requires some simple data analysis to answer. Where should we begin? First, let's review what we know about Stack Overflow. We know that it is a question-and-answer website for programmers, and we can assume that programmers probably use a lot of source code, error logs, and configuration files in the questions they are asking and answering. Furthermore, we know that sometimes posting these kinds of long text dumps on a web-based platform like Stack Overflow can be awkward because of line lengths, formatting, and other readability issues.

Seeing so many questions and answers with frustratingly large amounts of text made me wonder whether programmers on Stack Overflow ever link to their code or log files through an external **paste site** such as Pastebin or JSFiddle, for example `http://www.Pastebin.com` is a website where you can paste in large amounts of text, such as source code or a log file, and the site gives you back a short URL that you can share with others. Most paste sites also allow for source code syntax highlighting, which Stack Overflow does not do by default.

Using paste sites is very common on IRC and e-mail, but what about on Stack Overflow? On one hand, just like in IRC or e-mail, providing a link could make a question or an answer shorter, and therefore the rest of the question is much easier to read. But on the other hand, depending on the paste site being used, the URL is not guaranteed to be functional forever. This means that a question or an answer could lose its value over time due to **link rot**.

Tools like JSFiddle complicate this issue in one additional way. On an **interactive paste** site like JSFiddle, not only can you paste in your source code and get a URL for it, but you can also allow others to edit and run the code right in the browser. This could be extremely helpful in a question-and-answer scenario on Stack Overflow, especially in a browser-based language like JavaScript. However, the issue of link rot still exists. Additionally, JSFiddle is a little trickier to use for beginners than a simple code dump site like Pastebin.

JSFiddle has four windows, one each for HTML, CSS, JavaScript, and the result.

> In the community discussion area for Stack Overflow, there has been quite a bit of debate about whether paste sites should be used at all, and what the policy should be for questions or answers that include paste site links and no actual code. In general, even though people tend to agree that a paste site can be useful, they also recognize that it is important to protect the longevity and utility of Stack Overflow itself. The community has decided that posting questions or answers with only links and no code should be avoided. A good place to start if you want to recap that discussion is this link: `http://meta.stackexchange.com/questions/149890/`.

For our purposes here, we do not need to choose sides in this debate. Instead, we can just ask some simple data-driven questions like:

1. How frequently do people use tools like Pastebin and JSFiddle (and other similar paste sites) on Stack Overflow?
2. Do they use paste sites more in questions or in answers?
3. Do posts that reference a paste site URL tend to also include source code; if so, how much?

We can use these questions for our motivation as we collect, store, and clean our Stack Overflow data. Even if it turns out that some of these questions are too hard or impossible to answer, remembering what our overall purpose is will help direct the type of cleaning we need to do. Keeping our questions in the forefront of our minds will stop us from getting too far off track or performing tasks that will turn out to be pointless or a waste of time.

Step two – collecting and storing the Stack Overflow data

At the time of writing, Stack Exchange provides the data for their entire family of websites—including Stack Overflow—as XML files free for anyone to download. In this section, we will download the Stack Overflow files, and import the data into a database on our MySQL server. Finally, we will create a few smaller versions of these tables for testing purposes.

Downloading the Stack Overflow data dump

All the data available from Stack Exchange can be downloaded at the Internet Archive. The September 2014 dump is the latest one available at the time of writing. Each Stack Exchange site has one or more files for it, each of which is linked to this details page: `https://archive.org/details/stackexchange`.

We are only interested in the eight Stack Overflow files that appear alphabetically as shown in the following list:

stackoverflow.com-Badges.7z	77.8 MB
stackoverflow.com-Comments.7z	1.8 GB
stackoverflow.com-PostHistory.7z	9.4 GB
stackoverflow.com-PostLinks.7z	26.4 MB
stackoverflow.com-Posts.7z	5.7 GB
stackoverflow.com-Tags.7z	508.1 KB
stackoverflow.com-Users.7z	100.5 MB
stackoverflow.com-Votes.7z	385.0 MB

Archive.org listing showing the eight Stack Overflow files we are interested in.

For each file in the list, right-click the link and direct your browser to save the file to disk.

Unarchiving the files

Notice that each file has a `.7z` extension. This is a compressed archive format. It can be uncompressed and unarchived using the matching 7-Zip software, or another compatible software package. 7-Zip was not one of the more common file archivers that we discussed in *Chapter 2, Fundamentals – Formats, Types, and Encodings* and you may not already have a compatible unarchiver installed on your computer, so we can consider this our first small wrinkle that we need to work around. Try double-clicking on the file to open it, but if you have no installed software associated with the `.7z` extension, you will need to install an appropriate 7-Zip unarchiver.

- For Windows, you can download the 7-Zip software from their website: `http://www.7-zip.org`
- For Mac OS X, you can download and install The Unarchiver, a no-cost utility available at `http://unarchiver.c3.cx`

Once you have the software installed, unpack each file in turn. The uncompressed files are quite large, so make sure you have disk space that is large enough to hold them.

> On my system right now, comparing the compressed to uncompressed file sizes shows that the uncompressed versions are about ten times larger than the compressed versions. These files also take several minutes each to unarchive, depending on the specifications of the system you are working on, so set aside time for this step.

Creating MySQL tables and loading data

We now have eight `.xml` files, each of which will map to one table in the database we are about to build. To create the database and tables, we could either point and click our way through it using phpMyAdmin or some other graphical tool, or we can run the following simple SQL written by Georgios Gousios and available at `https://gist.github.com/gousiosg/7600626`. This code includes `CREATE` and `LOAD INFILE` statements for the first six tables, but since this script was written, the database dump has had two additional tables added to it.

To build the new table structure, we can run the `head` command in our Terminal window or shell in order to inspect the first few lines of this file. From Terminal, run it on the smallest of the XML files, `PostLinks.xml`, as follows:

```
head PostLinks.xml
```

The first four lines from the results are shown here:

```
<?xml version="1.0" encoding="utf-8"?>
<postlinks>
  <row Id="19" CreationDate="2010-04-26T02:59:48.130" PostId="109"
  RelatedPostId="32412" LinkTypeId="1" />
  <row Id="37" CreationDate="2010-04-26T02:59:48.600" PostId="1970"
  RelatedPostId="617600" LinkTypeId="1" />
```

Each row in our new database table should correspond to one of the XML `<row>` lines, and each attribute shown in the row line represents one column in the database table. We can perform the same `head` command on the `Tags.xml` file to see what its columns should be. The following SQL code will handle the `CREATE` statements and the `LOAD` statements for the two additional tables:

```
CREATE TABLE post_links (
  Id INT NOT NULL PRIMARY KEY,
  CreationDate DATETIME DEFAULT NULL,
  PostId INT NOT NULL,
  RelatedPostId INT NOT NULL,
  LinkTypeId INT DEFAULT NULL
);

CREATE TABLE tags (
  Id INT NOT NULL PRIMARY KEY,
  TagName VARCHAR(50) DEFAULT NULL,
  Count INT DEFAULT NULL,
  ExcerptPostId INT DEFAULT NULL,
  WikiPostId INT DEFAULT NULL
);

LOAD XML LOCAL INFILE 'PostLinks.xml'
INTO TABLE post_links
ROWS IDENTIFIED BY '<row>';

LOAD XML LOCAL INFILE 'Tags.xml'
INTO TABLE tags
ROWS IDENTIFIED BY '<row>';
```

> Note that the `LOAD XML` syntax is slightly changed, so that we can keep our files locally. If your `.xml` files are on your local machine rather than on the database server itself, simply add the word `LOCAL` to the `LOAD XML` statements, as shown in the preceding code, and you can reference the full path to your file.
>
> More information about the MySQL `LOAD XML` syntax is described in the MySQL documentation here: `http://dev.mysql.com/doc/refman/5.5/en/load-xml.html`.

At this point, we have a fully functional MySQL database comprised of eight tables, each of which is filled with data. However, these tables are very large. There are over 190 million rows in only eight tables. One thing we will notice as we start to clean the data and prepare it for analysis, is that if we make a mistake on a very large table like `posts`, `comments`, `votes`, or `post_history`, rebuilding the table will take a long time. In the next step, we learn how to create test tables, so that we contain the damage if one of our programs or queries goes awry.

Building test tables

In this section, we will build eight smaller versions of our original tables, each randomly populated with data from the original tables.

Our first step is to re-run the `CREATE` statements, but this time prefix each table name with `test_`, as shown with one table here:

```
DROP TABLE IF EXISTS test_post_links;
CREATE TABLE test_post_links (
  Id INT NOT NULL PRIMARY KEY,
  CreationDate INT,
  PostId INT,
  RelatedPostId INT,
  LinkTypeId INT
);
```

Other than the addition of `test_` to the front of the table name, these eight test tables will be identical to the others we made earlier.

Next, we need to populate our new test tables with data. We could simply select the first 1,000 rows from each table and load those into our test tables. However, the downside of doing that is that the rows are in order based on when they were inserted into the Stack Overflow database, so we will not have a good sample of rows from different dates and time in our subset if we just ask for the first 1,000 rows. We would like the rows we select to be of a fairly random distribution. How can we select a set of rows randomly? We have not had to tackle this question before in this book, so here is another case where we have to be ready to try new things in order to have our data science dinner party go off without a hitch.

There are a few possibilities for selecting random rows, some of which are more efficient than others. Efficiency will be important to us in this project, since the tables we are working with are quite large. One thing that makes our random row selection a little trickier than expected, is that while our tables do have a numeric primary key as the `Id` column, these `Id` numbers are not sequential. There are many holes, for example, in the `post_links` table, the first few values in the `Id` column are 19, 37, 42, and 48.

Holes in the data are problematic because a simple randomizer operates like this:

1. Construct a PHP script that asks for the lowest and highest `Id` values in the table, like this:

   ```
   SELECT min(Id) FROM post_links;
   SELECT max(Id) FROM post_links;
   ```

2. Then, still in the script, generate some random number between the `min` and the `max` value, and request the row with that random value:

   ```
   SELECT * FROM post_links WHERE Id = [random value];
   ```

3. Repeat step 2 for as many rows as you need.

Unfortunately, doing this in the Stack Overflow database tables, for example, on our `post_links` table, will result in many failed queries, since our data has so many holes in the `Id` column, for example, what if step 2 in the preceding example generated the number 38? There is no `Id` of 38 in our `post_links` table. This means we will need to detect this error and try again with a new random value.

> At this point, someone who knows a little SQL — but not a lot — will usually suggest that we just ask MySQL to `ORDER BY rand()` on the column with the `Id` in it, and then perform a `LIMIT` command to skim off the number of records we want. The problem with this idea is that even if the column we are ordering is an indexed column, `ORDER BY rand()` has to read every row in order to assign a new random number to it. So, on a very large table, like the tables we have in the Stack Overflow database, this does not scale at all. We will be waiting way too long for an `ORDER BY rand()` query to finish. `ORDER BY rand()` is a tolerable solution for small tables, but not for the sizes we are working with here.

The following PHP script shows how our final random row selection process will work to build eight test tables, each with exactly 1,000 rows. Each table will be populated by row values that are selected as randomly as possible with as little effort as possible, and without us over-engineering this simple problem:

```
<?php //randomizer.php
// how many rows should be in each of the test tables?
```

```
$table_target_size = 1000;

// connect to db, set up query, run the query
$dbc = mysqli_connect('localhost','username','password','stackoverfl
ow')
       or die('Error connecting to database!' . mysqli_error());
$dbc->set_charset("utf8");

$tables = array("badges",
    "comments",
    "posts",
    "post_history",
    "post_links",
    "tags",
    "users",
    "votes");

foreach ($tables as $table)
{
  echo "\n=== Now working on $table ===\n";
    $select_table_info = "SELECT count(Id) as c, min(Id) as mn,
    max(Id) as mx FROM $table";
    $table_info = mysqli_query($dbc, $select_table_info);
    $table_stuff = mysqli_fetch_object($table_info);
    $table_count = $table_stuff->c;
    $table_min = $table_stuff->mn;
    $table_max = $table_stuff->mx;

    // set up loop to grab a random row and insert into new table
    $i=0;
    while($i < $table_target_size)
    {
        $r = rand($table_min, $table_max);
        echo "\nIteration $i: $r";
        $insert_rowx = "INSERT IGNORE INTO test_$table (SELECT *
        FROM $table WHERE Id = $r)";
        $current_row = mysqli_query($dbc, $insert_rowx);

        $select_current_count = "SELECT count(*) as rc FROM
        test_$table";
        $current_count= mysqli_query($dbc, $select_current_count);
        $row_count = mysqli_fetch_object($current_count)->rc;
        $i = $row_count;
    }
}
?>
```

After running that code, we can see we have a nice selection of eight test tables to work with if we need them. Testing with these smaller tables ensures that our cleaning exercises will go more smoothly and mistakes can be contained. If we find that we need more rows in our random tables, we can simply raise the `$table_target_size` command and run this again.

Building test tables is a great habit to get into, once you know how easy it is to create them in a simple and useful way.

Step three – cleaning the data

Remembering that our goal is to begin analyzing how frequently certain URLs are referenced in questions, answers, and comments, it makes sense to begin in the text of the Stack Overflow `posts` and `comments` tables. However, since those tables are so large, we will use the `test_posts` and `test_comments` tables that we just created instead. Then, once we are confident that the queries work perfectly, we can re-run them on the larger tables.

This cleaning task is very similar to the way we stored the URLs extracted from tweets in *Chapter 7, RDBMS Cleaning Techniques*. However, this project has its own set of specific rules:

- Since posts and comments are different entities to begin with, we should make separate tables for the URLs that come from posts (including questions and answers) and the URLs that come from comments.
- Each question, answer, or comment can have multiple URLs inside it. We should store all of the URLs, and we should also track the unique identifier for which post or comment that URL came from.
- Each question and answer can also have formatted source code in it. The <code> tag is used to delimit source code in the Stack Overflow posts. Separating code from posts will help us answer questions about the co-existence of paste site URLs and source code. How much code will typically accompany such a link, if any?

> Technically, posts *can* be created without the <code> tags, but usually someone will quickly edit the errant post to include these useful tags, and will get the Stack Overflow points for doing so. For brevity's sake, in this project, we will assume that code is included in the <code> tags.

- According to the Stack Overflow database dump documentation (available at `http://meta.stackexchange.com/questions/2677/`), there are actually eight types of posts, of which questions and answers are just two types. So, we will need to limit our queries to posts that have `postTypeId=1` for questions and `postTypeId=2` for answers.
- To ensure that we are only extracting URLs from comments made to questions or answers, and not other types of posts, we will need to do a join back to the posts table and limit our results to `postTypeId=1` or `postTypeId=2`.

Creating the new tables

The SQL query to create the database tables we need to store these URLs is as follows:

```
CREATE TABLE clean_comments_urls (
  id INT NOT NULL AUTO_INCREMENT PRIMARY KEY,
  commentId INT NOT NULL,
  url VARCHAR(255) NOT NULL
) ENGINE=MyISAM  DEFAULT CHARSET=utf8;

CREATE TABLE IF NOT EXISTS clean_posts_urls (
  id INT NOT NULL AUTO_INCREMENT PRIMARY KEY,
  postId INT NOT NULL,
  url VARCHAR(255) NOT NULL
) ENGINE=MyISAM  DEFAULT CHARSET=utf8;
```

We also need to create a table that can hold the code we stripped out of the posts:

```
CREATE TABLE clean_posts_code (
  id INT NOT NULL AUTO_INCREMENT PRIMARY KEY,
  postId INT NOT NULL,
  code TEXT NOT NULL
) ENGINE=MyISAM DEFAULT CHARSET=utf8;
```

At this point, we have three new tables that will store our cleaned URLs and cleaned source code. In the next section, we will extract URLs and code and fill up these new tables.

Extracting URLs and populating the new tables

We can modify the scripts we wrote earlier in *Chapter 7, RDBMS Cleaning Techniques*, to extract URLs in this new Stack Overflow environment as follows:

```
<?php // urlExtractor.php
// connect to db
$dbc = mysqli_connect('localhost', 'username', 'password',
  'stackoverflow')
    or die('Error connecting to database!' . mysqli_error());
$dbc->set_charset("utf8");

// pull out the text for posts with
// postTypeId=1 (questions)
// or postTypeId=2 (answers)
$post_query = "SELECT Id, Body
    FROM test_posts
    WHERE postTypeId=1 OR postTypeId=2";

$comment_query = "SELECT tc.Id, tc.Text
    FROM test_comments tc
    INNER JOIN posts p ON tc.postId = p.Id
    WHERE p.postTypeId=1 OR p.postTypeId=2";

$post_result = mysqli_query($dbc, $post_query);
// die if the query failed
if (!$post_result)
    die ("post SELECT failed! [$post_query]" .  mysqli_error());

// pull out the URLS, if any
$urls = array();
$pattern  = '#\b(([\w]+://?|www[.])[^\s()<>]+(?:\([\w\d]+\)
  |([^[:punct:]\s]|/)))#';

while($row = mysqli_fetch_array($post_result))
{
    echo "\nworking on post: " . $row["id"];
    if (preg_match_all(
        $pattern,
        $row["Body"],
        $urls
    ))
    {
```

```
        foreach ($urls[0] as $url)
        {
          $url = mysqli_escape_string($dbc, $url);
            echo "\n----url: ".$url;
            $post_insert = "INSERT INTO clean_posts_urls (id,
            postid, url)
                VALUES (NULL," . $row["Id"] . ",'$url')";
            echo "\n$post_insert";
            $post_insert_result = mysqli_query($dbc,
            $post_insert);
        }
    }
}

$comment_result = mysqli_query($dbc, $comment_query);
// die if the query failed
if (!$comment_result)
    die ("comment SELECT failed! [$comment_query]" .
    mysqli_error());

while($row = mysqli_fetch_array($comment_result))
{
    echo "\nworking on comment: " . $row["id"];
    if (preg_match_all(
        $pattern,
        $row["Text"],
        $urls
    ))
    {
        foreach ($urls[0] as $url)
        {
            echo "\n----url: ".$url;
            $comment_insert = "INSERT INTO clean_comments_urls
            (id, commentid, url)
                VALUES (NULL," . $row["Id"] . ",'$url')";
            echo "\n$comment_insert";
            $comment_insert_result = mysqli_query($dbc,
            $comment_insert);
        }
    }
}
?>
```

We now have fully populated `clean_post_urls` and `clean_comment_urls` tables. For my randomly filled test tables, running this script only yields around 100 comment URLs and 700 post URLs. Still, that is enough to test out our ideas before running them on the full dataset.

Extracting code and populating new tables

To extract the text embedded in `<code>` tags and populate our new `clean_posts_code` table, we can run the following script. It is similar to the URL extractor, except that it does not need to search comments, because those do not have code delimited with a `<code>` tag.

In my version of the randomly selected test table, the initial `SELECT` yields about 800 rows out of 1,000 total rows in the `test_post` table. However, each post can have multiple code snippets in it, so the final table ends up having over 2,000 rows in it. The following PHP code extracts the text embedded in the `<code>` tag:

```
<?php // codeExtractor.php
// connect to db
$dbc = mysqli_connect('localhost', 'username, 'password',
  'stackoverflow')
    or die('Error connecting to database!' . mysqli_error());
$dbc->set_charset("utf8");

// pull out the text for posts with
// postTypeId=1 (questions)
// or postTypeId=2 (answers)
$code_query = "SELECT Id, Body
    FROM test_posts
    WHERE postTypeId=1 OR postTypeId=2
    AND Body LIKE '%<code>%'";

$code_result = mysqli_query($dbc, $code_query);
// die if the query failed
if (!$code_result)
    die ("SELECT failed! [$code_query]" .  mysqli_error());

// pull out the code snippets from each post
$codesnippets = array();
$pattern  = '/<code>(.*?)<\/code>/';

while($row = mysqli_fetch_array($code_result))
{
```

```
        echo "\nworking on post: " . $row["Id"];
        if (preg_match_all(
            $pattern,
            $row["Body"],
            $codesnippets
        ))
        {
          $i=0;
            foreach ($codesnippets[0] as $code)
            {
              $code = mysqli_escape_string($dbc, $code);
                $code_insert = "INSERT INTO clean_posts_code (id,
                postid, code)
                    VALUES (NULL," . $row["Id"] . ",'$code')";
                $code_insert_result = mysqli_query($dbc,
                $code_insert);
                if (!$code_insert_result)
                    die ("INSERT failed! [$code_insert]" .
                    mysqli_error());
                $i++;
            }
            if($i>0)
            {
              echo "\n   Found $i snippets";
            }
        }
    }
    ?>
```

We now have a list of all the code that has been printed in each post, and we have stored that in the `clean_post_code` table.

Step four – analyzing the data

In this section, we write some code to answer our three questions from the beginning of this chapter. We were interested in finding:

- The counts of different paste sites mentioned by URLs in posts and comments
- The counts of paste site URLs in questions compared to answers
- Statistics about `<code>` prevalence in posts with a paste site URL

Which paste sites are most popular?

To answer this first question, we will generate a JSON representation of the paste site URLs and counts using the `clean_posts_urls` and `clean_comments_urls` tables. This simple analysis will help us find out which pastebin websites are popular in this Stack Overflow data dump. The following PHP queries the database for the paste sites we have prelisted in the `$pastebins` array and then performs a count of the matching URLs from the posts and comments. It uses the test tables, so the numbers are much smaller than they would be if we used the real tables:

```
<?php // q1.php
// connect to db
$dbc = mysqli_connect('localhost', 'username', 'password',
  'stackoverflow')
    or die('Error connecting to database!' . mysqli_error());
$dbc->set_charset("utf8");

// these are the web urls we want to look for and count
$pastebins = array("pastebin",
    "jsfiddle",
    "gists",
    "jsbin",
    "dpaste",
    "pastie");
$pastebin_counts = array();

foreach ($pastebins as $pastebin)
{
    $url_query = "SELECT count(id) AS cp,
          (SELECT count(id)
          FROM clean_comments_urls
          WHERE url LIKE '%$pastebin%') AS cc
        FROM clean_posts_urls
        WHERE url LIKE '%$pastebin%'";
    $query = mysqli_query($dbc, $url_query);
    if (!$query)
        die ("SELECT failed! [$url_query]" .  mysqli_error());
    $result = mysqli_fetch_object($query);
    $countp = $result->cp;
    $countc = $result->cc;
    $sum = $countp + $countc;

    array_push($pastebin_counts, array('bin' => $pastebin,
                                       'count' => $sum));
}
// sort the final list before json encoding it
// put them in order by count, high to low
foreach ($pastebin_counts as $key => $row)
{
```

```
        $first[$key]   = $row['bin'];
        $second[$key]  = $row['count'];
    }

    array_multisort($second, SORT_DESC, $pastebin_counts);
    echo json_encode($pastebin_counts);
    ?>
```

We can view the JSON output from this script when run against the test tables by looking at the output of the script. My random rows produced the following counts:


```
[{"bin":"jsfiddle","count":44},{"bin":"jsbin","count":4},{"bin":"paste
bin","count":3},{"bin":"dpaste","count":0},{"bin":"gists","count":0},{
"bin":"pastie","count":0}]
```


[Remember that your values may be different since you have a different set of randomly selected URLs.]

When we move to the *Step 5 – visualizing the data* section of this chapter, we will use this JSON code to build a bar graph. But first, let's answer the other two questions we posed earlier.

Which paste sites are popular in questions and which are popular in answers?

Our second question was whether the pastebin URLs are more prevalent in question posts or answer posts. To start to develop this answer, we will run a series of SQL queries. The first query simply asks how many posts are in the `clean_posts_urls` table of each type, both questions and answers:

```
SELECT tp.postTypeId, COUNT(cpu.id)
FROM test_posts tp
INNER JOIN clean_posts_urls cpu ON tp.Id = cpu.postid
GROUP BY 1;
```

The results show that in my randomly selected test set, I have 237 questions and 440 answers:

postTypeId	COUNT(cpu.id)
1	237
2	440

phpMyAdmin shows the count of question URLs and answer URLs.

Now, we would want to know the answer to this question: of those 677 URLs, divided by questions and answers, how many reference specifically one of the six pastebin URLs? We can run the following SQL code to find out:

```
SELECT  tp.postTypeId, count(cpu.id)
FROM test_posts tp
INNER JOIN clean_posts_urls cpu ON tp.Id = cpu.postId
WHERE cpu.url LIKE '%jsfiddle%'
OR cpu.url LIKE '%jsbin%'
OR cpu.url LIKE '%pastebin%'
OR cpu.url LIKE '%dpaste%'
OR cpu.url LIKE '%gist%'
OR cpu.url LIKE '%pastie%'
GROUP BY 1;
```

The results look like the following table. A total of 18 questions reference one of the paste sites, whereas 24 answers reference one of the paste sites.

postTypeId	count(cpu.id)
1	18
2	24

phpMyAdmin shows the count of question and answer URLs referencing a pastebin.

One thing to keep in mind about these queries is that they count individual URLs. So, if a particular `postId` referenced five URLs, those get counted five times. If I am interested in how many posts used a paste site URL once or more, I need to modify the first line of both queries as follows. This query counts distinct postings in the URLs table:

```
SELECT tp.postTypeId, COUNT(DISTINCT cpu.postId)
FROM test_posts tp
INNER JOIN clean_posts_urls cpu ON tp.Id = cpu.postId
GROUP BY 1;
```

The following screenshot shows how many questions and answers include a URL:

postTypeId	COUNT(DISTINCT cpu.postid)
1	81
2	222

phpMyAdmin shows how many questions and answers include any URL.

This query counts the particular posts in the URLs table that mention a paste site:

```
SELECT  tp.postTypeId, count(DISTINCT cpu.postId)
FROM test_posts tp
INNER JOIN clean_posts_urls cpu ON tp.Id = cpu.postId
WHERE cpu.url LIKE '%jsfiddle%'
OR cpu.url LIKE '%jsbin%'
OR cpu.url LIKE '%pastebin%'
OR cpu.url LIKE '%dpaste%'
OR cpu.url LIKE '%gist%'
OR cpu.url LIKE '%pastie%'
GROUP BY 1;
```

The results for this paste site query are as follows, and, as expected, the numbers are smaller. In our test set, **11** questions used at least one pastebin URL, and so did **16** answers. Combined, 37 posts reference a pastebin URL at least once.

postTypeId	count(distinct cpu.postid)
1	11
2	16

PhpMyAdmin shows how many questions and answers include any paste site URL.

Even though these results seem to show that people reference paste site URLs more in answers than questions, we need to compare them in terms of the overall number of questions and answers. We should report our result values as a percentage of the total for that post type, question or answer. Taking the totals into account, we can now say something like this: "Considering only the questions and answers that used any kind of URL at least once, 11 questions out of 81 used at least one paste site URL (13.6 percent), and 16 answers out of 222 used at least one paste site URL (7.2 percent)." With that in mind, it appears that the questions actually outstripped answers in referencing a paste site, almost two to one.

At this point in any data analysis project, you must have a flood of questions, like:

- How has the usage of paste site URLs in questions and answers changed over time?
- How do questions with paste site URLs fare on voting and favorites?
- What are the characteristics of users who post questions with paste site URLs?

But since this is a book about data cleaning, and since we still have not even visualized this data, I will restrain myself and not answer these for the time being. We still have one of our original three questions to answer, and then we will move on to visualizing some of our results.

Do posts contain both URLs to paste sites and source code?

Answering our third question requires us to compare the amount of code in the Stack Overflow questions to the amount in the Stack Overflow answers, paying particular attention to the posts that include some sort of source code, delimited by the `<code>` tags. In the *Step three – cleaning the data* section, we extracted all code from the posts in our test tables, and created a new table to hold these code snippets. Now, a simple query to figure out how many code-containing posts there are is as follows:

```
SELECT count(DISTINCT postid)
FROM clean_posts_code;
```

In my sample set, this yields 664 code-containing posts, out of the total 1,000 test posts. Another way to put this is: 664 out of 1,000 posts contain at least one <code> tag.

To figure out how many of these code-containing posts also contained any URL, we can run the following SQL query:

```
SELECT count(DISTINCT cpc.postid)
FROM clean_posts_code cpc
INNER JOIN clean_posts_urls cpu
ON cpu.postId = cpc.postId;
```

My sample set yields 175 rows for this. We can interpret that by saying that 17.5 percent of the original test set of 1,000 posts contains code and a URL.

Now, to figure out how many of the code-containing posts also contained a paste site URL, we will narrow down the SQL query even further:

```
SELECT count(DISTINCT cpc.postid)
FROM clean_posts_code cpc
INNER JOIN clean_posts_urls cpu
ON cpu.postId = cpc.postId
WHERE cpu.url LIKE '%jsfiddle%'
OR cpu.url LIKE '%jsbin%'
OR cpu.url LIKE '%pastebin%'
OR cpu.url LIKE '%dpaste%'
OR cpu.url LIKE '%gist%'
OR cpu.url LIKE '%pastie%';
```

From these results, we can see that only a tiny set of 25 posts contained both source code and a paste site URL. From the second question, we know that 37 distinct posts (both questions and answers) used some sort of paste site URL at least once. So, 25 out of 37 is about 68 percent. It will be interesting to run these queries on the larger dataset to see how those values come out.

In the meantime, we will carry out some simple visualizations of at least one of our questions so that we can close the loop on one complete round of the data science six-step process.

Step five – visualizing the data

The visualization step is sort of like the dessert course in our dinner party. Everyone loves a rich graphic and they look so nice. However, since our focus in this book is on cleaning rather than analysis and visualization, our graphics here will be very simple. In the code that follows, we will use the JavaScript D3 visualization libraries to display the results of the first question graphically. This visualization will be much simpler than the D3 visualization we did in *Chapter 4, Speaking the Lingua Franca – Data Conversions*. In that chapter, you will recall that we built a fairly complicated network diagram, but here, a simple bar graph will suffice since all we have to display is just a few labels and counts.

The HTML and JavaScript/D3 code is as follows. This code extends the *Let's Build a Bar Graph* tutorial by Mike Bostock, available at `http://bl.ocks.org/mbostock/3885304`. One of the ways that I extended this code was to make it read the JSON file we generated earlier in our `q1.php` script. Our JSON file printed really nicely, and was already sorted high to low, so building a little bar graph from that will be easy:

```
<!DOCTYPE html>
<meta charset="utf-8">
<!--
this code is modeled on mbostock's
"Let's Make a Bar Chart" D3 tutorial
available at http://bl.ocks.org/mbostock/3885304
My modifications:
* formatting for space
* colors
* y axis labels
* changed variable names to match our data
* loads data via JSON rather than .tsv file
-->
```

```
<style>
.bar {fill: lightgrey;}
.bar:hover {fill: lightblue;}
.axis {font: 10px sans-serif;}
.axis path, .axis line {
  fill: none;
  stroke: #000;
  shape-rendering: crispEdges;
}
.x.axis path {display: none;}
</style>
<body>
<script src="d3.min.js"></script>
<script>

var margin = {top: 20, right: 20, bottom: 30, left: 40},
    width = 960 - margin.left - margin.right,
    height = 500 - margin.top - margin.bottom;

var x = d3.scale.ordinal()
    .rangeRoundBands([0, width], .1);

var y = d3.scale.linear()
    .range([height, 0]);

var xAxis = d3.svg.axis()
    .scale(x)
    .orient("bottom");

var yAxis = d3.svg.axis()
    .scale(y)
    .orient("left");

var svg = d3.select("body").append("svg")
    .attr("width", width + margin.left + margin.right)
    .attr("height", height + margin.top + margin.bottom)
  .append("g")
    .attr("transform", "translate(" + margin.left + "," + margin.top +
")");

d3.json("bincounter.php", function(error, json)
{
```

```
    data = json;
    draw(data);
});

function draw(data)
{
  x.domain(data.map(function(d) { return d.bin; }));
  y.domain([0, d3.max(data, function(d) { return d.count; })]);

  svg.append("g")
      .attr("class", "x axis")
      .attr("transform", "translate(0," + height + ")")
      .call(xAxis);

  svg.append("g")
      .attr("class", "y axis")
      .call(yAxis)
    .append("text")
      .attr("transform", "rotate(-90)")
      .attr("y", 6)
      .attr("dy", ".71em")
      .style("text-anchor", "end")
      .text("Frequency");

  svg.selectAll(".bar")
      .data(data)
    .enter().append("rect")
      .attr("class", "bar")
      .attr("x", function(d) { return x(d.bin) ; })
      .attr("width", x.rangeBand())
      .attr("y", function(d) { return y(d.count); })
      .attr("height", function(d) { return height - y(d.count); });
}

</script>
</body>
</html>
```

We can save this as `q1chart.html`, and view it in the browser. The code calls our `q1.php` script, which generates the JSON file that D3 then uses to build this chart, the left-hand-side of which is shown here:

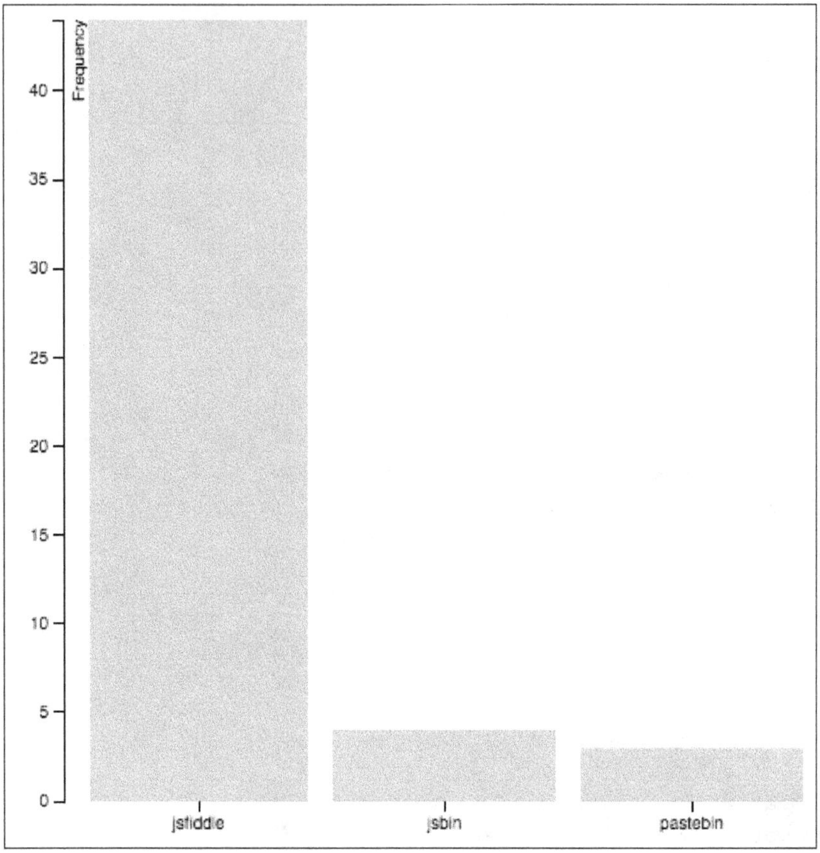

D3 visualization of the JSON produced from a count of three URLs.

The bar graph shows that the URLs pointing to JSFiddle seem to be the most common, at least in my version of the randomly selected test dataset. We knew that just from looking at the JSON output from `q1.php`, but it is nice to see it graphically as well. In the next section, we will summarize the results and our procedure, and talk about where to go next with this project.

Step six – problem resolution

From the queries and visualizations we developed in the *Step four – analyzing the data* and *Step five – visualizing the data* sections, we can now attempt to answer each of the three questions that prompted this project in the first place.

With our first question, we wanted to find counts of the different paste sites mentioned by URL in posts and comments. The `q1.php` script and bar graph we made to visualize the data show that, at least in the test data, JSFiddle was the most commonly referenced of the six paste site URLs we looked at.

The second question was about whether paste site URLs were more prevalent in questions or answers. Our queries show that paste site URLs were about twice as likely to occur in questions as opposed to answers, but the numbers for both were very small, at least in our test set.

For the third question, we wanted to look for whether people were actually heeding the advice of Stack Overflow and posting code in addition to a paste site URL. In our test set, the queries show that 25 postings (out of 37) include both a paste site URL and the recommended accompanying source code. This is a rate of about 68 percent compliance.

There are many additional questions we could ask and answer at this point, and many exciting ways we could extend this simple study into something that could be even more interesting. For now though, we will focus on the storage and cleaning procedures needed to extend this project to use the full dataset.

Moving from test tables to full tables

At the beginning of this project, we made a set of test tables so that we could develop our project in a stress-free environment using tables with only 1,000 rows each. Using small tables with manageable numbers of rows is important in cases where we are not sure that our queries will work as we want them to, or where we want to experiment with tricky joins, subqueries, weird regular expressions, and so on. At this point, though, if we feel good about the queries and scripts we have written, it is time to rewrite our procedures to use the full-size tables.

Here are the steps we will follow to move the project over to full-size tables:

1. `DROP` the test tables:

   ```
   DROP TABLE IF EXISTS test_badges;
   DROP TABLE IF EXISTS test_comments;
   DROP TABLE IF EXISTS test_posts;
   DROP TABLE IF EXISTS test_post_history;
   DROP TABLE IF EXISTS test_post_links;
   DROP TABLE IF EXISTS test_tags;
   DROP TABLE IF EXISTS test_users;
   DROP TABLE IF EXISTS test_votes;
   ```

2. Empty the `cleaned_posts_code`, `cleaned_posts_urls`, and `cleaned_comments_urls` tables as follows:

   ```
   TRUNCATE TABLE cleaned_posts_code;
   TRUNCATE TABLE cleaned_posts_urls;
   TRUNCATE TABLE cleaned_comments_urls;
   ```

3. Edit the `urlExtractor.php` and `codeExtractor.php` scripts to `SELECT` from the `posts` table rather than the `test_posts` table. These queries can be edited as follows:

   ```
   SELECT Id, Body FROM posts
   ```

4. Re-run the `urlExtractor.php` and `codeExtractor.php` scripts so that they will repopulate the clean code and URL tables we emptied (truncated) earlier.

At this point, we have the cleaned code and URL tables ready to be analyzed and visualized. Take your time when performing these steps, and know that many of these queries and scripts will likely take a long time to finish. The posts table is quite large and many of the queries we are writing are selected against a text column using wildcards.

Summary

In this project, we posed a few questions about the prevalence of URLs on Stack Overflow, specifically those related to paste sites like `http://www.Pastebin.com` and `http://www.JSFiddle.net`. To get started answering these questions, we downloaded data from the Stack Overflow postings (and other Stack Overflow data as well) from the Stack Exchange public file release. We built a MySQL database and eight tables to hold this data. We then created smaller 1,000-row versions of each of those tables for testing purposes, populated with a randomly selected sample of the data. From these test tables, we extracted the URLs mentioned in each question, answer, and comment, and saved them to a new clean table. We also extracted the source code found in the questions and answers, and saved those snippets to a new table as well. Finally, we were able to build some simple queries and visualizations to help us answer the questions we posed at the beginning.

Despite its modest results, from a data cleaning perspective, our dinner party was a success. We were able to make a coherent plan, and take methodical steps to put the plan into action and alter it when needed. We are now ready for our final project, and a completely different dinner party menu.

In the next chapter, we will collect and clean our own version of a famous Twitter dataset.

10
Twitter Project

As with the project we completed in *Chapter 9, Stack Overflow Project*, our next full-length chapter dinner party is designed to show off our data cleaning skills in particular, while still completing each stage of the overall data science process. Our previous project used Stack Overflow data, a combination of MySQL and PHP to clean it, and JavaScript D3 to visualize it. In this chapter, we will use Twitter data, MySQL and Python to collect and clean it, and JavaScript and D3 to visualize it. As with our previous project, in this project, the data science process is still the same:

1. Decide what kind of problem we are trying to solve — why do we need to examine this data?
2. Collect and store our data, which consists of downloading and extracting a publicly-available set of tweet identification numbers, and then using a program to redownload the original tweets. This step also includes creating smaller sets of data for testing purposes.
3. Clean data by extracting and storing only the parts that we need. In this step, we write a quick Python program to load in the data, pull out the fields we want, and write those to a small set of database tables.
4. Analyze the data. Do we need to perform any calculations on the data? Should we write some aggregate functions to count or sum the data? Do we need to transform the data in some way?
5. Provide visualizations of the data, if possible.
6. Resolve the problem we set out to investigate. Did our process work? Were we successful?

As with our previous project, the bulk of the work will be in the collection, storage, and cleaning tasks. In this project, we will notice that we store different versions of our data several times, first as a text file, then as a hydrated JSON file, then as a MySQL database. Each of these different formats results from a different collection or cleaning process and feeds into the next. In this way, we start to see how the collection, storage, and cleaning steps can be **iterative** – feeding back to one another – rather than just linear.

Step one – posing a question about an archive of tweets

Twitter is a popular **microblogging** platform used by millions of people around the world to share their thoughts or communicate about current events. Because of Twitter's relative ease of access for both posting and reading, especially from mobile devices, it has emerged as an important platform for sharing information during public events, such as political crises and protests, or to track the emergence of an issue in the public consciousness. Saved tweets become a sort of time capsule, providing a wealth of insight into public sentiment at the time of the event. Frozen in time, the tweets themselves are unaffected by memory lapses or subsequent reversals in public opinion. Scholars and media experts can collect and study these topical **tweet archives** to attempt to learn more about what the public opinion was at the time, or about how information traveled, or even about what happened in an event, when it happened, and why.

Many people have now started making their tweet collections public. Some of the tweet archives that are now available for public download include:

- Tweets that are in reference to protest and unrest following events in Ferguson, Missouri, USA, between August 10 and August 27, 2014. These are available at `https://archive.org/details/ferguson-tweet-ids`.
- Tweets from a number of countries during the Arab Spring events of 2011, including Libya, Bahrain, Egypt, and others. These are available at `http://dfreelon.org/2012/02/11/arab-spring-twitter-data-now-available-sort-of/`.
- Tweets that mention **#YesAllWomen** hashtag and the related hashtag **#NotAllMen**, between May and June 2014. These are available at `http://digital.library.unt.edu/ark:/67531/metadc304853/`.

In the next step, we will need to choose one of these to download and begin to work with. Since the Ferguson tweets are the newest and the most complete of those three example data sets, I have designed the rest of this chapter around it. However, no matter what set you use, the concepts and basic procedures here will apply.

The basic question we want to ask in this chapter is quite simple: when people tweeted about Ferguson, which Internet domains did they tweet about most? Compared to our set of questions in *Chapter 9, Stack Overflow Project*, this is a very simple question, but the data collection process is somewhat different here, so a simple question is enough to motivate our data science dinner party.

Step two – collecting the data

Unlike the small sentiment tweet archive that we studied in *Chapter 7, RDBMS Cleaning Techniques*, the newer tweet archives, like those mentioned, no longer contain the actual text of the tweets themselves. Twitter's **Terms of Service** (**ToS**) have changed as of 2014, and distributing other people's tweets is now a violation of this ToS. Instead, what you will find in a newer tweet archive is actually just the tweet identification (ID) numbers. Using these numbers, we will have to collect the actual tweets individually. At that point, we can store and analyze the tweets ourselves. Note that at any point during or after this process, we cannot redistribute the tweet text or their metadata, only the tweet identification numbers.

> Even though it is inconvenient for the researcher who wants to collect the tweets, the stated reason for Twitter's change to their ToS is to honor the notion of copyright by the original person who posted the tweet. This is especially important in terms of deleting a tweet. If a tweet has been copied and redistributed all around the Web and stored in data files by third parties, the tweet cannot really be deleted. By asking that researchers copy only the tweet ID, Twitter attempts to protect the user's ability to delete his or her own content. A request for a deleted tweet ID will return no result.

Download and extract the Ferguson file

The Ferguson-related tweets are available at the Internet Archive as a set of archived, compressed text files. Point your browser to `https://archive.org/details/ferguson-tweet-ids` and download the 147 MB ZIP file.

We can extract the files as follows:

```
unzip ferguson-tweet-ids.zip
```

The `ls` command shows that a directory is created called `ferguson-tweet-ids`, and there are two zipped files inside that directory as well: `ferguson-indictment-tweet-ids.zip` and `ferguson-tweet-ids.zip`. We really only need to unzip one of these to perform this project, so I chose this one:

```
unzip ferguson-tweet-ids.zip
```

Unzipping this file exposes several manifest text files, as well as a data folder. Inside the `data` folder is a gzipped file. Unzip it as follows:

```
gunzip ids.txt.gz
```

This yields a file called `ids.txt`. This is the file we are actually after. Let's explore this file.

To see the size of the file, we can run the `wc` command. When run from the command prompt as shown here, `wc` shows how many lines, words, and characters are in the file, in that order:

```
megan$ wc ids.txt
 13238863 13238863 251538397 ids.txt
```

The first number indicates how many lines are in the `ids.txt` file, just over 13 million. Next, we can peek inside the file with the `head` command:

```
megan$ head ids.txt
501064188211765249
501064196642340864
501064197632167936
501064196931330049
501064198005481472
501064198009655296
501064198059597824
501064198513000450
501064180468682752
501064199142117378
```

The `head` command shows the first ten lines of the file so we can see that each line is comprised of an 18-digit tweet ID.

Create a test version of the file

In this stage, we will create a small test file to work with for the remainder of this project. The reasons we want to do this are the same reasons why we worked with test tables in the *Chapter 9, Stack Overflow Project*. Because the original files are extremely large, we want to work with a subset of the data in case we make a mistake. We also want to be able to test our code without taking too long to complete each step.

Unlike in previous exercises, it probably does not matter if we select our test data lines randomly in this case. Just by looking at the result of the `head` command we ran earlier, we can see that the lines are not really in low-to-high order. In fact, we have no information about what order the original set of lines are in. Therefore, let's just grab the first 1,000 tweet IDs and save them to a file. This will become our test set:

```
head -1000 ids.txt > ids_1000.txt
```

Hydrate the tweet IDs

We will now use this test set of 1,000 tweet IDs to test our procedure for collecting the original tweets based on their identification number. This process is called **hydrating** the tweets. To do this, we will use a handy Python tool called **twarc**, which was written by Ed Summers, the same person who archived all the Ferguson tweets. It works by taking a list of tweet IDs and fetching each original tweet from the Twitter API one by one. To do anything with the Twitter API, we must have a Twitter developer account already set up. Let's make our Twitter account first, and then we can install twarc and use it.

Setting up a Twitter developer account

To set up a Twitter developer account, go to `https://apps.twitter.com` and log in with your Twitter account. If you do not already have a Twitter account, you will need to make one of those in order to complete the rest of these steps.

Once you are logged in with your Twitter account, from the `http://apps.twitter.com` page, click on **Create New App**. Fill in the required details to create your application (give it a name, perhaps something like `My Tweet Test`; a short description; and a URL, which does not have to be permanent). My filled-in app creation form is shown here for your reference:

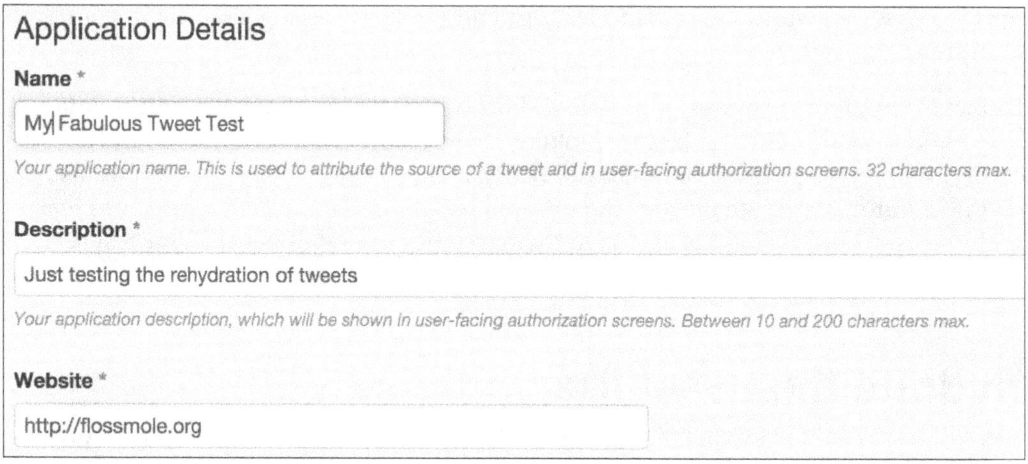
Application Details
Name *
My Fabulous Tweet Test
Your application name. This is used to attribute the source of a tweet and in user-facing authorization screens. 32 characters max.
Description *
Just testing the rehydration of tweets
Your application description, which will be shown in user-facing authorization screens. Between 10 and 200 characters max.
Website *
http://flossmole.org

Twitter's Create New App form, filled in with sample data

Click on the checkbox indicating that you agree to the developer agreement, and you will be returned to the screen listing all your Twitter apps, with your new app at the top of the list.

Next, to use this app, we will need to get a few key pieces of information that are required for it to work. Click on the app you just created, and you will see four tabs across the top of the next screen. We are interested in the one that says **Keys and Access Tokens**. It looks like this:

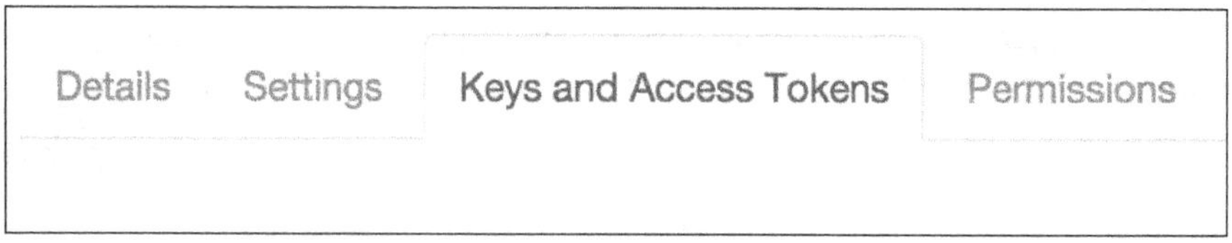
Details
Settings
Keys and Access Tokens
Permissions

The tab interface within your newly created Twitter app.

There are a lot of numbers and secret codes on this screen, but there are four items that we need to pay particular attention to:

- **CONSUMER_KEY**
- **CONSUMER_SECRET**
- **ACCESS_TOKEN**
- **ACCESS_TOKEN_SECRET**

No matter what kind of Twitter API programming you are doing, at least for the time being, you will always need these same four items. This is true whether you are using twarc or some other tool. These credentials are how Twitter authenticates you and makes sure that you have the access rights needed to see whatever it is that you are requesting.

> These API credentials are also how Twitter limits how many requests you can send and how quickly you can make your requests. The twarc tool handles all of this on our behalf, so we do not have to worry too much about exceeding our rate limits. For more information on Twitter's rate limits, check out their developer documentation at `https://dev.twitter.com/rest/public/rate-limiting`.

Installing twarc

Now that we have access to our Twitter credentials, we can install twarc.

The twarc download page is available on GitHub at `https://github.com/edsu/twarc`. On that page, there is documentation about how to use the tool and what options are available.

To install twarc in your Canopy Python environment, start up Canopy and then choose **Canopy Command Prompt** from the **Tools** menu.

At the command prompt, type in:

```
pip install twarc
```

This command will install twarc and make it available to be called as a command-line program, or from within your own Python programs.

Running twarc

We can now use twarc from the command line to hydrate the `ids_1000.txt` file that we created earlier. The command line for this is very long, since we have to pass in those four long secret tokens that we created earlier on the Twitter site. To save myself from making errors, I used my text editor, Text Wrangler, to create the command line first, and then I pasted it into my Command Prompt. Your final command line will look like the one that follows, except everywhere that it says `abcd`, you should instead fill in your appropriate secret token or secret key:

```
twarc.py --consumer_key abcd --consumer_secret abcd --access_token
abcd --access_token_secret abcd --hydrate ids_1000.txt >
tweets_1000.json
```

Note that this command line will redirect its output to a JSON file called `tweets_1000.json`. Inside that file is a JSON representation of each tweet that we only had the ID for previously. Let's check how long the new file is:

```
wc tweets_1000.json
```

The `wc` utility indicates that my file is 894 lines long, which indicates that some of the tweets were unable to be found (since I originally had 1,000 tweets in my dataset). If tweets have been deleted in the time since I have written this, your file might be even smaller.

Next, we can also peek inside the file:

```
less tweets_1000.json
```

We could also open it in a text editor to view it.

Each line in the JSON file represents a single tweet, each of which looks like the example that follows. However, this example tweet is not from the Ferguson dataset, since I do not have the rights to distribute those tweets. Instead, I used one of the tweets I created back in *Chapter 2, Fundamentals – Formats, Types, and Encodings*, for our discussion on UTF-8 encoding. Since this tweet was created just for this book, and I own the content, I can show you the JSON format without violating Twitter's ToS. Here is what my tweet looked like through the Twitter web interface:

megan squire
@MeganSquire0
Another test. Ég elska gögn. #datacleaning
8:09 PM - 9 Dec 2014

An example of a tweet, as shown in Twitter's web interface.

The following is what the tweet looks like in its JSON representation after twarc hydrates it. I have added newlines in between each JSON element so we can see what attributes are available in each tweet more easily:


```
{"contributors": null,
"truncated": false,
"text": "Another test. \u00c9g elska g\u00f6gn. #datacleaning",
"in_reply_to_status_id": null,
"id": 542486101047275520,
"favorite_count": 0,
"source": "<a href=\"http://twitter.com\" rel=\"nofollow\">Twitter Web
Client</a>",
"retweeted": false,
"coordinates": null,
"entities":
{"symbols": [],
"user_mentions": [],
"hashtags":
[{"indices": [29, 42],
"text": "datacleaning"}],
"urls": []},
"in_reply_to_screen_name": null,
"id_str": "542486101047275520",
"retweet_count": 0,
"in_reply_to_user_id": null,
"favorited": false,
"user":
```

```
{"follow_request_sent": false,
"profile_use_background_image": false,
"profile_text_color": "333333",
"default_profile_image": false,
"id": 986601,
"profile_background_image_url_https": "https://pbs.twimg.com/profile_
background_images/772436819/b7f7b083e42c9150529fb13971a52528.png",
"verified": false,
"profile_location": null,
"profile_image_url_https": "https://pbs.twimg.com/profile_
images/3677035734/d8853be8c304729610991194846c49ba_normal.jpeg",
"profile_sidebar_fill_color": "F6F6F6",
"entities":
{"url":
{"urls":
[{"url": "http://t.co/dBQNKhR6jY",
"indices": [0, 22],
"expanded_url": "http://about.me/megansquire",
"display_url": "about.me/megansquire"}]},
"description": {"urls": []}},
"followers_count": 138,
"profile_sidebar_border_color": "FFFFFF",
"id_str": "986601",
"profile_background_color": "000000",
"listed_count": 6,
"is_translation_enabled": false,
"utc_offset": -14400,
"statuses_count": 376,
"description": "Open source data hound. Leader of the FLOSSmole
project. Professor of Computing Sciences at Elon University.",
"friends_count": 82,
"location": "Elon, NC",
"profile_link_color": "038543",
"profile_image_url": "http://pbs.twimg.com/profile_images/3677035734/
d8853be8c304729610991194846c49ba_normal.jpeg",
"following": false,
"geo_enabled": false,
"profile_banner_url": "https://pbs.twimg.com/profile_
banners/986601/1368894408",
"profile_background_image_url": "http://pbs.twimg.com/profile_
background_images/772436819/b7f7b083e42c9150529fb13971a52528.png",
"name": "megan squire",
"lang": "en",
"profile_background_tile": false,
```

```
    "favourites_count": 64,
    "screen_name": "MeganSquire0",
    "notifications": false,
    "url": "http://t.co/dBQNKhR6jY",
    "created_at": "Mon Mar 12 05:01:55 +0000 2007",
    "contributors_enabled": false,
    "time_zone": "Eastern Time (US & Canada)",
    "protected": false,
    "default_profile": false,
    "is_translator": false},
    "geo": null,
    "in_reply_to_user_id_str": null,
    "lang": "is",
    "created_at": "Wed Dec 10 01:09:00 +0000 2014",
    "in_reply_to_status_id_str": null,
    "place": null}
```

Not only does each JSON object include facts about the tweet itself, for example, the text, the date, and the time that it was sent out, it also includes a wealth of information about the person who tweeted it.

> The hydration process results in a *lot* of information about a single individual tweet – and this is a dataset with 13 million tweets in all. Keep this in mind when you get ready to hydrate the entire Ferguson dataset at the end of this chapter.

Step three – data cleaning

At this point, we are ready to begin cleaning the JSON file, extracting the details of each tweet that we want to keep in our long-term storage.

Creating database tables

Since our motivating question only asks about URLs, we really only need to extract those, along with the tweet IDs. However, for the sake of practice in cleaning, and so that we can compare this exercise to what we did earlier in *Chapter 7, RDBMS Cleaning Techniques*, with the `sentiment140` data set, let's design a small set of database tables as follows:

- A `tweet` table, which only holds information about the tweets
- A `hashtag` table, which holds information about which tweets referenced which hashtags

- A `URL` table, which holds information about which tweets referenced which URLs
- A `mentions` table, which holds information about which tweets mentioned which users

This is similar to the structure we designed in *Chapter 7, RDBMS Cleaning Techniques,* except in that case we had to parse out our own list of hashtags and URLs and user mentions from the tweet text. The twarc tool has definitely saved us some effort as we complete this project in this chapter.

The `CREATE` statements to make our four tables are as follows:

```
CREATE TABLE IF NOT EXISTS ferguson_tweets (
  tid bigint(20) NOT NULL,
  ttext varchar(200) DEFAULT NULL,
  tcreated_at varchar(50) DEFAULT NULL,
  tuser bigint(20) DEFAULT NULL,
  PRIMARY KEY (tid)
) ENGINE=MyISAM DEFAULT CHARSET=utf8mb4;

CREATE TABLE IF NOT EXISTS ferguson_tweets_hashtags (
  tid bigint(20) NOT NULL,
  ttag varchar(200) NOT NULL,
  PRIMARY KEY (tid, ttag)
) ENGINE=MyISAM DEFAULT CHARSET=utf8;

CREATE TABLE IF NOT EXISTS ferguson_tweets_mentions (
  tid bigint(20) NOT NULL,
  tuserid bigint(20) NOT NULL,
  tscreen varchar(100) DEFAULT NULL,
  tname varchar(100) DEFAULT NULL,
  PRIMARY KEY (tid,tuserid)
) ENGINE=MyISAM DEFAULT CHARSET=utf8;

CREATE TABLE IF NOT EXISTS ferguson_tweets_urls (
  tid bigint(20) NOT NULL,
  turl varchar(200) NOT NULL,
  texpanded varchar(255) DEFAULT NULL,
  tdisplay varchar(200) DEFAULT NULL,
  PRIMARY KEY (tid,turl)
) ENGINE=MyISAM DEFAULT CHARSET=utf8;
```

One thing to note about the tweets table is that it was created with the **utf8mb4** collation. This is because the tweets themselves may include characters that are very high in the UTF-8 range. In fact, some characters in these tweets will require more space than the 3-byte limit that the native MySQL UTF-8 character set can hold. Therefore, we designed the main tweet table to hold data in MySQL's utf8mb4 collation, which is included in MySQL 5.5 or higher. If you are working on a MySQL version older than that, or for some other reason, you do not have access to the utf8mb4 collation, you can use MySQL's older UTF-8-general collation, but be aware that you may generate encoding errors with an emoji here or there. If you do run into this error, MySQL will likely yield a message about Error 1366 and *incorrect string value* when you are trying to `INSERT` the record.

Now that each table is created, we can begin to select and load the data in.

Populating the new tables in Python

The Python script that follows will load in the JSON file, extract the values from the fields we are interested in, and populate the four tables described previously. There are a few additional, important notes about this script, which I will go through now.

This script does require the `MySQLdb` Python modules to be installed. As a Canopy Python user, these modules are easy to install through the package manager. Simply run a search for `MySQLdb` in the **Package Manager** and click to install:

```
#jsonTweetCleaner.py
import json
import MySQLdb

# Open database connection
db = MySQLdb.connect(host="localhost",\
    user="username", \
    passwd="password", \
    db="ferguson", \
    use_unicode=True, \
    charset="utf8")
cursor = db.cursor()
cursor.execute('SET NAMES utf8mb4')
cursor.execute('SET CHARACTER SET utf8mb4')
cursor.execute('SET character_set_connection=utf8mb4')
```

```
# open the file full of json-encoded tweets
with open('tweets_1000.json') as f:
    for line in f:
        # read each tweet into a dictionary
        tweetdict = json.loads(line)

        # access each tweet and write it to our db table
        tid    = int(tweetdict['id'])
        ttext  = tweetdict['text']
        uttext = ttext.encode('utf8')
        tcreated_at = tweetdict['created_at']
        tuser  = int(tweetdict['user']['id'])

        try:
            cursor.execute(u"INSERT INTO ferguson_tweets(tid,
ttext, tcreated_at, tuser) VALUES (%s, %s, %s, %s)", \
(tid,uttext,tcreated_at,tuser))
            db.commit() # with MySQLdb you must commit each change
        except MySQLdb.Error as error:
            print(error)
            db.rollback()

        # access each hashtag mentioned in tweet
        hashdict = tweetdict['entities']['hashtags']
        for hash in hashdict:
            ttag = hash['text']
            try:
                cursor.execute(u"INSERT IGNORE INTO
ferguson_tweets_hashtags(tid, ttag) VALUES (%s, %s)",(tid,ttag))
                db.commit()
            except MySQLdb.Error as error:
                print(error)
                db.rollback()

        # access each URL mentioned in tweet
        urldict = tweetdict['entities']['urls']
        for url in urldict:
            turl      = url['url']
            texpanded = url['expanded_url']
            tdisplay  = url['display_url']

            try:
                cursor.execute(u"INSERT IGNORE INTO  ferguson_tweets_
urls(tid, turl, texpanded, tdisplay)
```

```
VALUES (%s, %s, %s, %s)", (tid,turl,texpanded,tdisplay))
                db.commit()
            except MySQLdb.Error as error:
                print(error)
                db.rollback()

        # access each user mentioned in tweet
        userdict = tweetdict['entities']['user_mentions']
        for mention in userdict:
            tuserid = mention['id']
            tscreen = mention['screen_name']
            tname   = mention['name']

            try:
                cursor.execute(u"INSERT IGNORE INTO
ferguson_tweets_mentions(tid, tuserid, tscreen, tname)
VALUES (%s, %s, %s, %s)", (tid,tuserid,tscreen,tname))
                db.commit()
            except MySQLdb.Error as error:
                print(error)
# disconnect from server
db.close()
```

For more information on each of the fields provided in the JSON representation of a tweet, the Twitter API documentation is very helpful. The sections on Users, Entities, and Entities in Tweets are particularly instructive when planning which fields to extract from the JSON tweet. You can get started with the documentation at `https://dev.twitter.com/overview/api/`.

Once this script is run, the four tables are populated with data. On my MySQL instance, after running the preceding script against my `ids_1000.txt` file, I ended up with 893 rows in the tweets table; 1,048 rows in the hashtags table; 896 rows in the user mentions table; and 371 rows in the URLs table. If you have fewer rows here or there, check to see whether it is because tweets have been deleted.

Step four – simple data analysis

Suppose we want to learn which web domains were linked the most in the Ferguson dataset. We can answer this question by extracting just the domain portion of the URL stored in the `tdisplay` column in our `ferguson_tweets_urls` table. For our purposes, we will consider everything before the first slash (/) as the interesting part of the URL.

The following SQL query gives us the domain and count of posts that reference that domain:

```
SELECT left(tdisplay,locate('/',tdisplay)-1) as url,
  count(tid) as num
FROM ferguson_tweets_urls
GROUP BY 1 ORDER BY 2 DESC;
```

The result of this query is a dataset that looks something like the following (run on the sample set of 1,000 rows):

url	num
bit.ly	47
wp.me	32
dlvr.it	18
huff.to	13
usat.ly	9
ijreview.com	8
latimes.com	7
gu.com	7
ift.tt	7

This snippet of the dataset shows just the first few rows, but we can already see some of the more popular results are URL-shortening services, such as `bit.ly`. We can also see that we are able to remove all those shortened URLs created by Twitter's own shortener, `t.co`, simply by using the display column rather than the main URL column.

In the next section, we can use these counts to build a bar graph, in a similar manner to the way we built a simple graph in Chapter 9, *Stack Overflow Project*.

Step five – visualizing the data

To build a little D3-enabled graph, we could follow the same procedure we used in *Chapter 9, Stack Overflow Project*, in which we made a PHP script that queries the database, and then our JavaScript uses the results as the live input to a bar graph. Alternatively, we could generate a CSV file with Python and let D3 generate its graph from those results. Since we already performed the PHP method in the previous chapter, let's use the CSV file method here, just for variety. This is also a good excuse to continue on with Python in this chapter, since this is already the language we have been using.

The following script connects to the database, selects out the top 15 most-used URLs and their counts, and writes the entire thing to a CSV file:

```
import csv
import MySQLdb

# Open database connection
db = MySQLdb.connect(host="localhost",
    user="username",
    passwd="password",
    db="ferguson",
    use_unicode=True,
    charset="utf8")
cursor = db.cursor()

cursor.execute('SELECT left(tdisplay, LOCATE(\'/\',
    tdisplay)-1) as url, COUNT(tid) as num
    FROM ferguson_tweets_urls
    GROUP BY 1 ORDER BY 2 DESC LIMIT 15')

with open('fergusonURLcounts.tsv', 'wb') as fout:
    writer = csv.writer(fout)
    writer.writerow([ i[0] for i in cursor.description ])
    writer.writerows(cursor.fetchall())
```

Once we have this CSV file, we can feed it into a stock D3 bar graph template, just to see what it looks like. The following can be called `buildBarGraph.html` or the like:

> Make sure you have the D3 libraries in your local folder, just as you did in previous chapters, along with the CSV file you just made.

```
<!DOCTYPE html>
<meta charset="utf-8">
<!--
this code is modeled on mbostock's
"Let's Make a Bar Chart" D3 tutorial
available at http://bl.ocks.org/mbostock/3885304
My modifications:
* formatting for space
* colors
* y axis label moved
* changed variable names to match our data
* loads data via CSV rather than TSV file
```

```
-->

<style>
.bar {fill: lightgrey;}
.bar:hover {fill: lightblue;}
.axis {font: 10px sans-serif;}
.axis path, .axis line {
  fill: none;
  stroke: #000;
  shape-rendering: crispEdges;
}
.x.axis path {display: none;}
</style>
<body>
<script src="d3.min.js"></script>
<script>

var margin = {top: 20, right: 20, bottom: 30, left: 40},
    width = 960 - margin.left - margin.right,
    height = 500 - margin.top - margin.bottom;

var x = d3.scale.ordinal()
    .rangeRoundBands([0, width], .1);

var y = d3.scale.linear()
    .range([height, 0]);

var xAxis = d3.svg.axis()
    .scale(x)
    .orient("bottom");

var yAxis = d3.svg.axis()
    .scale(y)
    .orient("left");

var svg = d3.select("body").append("svg")
    .attr("width", width + margin.left + margin.right)
    .attr("height", height + margin.top + margin.bottom)
  .append("g")
    .attr("transform", "translate(" + margin.left + "," + margin.top +
")");
```

```
d3.csv("fergusonURLcounts.csv", type, function(error, data) {
  x.domain(data.map(function(d) { return d.url; }));
  y.domain([0, d3.max(data, function(d) { return d.num; })]);

  svg.append("g")
      .attr("class", "x axis")
      .attr("transform", "translate(0," + height + ")")
      .call(xAxis);

  svg.append("g")
      .attr("class", "y axis")
      .call(yAxis)
    .append("text")
      .attr("transform", "rotate(-90)")
      .attr("y", 6)
      .attr("dy", "-3em")
      .style("text-anchor", "end")
      .text("Frequency");

  svg.selectAll(".bar")
      .data(data)
    .enter().append("rect")
      .attr("class", "bar")
      .attr("x", function(d) { return x(d.url) ; })
      .attr("width", x.rangeBand())
      .attr("y", function(d) { return y(d.num); })
      .attr("height", function(d) { return height - y(d.num); });
});

function type(d) {
  d.num = +d.num;
  return d;
}

</script>
</body>
</html>
```

The resulting bar graph looks like the one shown here. Again, remember that we are using the test dataset so the numbers are quite small:

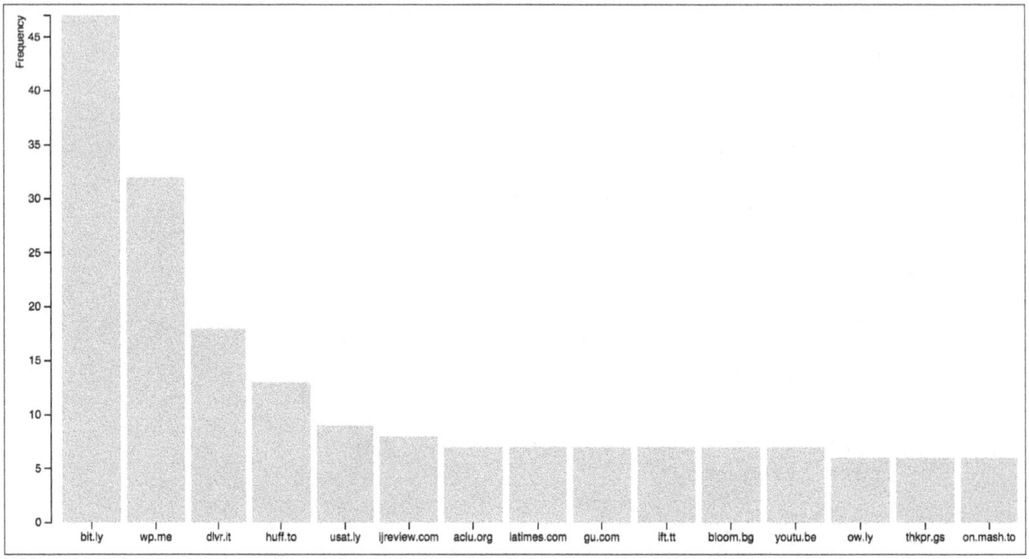

A simple bar graph drawn in D3 using our CSV file.

Step six – problem resolution

Since data visualization is not the main purpose of this book, we are not overly concerned with how sophisticated the diagram from the section is, and suffice it to say that there are many, many more interesting patterns to be uncovered in the Ferguson data set than just which URLs were pointed to the most. Now that you know how to easily download and clean this massive data set, perhaps you can let your imagination work to uncover some of these patterns. Remember that when you release your findings to your adoring public, you must not release the tweets themselves or their metadata. But you can release the tweet IDs, or a subset of them, if that is what your question required.

Moving this process into full (non-test) tables

Just like in *Chapter 9, Stack Overflow Project*, we made test tables so that we could develop our project in a stress-free environment with a manageable number of tweets to collect. When you are ready to collect the full list of tweets, be ready to spend some time doing so. Twitter's rate limits will kick in, and twarc will take a long time to run. Ed Summers indicates on this blog post that it will take about one week to run the Ferguson tweets: `http://inkdroid.org/journal/2014/11/18/on-forgetting/`. Of course, if you are careful, you will only have to run it once.

Another thing you could do to speed up the time it takes to hydrate the tweet IDs is to work as a team with someone else. You can divide the tweet ID file in half and each work on your portion of the tweets. During the data cleaning process, make sure you `INSERT` both into the same final database table.

Here are the steps we will follow to change our project to collect the full set of tweets rather than the 1,000-tweet sample:

1. Empty the `ferguson_tweets`,`ferguson_tweets_hashtags`, `ferguson_tweets_mentions`, and `ferguson_tweets_urls` tables as follows:

   ```
   TRUNCATE TABLE ferguson_tweets;
   TRUNCATE TABLE ferguson_tweets_hashtags;
   TRUNCATE TABLE ferguson_tweets_mentions;
   TRUNCATE TABLE ferguson_tweets_urls;
   ```

2. Run twarc on the full `ids.txt` file rather than the `ids_1000.txt` file as follows:

   ```
   twarc.py --consumer_key abcd --consumer_secret abcd --access_token
   abcd --access_token_secret abcd --hydrate ids.txt > tweets.json
   ```

3. Re-run the `jsonTweetCleaner.py` Python script.

At this point, you will have a cleaned database full of tweets, hashtags, mentions, and URLs, ready for analysis and visualization. Since there are so many more rows now in each table, be aware that each of the visualization steps could take much longer to run, depending on what kind of queries you are running.

Summary

In this project, we learned how to reconstruct a list of tweets based on their identification numbers. First, we located high-quality archived tweet data that conforms to Twitter's latest ToS. We learned how to split it into a set small enough for testing purposes. Then, we learned how to hydrate each tweet into a full JSON representation of itself, using the Twitter API and the twarc command-line tool. Next, we learned how to extract pieces of the JSON entities in Python, saving the fields to a new set of tables in our MySQL database. We then ran some simple queries to count the most common URLs, and we drew a bar graph using D3.

In this book, we have learned how to perform a variety of data cleaning tasks, both simple and complex. We used a variety of languages, tools, and techniques to get the job done, and along the way, I hope you were able to perfect your existing skills while learning many new ones.

At this point, our final dinner party is complete, and you are now ready to begin your own cleaning projects in your fully stocked — and very clean — data science kitchen. Where should you begin?

- Do you like contests and prizes? Kaggle hosts frequent data analysis competitions at their website, `http://kaggle.com`. You can work alone or as part of a team. Many teams need clean data, so that is a fantastic way to pitch in.
- If you are more of a public service kind of person, may I suggest School of Data? Their website is at `http://schoolofdata.org`, and they host courses and *Data Expeditions* where experts and amateurs from around the world get together and solve real-world problems using data.
- To extend your data cleaning practice, I highly recommend getting your hands dirty with some of the many publicly-available data sets out there. KDnuggets has a nice list of them here, including some lists of lists: `http://www.kdnuggets.com/datasets/`.

- Did you like the Stack Overflow examples in *Chapter 9, Stack Overflow Project*? The *Meta* Stack Exchange, available at `http://meta.stackexchange.com`, is a site just for discussing the way StackExchange sites work. Users discuss hundreds of amazing ideas for how to query Stack Overflow data and what to do with what they find. Or, you can always contribute to the large body of questions on Stack Overflow itself that are related to data cleaning. Finally, there are several other Stack Exchange sites that are also related to data cleaning. One useful site is the Open Data Stack Exchange, available at `http://opendata.stackexchange.com`.
- Twitter data is extremely popular right now. If you liked working with Twitter data, consider taking our *Chapter 10, Twitter Project*, project to the next level by asking and answering your own questions about one of those publicly-available tweet collections. Or, how about collecting and curating a new set of tweet IDs of your own? If you build clean collections of tweet IDs on some topic of interest, you can distribute those and researchers and other data scientists will be extremely grateful.

Good luck in your data cleaning adventures, and *bon apetit!*

Index

Symbols

A

B

C

E

F

S

T

U

V

W

Z

[PACKT] PUBLISHING

Thank you for buying
Clean Data

About Packt Publishing

Packt, pronounced 'packed', published its first book, *Mastering phpMyAdmin for Effective MySQL Management*, in April 2004, and subsequently continued to specialize in publishing highly focused books on specific technologies and solutions.

Our books and publications share the experiences of your fellow IT professionals in adapting and customizing today's systems, applications, and frameworks. Our solution-based books give you the knowledge and power to customize the software and technologies you're using to get the job done. Packt books are more specific and less general than the IT books you have seen in the past. Our unique business model allows us to bring you more focused information, giving you more of what you need to know, and less of what you don't.

Packt is a modern yet unique publishing company that focuses on producing quality, cutting-edge books for communities of developers, administrators, and newbies alike. For more information, please visit our website at `www.packtpub.com`.

Writing for Packt

We welcome all inquiries from people who are interested in authoring. Book proposals should be sent to `author@packtpub.com`. If your book idea is still at an early stage and you would like to discuss it first before writing a formal book proposal, then please contact us; one of our commissioning editors will get in touch with you.

We're not just looking for published authors; if you have strong technical skills but no writing experience, our experienced editors can help you develop a writing career, or simply get some additional reward for your expertise.

www.ingramcontent.com/pod-product-compliance
Lightning Source LLC
Chambersburg PA
CBHW060531060326
40690CB00017B/3453